ANTIQUE TRADER BOOKS

Metalwares
Price Guide

Edited by
Marilyn E. Dragowick

An Illustrated comprehensive price guide
to all types of antique and collectible metalwares.

Antique Trader Books
P.O. Box 1050
Dubuque, IA 52004

STAFF

EDITORIAL
Managing Editor - Books/Price Guides..............................Kyle Husfloen
Assistant Editor..Elizabeth Stephan
Editorial Assistant..Ruth Willis

ART & PRODUCTION
Art Director...Jaro Sebek
Design Associate..Aaron J. Roeth
Design Assistant...Karen Bartch
Design Assistant ....Lynn Bradshaw

CUSTOMER SERVICE/
ORDER FULFILLMENT ....Bonnie Rojemann

ISBN: 0-930625-39-0
Library of Congress Catalog Card No. 95-076093

Other books and magazines published by
Antique Trader Publications

American Pressed Glass & Bottles Price Guide
American & European Decorative & Art Glass Price Guide
American & European Art Pottery Price Guide
American & European Furniture Price Guide
American Military Collectibles Price Guide
German Military Collectibles Price Guide
Japanese & Other Foreign Military Collectibles Price Guide

Ceramics Price Guide	The Antique Trader Weekly
Toy Trader	Collector Magazine & Price Guide
DISCoveries	The Big Reel
Postcard Collector	Baby Boomer Collectibles
Maloney's Resoure Directory	Military Trader
Rockin' Records	White Ironstone: A Collector's Guide
Comics Values Annual	Garage Sale Manual & Price Guide

To order additional copies of this book or
other publications listed above, contact:

Antique Trader Publications
P.O. Box 1050
Dubuque, Iowa 52004
1-800-334-7165

TABLE OF CONTENTS

INTRODUCTION

Recently, when I decided to take early retirement from my position as Assistant Editor of the *Antique Trader Price Guide* I was filled with mixed emotions. On the one hand, I would have time to read all those books I have been putting aside for so long and there would be the time to take long walks on the beach with my companion Timothy, the world's most wonderful golden retriever. On the other hand, I would have to give up the association with people who enjoy and respect antiques and it would, to some extent, mean giving up the daily need to do the never-ending research on the various antiques and collectibles that we included in our annual price guide.

Imagine my joy when the powers-that-be at Antique Trader Books asked me if I would be interested in compiling a price guide on metals as they felt there is a definite need for such a project. The subject matter fascinated me and it was a real pleasure to get to work on gathering the data.

You will note that the price listings have been divided alphabetically by metal from aluminum to zinc and each section begins with a brief introduction covering the pertinent facts about each metal. Under each category the various items have been listed alphabetically for ease in locating specific pieces. Although I have attempted to describe each entry in detail I have also included a large selection of photographs to further clarify the subject. In addition, you will find a glossary of terms used in the descriptions, a section of various marks and their identification and a bibliography that includes readings that will be useful in your pursuit of further information about metals.

The prices and photographs included in this volume have been largely obtained from the major auction houses in this country. You should be aware, however, that this book should be used only as a *guide* and is not intended to set prices. Prices can vary significantly from one part of the country to another and auction prices can have an even greater variation. Although prices have been double-checked and every effort has been made to assure accuracy, we cannot be responsible for any losses that might be incurred as a result of consulting this guide, or of errors, typographical or otherwise.

Sincere appreciation is expressed to Ms. Dannie Woodard who prepared the special in-depth section on aluminum. It was grand to have an expert share her knowledge with us. Ms. Woodard is the author of two books on aluminum wares and these are listed in the Bibliography.

I hope you will find this guide a valuable addition to your library and helpful in your quest for metalworks. We're always interested in hearing from our readers so, if you have any questions or comments, please contact us and we'll do our best to respond personally.

May you find that elusive treasure in your searching.

Marilyn E. Dragowick

ABOUT THE EDITOR:

Marilyn Dragowick first became interested in antiques when she helped clean out her grandfather's home as a young woman and then discovered the joys of visiting antiques shops.

After her mother retired, they began visiting auctions and sales and eventually their collecting pursuits lead to the opening of their own antiques shop in Minnesota.

In 1983 Marilyn had the opportunity to join the staff of The Antique Trader Price Guide as Assistant Editor and remained in this position until her retirement in 1994.

PHOTOGRAPHY CREDITS

Photographers who have contributed to this volume include: Dorothy Beckwith, Platteville, Wisconsin; and Joe Hallahan, Dubuque, Iowa.

For other photographs, artwork, data or permission to photograph in their shops, we sincerely express appreciation to the following auctioneers, galleries, museums, individuals and shops:

Mrs. Tom Bender, Lancaster, Ohio; Butterfield & Butterfield, San Francisco, California; Christie's, New York, New York; Collector's Auction Services, Oil City, Pennsylvania; Katrina Ford, Tulsa, Texas; Garth's Auctions, Inc., Delaware, Ohio; Neal Auction Company, New Orleans, Weatherford, Texas; Dave Rago Arts & Crafts, Lambertville, New Jersey; Robert W. Skinner, Inc., Bolton, Massachusetts; Sotheby's, New York, New York; Doug Sutherland, Greenbelt, Maryland; George and Judy Swan, Dubuque, Iowa; Treadway Gallery, Cincinnati, Ohio; Wendell August Forge, Grove City, Pennsylvania; and Dannie Woodard, Weatherford, Texas.

On The Cover:	Top left - a mid-19th century American brass candlestick; center left - American pewter tall teapot by Roswell Gleason, ca. 1830-40; bottom right - large shallow hammered aluminum bowl decorated with thistles and produced by Buenilum.
Back Cover:	Upper left - small 19th century copper teapot; lower right - late Victorian silver plate center bowl on footed base, ca. 1875-80.
Cover Design:	Jaro Sebek

Special Report:
ALUMINUM

by Dannie Woodard
Author of "Hammered Aluminum
Hand Wrought Collectibles," Book
One & Two

Once an object in great demand, the aluminum giftware of the 1930s and '40s faded into obscurity and lay dormant for forty years before it began to attract the attention of collectors. Both the appearance of the metal and its low price boosted its popularity, but today, some collectors pay hundreds of dollars for a choice item.

Aluminum giftware and accessories have been made by numerous processes. The predecessors of some of the popular collectibles of today were small items such as memo pad covers, combs, eyeglass holders and even large hairpins. Many of these pieces were decorated with delicate bright-cut designs of flowers or monograms.

In the late 1920s the Wendell August Forge, a manufacturer of decorative wrought iron, became interested in adapting aluminum to hand-wrought architectural use and to the production of giftwares. This production continues, interrupted only by World War II. The popularity of these items spurred the formation of numerous other companies, but most were short-lived.

There were probably several hundred makers of hammered aluminum but very few of them continued production after World War II. The wartime use of aluminum in defense products stopped its use for gift items and post-war mass-production affected its desirability. Only the companies using start-to-finish hand-production methods survived. The forges of Wendell August, Arthur Armour and DePoncea were survivors and their products are choice collectibles today.

The firms of Palmer-Smith, Continental, Rodney Kent, Cellini Craft and Everlast were other producers of some of today's most popular aluminum wares. Quality pieces made by other companies are being discovered and many of these are gaining in popularity.

The enduring beauty of the hand-wrought, decorative articles was created by a meticulous process involving skilled and talented artisans. Each design was cut by hand by die cutters who, working on steel with small chisels, produced finely detailed designs ranging from the very simple to the extremely intricate.

To make the desired articles, the craftsman started with a piece of aluminum cut to the approximate size and shape that was needed. The material was then positioned onto the selected die and hammered to produce the repoussé design which is so attractive on hand-forged articles. Further shaping and working was done on a wooden form and, for some designs, smoke or carbon blackening was used to create the pattern's dark patina.

In addition to the popular repoussé style, several other techniques were employed. One, an incised or carved design known as *intaglio,* is found on several lines of aluminum ware. This method was not as widely used as that of repoussé.

Other giftware took on a wide variety of appearances. Brightly polished pieces, spun items, machine-embossed patterns and anodized aluminum were, for a brief time, popular accessories for the home. Cast aluminum has also become popular with many collectors. Items marked *Bruce Fox* or *Bruce Cox* account for most of this type. In addition, furniture, such as chairs, have become very popular with some collectors.

Usually a company's chosen design was used on an entire line of accessories with a variation of a leaf or flower featured on the pieces. Also, the techniques used to produce the finished appearance, whether brightly polished or lustrously hand-rubbed, became an integral part of the look and feel of each company's product. Even the appearance of the hammer marks is distinctive.

Today's rising prices should encourage collectors to be as knowledgeable and careful as possible when considering their purchases. Pitting and scratches decrease the value. Loose handles or missing glassware are also important in determining the value. Often lids and inserts are mismatched and even made by different companies. Some aluminum giftware was made by using a simulated hammered look and had machine embossing. Lightweight polished aluminum was also used in some products and these pieces do not have the value of the items made of thicker aluminum, hand-hammered and with repoussé or intaglio patterns. Although aluminum giftware was probably never produced as abundantly as Depression or Carnival Glass, it is becoming apparent that its variety of styles and patterns are as numerous. At present prices vary from region to region and even from shop to shop, enabling the collector to "shop around" for purchases which will best fit their budget.

Note: Ms. Woodard's books are available from Aluminum Collector's Books, P. O. Box 1346, Weatherford, TX 76086. Book One is $20; Book Two is $24.95, plus $1.50 postage for the two.

Price listings:

Ashtray, hammered, large center flower, wrap-around platform base forms cigarette rests, Buenilum, 4½" d. **$22.00**

Ashtray, hammered, bittersweet decoration, Wendell August #60, 5½" d. **35.00**

Ashtray, cast, horse head decoration, Bruce Fox, 5½ x 5½"....**35.00**

Basket, polished aluminum,

frame w/stamped rose pattern, twisted handle, pottery insert, Farber & Shlevin, 7" d. **18.00**

Basket, polished w/stamped flowers, unmarked, 7" d. **7.00**

Basket, hammered, double-style, handle w/square knot, fern & flowers decoration, Canterbury Arts, 9" w. **18.00**

Basket, polished aluminum frame w/stamped rose design, fluted, etched glass insert, double aluminum strand handle, twisted in center, Farber & Shlevin, 9½" d. **27.00**

Basket, hammered, twisted handle, sailing ship decoration, Hand Forged #29, 10" d. **12.00**

Basket, hammered, china plate insert, morning glories on frame, square w/rolled sides, looped diagonally-placed handle, Wrought Farberware, 12" w. **38.00**

Basket, hammered aluminum frame w/flower clusters, Paden City glass insert, looped handle, fluted edge, Cromwell, 14" d.....................................**35.00**

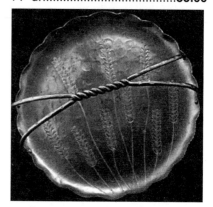

Basket with Wheat Design

Basket, flat round form w/upturned fluted rim, double handle w/twist design, wheat decoration, Milcraft, 14" d. ......**25.00** (Illustration)

Basket, bread, hammered, oval w/twisted handle, duck on pond decoration, Cromwell **12.00**

Aluminum Beverage Server & Stand

Beverage server, cover & stand, tapering cylindrical body w/wide upturned loop side handles & spigot near the base, low domed cover w/large loop handle, on a separate ring base w/twisted strap angled legs curving in to support a center burner, Buenilum, overall 20" h. ....**95.00** (Illustration)

Bowl, covered, hammered, cast aluminum "baker man" on cover, Cellini Craft..................**85.00**

Bowl, hammered, blackbird & fledglings decoration, De Ponceau, 5¾" d. **22.00**

Bowl, hammered, looped handles, Buenilum, 6" d. **8.00**

Bowl, machine-embossed pattern, Wrought Aluminum, 7" d..**7.00**

Bowl, simulated hammer marks, mums decoration, Federal Silver Co., 7½" d. **8.00**

Bowl, lightly scalloped cupped rim w/hammered design, small yellow & tan pottery insert in center decorated w/a crowing

Aluminum Bowl with Pottery Insert

rooster, Modern Hand Made #147, 7½" d. ....**25.00 to 35.00** (Illustration)

Bowl, hammered, Big Horn sheep decoration, Hand Forged #2, 8¾" d. **25.00**

Bowl, hammered, intaglio band of stylized dogwood, Everlast, 9" d..**10.00**

Bowl, hammered, Bromeliad-like flowers, Buenilum, 9¼" d. **15.00**

Shallow Bowl with Petal & Loop Design

Bowl, wide shallow form w/engraved four-petal & line loop decoration, Canterbury Arts, 11" d. ....**25.00** (Illustration)

Bowl, hammered, footed, flat, scalloped edge w/tiny berries between scallops, Cellini Craft, 11½" d. **85.00**

Bowl, hammered, fruits decoration, Everlast, 12½" d. **18.00**

Bowl, hammered, scalloped edge, oak leaves & acorns decoration, Everlast, 13" d. **22.00**

Bowl, hammered, hunter scene, LA Handwrought (bell symbol), 15" d. **95.00**

Bowl, hammered, petal design w/grape cluster in center, Wendell August #807 ....**85.00**

Bowl, polished, repoussé flower design in center, butterfly handles, Hand Forged **12.00**

Book ends, hammered, chopped corners, daisy decoration, Wendell August, pr.....**125.00**

Book ends, hammered, applied horseshoe, Everlast, pr. **85.00**

Box, cov., hammered, square w/sturdy hinged cover, schooner decoration, Arthur Armour **95.00**

Box, cov., cigarette, hammered, applied leaves & rosette on cover, World.............................**28.00**

Box, cov., cigarette, hammered, pine decoration, Wendell August...................................**85.00**

Bread tray, hammered, anchor decoration, Everlast **18.00**

Bread tray, hammered, chrysanthemum decoration, applied leaves, Continental.....**20.00**

Bread tray, hammered, grape clusters, handles w/leaves, World....................................**15.00**

Bread tray, machine-embossed, pansy decoration, National Silver Co. **8.00**

Bread tray, hammered, scal-

loped edges, tulip decoration, Rodney Kent **15.00**

Bread tray, hammered, wild rose decoration, Continental ...**15.00**

Bread tray, polished, stamped wild rose decoration, unmarked **7.00**

Butter dish, cov., polished, glass insert for ¼ lb., looped finial, Buenilum.......................**25.00**

Butter dish, cov., polished, round w/glass insert, looped finial on domed cover, undertray w/beaded edge, Buenilum, 6½" d. **27.00**

Butter dish, cov., machine-embossed chrysanthemum on aluminum cover, floret finial, pressed glass base, Forman Family **15.00**

Butter dish, cov., polished, stamped Bali Bamboo patt., crisscross patterned glass insert for ¼ lb., Everlast #B55......................................**22.00**

Butter dish, cov., deep glass dish in crisscross design, aluminum undertray & cover w/tulip finial, Rodney Kent.......**20.00**

Candlestick, hammered, scalloped base, Everlast, 4" w., 3½" h................................**25.00**

Candlestick, hammered, flower sprigs, Findley, 5" w., 3½" h....................................**20.00**

Candlestick, applied leaves on stem, Continental, 4½" h.........**25.00**

Candlestick, hammered, deep saucer base, twisted stem, Wendell August, 6" w., 8" h.....**75.00**

Candlestick, anodized (polished), crystal ball, Kensington **35.00**

Candlesticks, hammered, holds three candles on a thick bar w/large center loop, Buenilum, 14" w., 6" h., pr. **75.00**

Candlesticks, two-light, hammered, rectangular base w/scrolled band, Wendell August #840, pr....................**135.00**

Candlesticks, hammered, double platform base, three cupped lotus leaves, holds one candle, Wendell August, pr. **175.00**

Candy dish, cov., hammered aluminum cover w/chrysanthemum & floret, footed pressed glass base dish, Continental, 6" d. **45.00**

Candy dish, cov., hammered aluminum cover w/flower sprigs & "spoon handle" curl, footed etched glass base dish, Buenilum, 6" d. **45.00**

Candy dish, cov., hammered aluminum holder & cover w/applied ribbon decoration, tulip finial, ribbon & flower decorative handles extending into feet, divided glass insert dish, Rodney Kent, 6" d. **35.00**

Candy dish, cov., hammered aluminum cover, fruits decoration, pear finial, thick glass base dish, unmarked Everlast **45.00**

Candy dish, open, square, hammered, curled side handle, flowers decoration, Kraftware, 4½" w. **6.00**

Casserole, cov., hammered, Bali Bamboo patt., baking dish insert, bamboo stylized cover finial, Everlast, 7" d. **15.00**

Casserole, cov., hammered, leafy vine & open pea pod cover finial, baking dish insert, Everlast #1038, 7" d. **15.00**

Casserole, cov., hammered, footed ring-style caddy, vegetables & wheat decoration, ridged fan-shaped handles & cover finial, Pyrex glass insert, Crown, 8½" d. **35.00**
(Illustration: top next column)

Aluminum Covered Casserole Dish

Casserole, cov., hammered, butterfly & dogwood decoration & ring handle on cover, baking dish insert, grooved handles, Arthur Armour, 9" d. **125.00**

Casserole, cov., hammered, intaglio design of stylized leaves & flowers, flattened cover knob, side handles, baking dish insert, Everlast, 9¼" d. **15.00**

Casserole, cover & undertray, hammered, Bittersweet patt., twisted bar handle on cover, baking dish insert, Wendell August #735, 9 x 13½" undertray, 3 pcs. **125.00**

Chafing dish, cov., hammered, grape cluster design around cover w/beaded knob surrounded w/leaves, baking dish insert, Everlast, 10" d. **35.00**

Chafing dish, cov., hammered, tulip decoration, decorative ribbon & flower handles & legs, baking dish insert, Rodney Kent..**27.00**

Chafing dish, cov., hammered, black handle & knob finial on cover, Spain **12.00**

Coaster, hammered, tropical fish decoration, Wendell August......................................**15.00**

Coasters, hammered, rose decoration, in caddy w/curled handle, Everlast, set of 6 ....**25.00**

Coasters, hammered, spiral design, Everlast, set of 6.........**18.00**

Coasters, polished, beaded edge, in caddy w/double looped handle, Buenilum, set of 8 ....**30.00**

Coasters, embossed chrysan- themum pattern, in caddy w/decorative leaves, Continental, set of 8 ....**35.00**

Coasters, embossed tulip motif, in caddy w/decorative ribbon & flower design handle, Rodney Kent, the set............................**35.00**

Cocktail shaker, cov., double looped finial on cover, Buenilum, 9½" h......................**85.00**

Cocktail Shaker with Chrysanthemum Design

Cocktail shaker, cov., chrysan- themum decoration, pouring spout on shoulder, handle w/decorative leaf, Continental #530, 12" h..............................**50.00** (Illustration)

Condiment server, hammered, apple blossom design on undertray & slotted cover on glass jar, Wendell August #592 ....**35.00**

Condiment server, hammered caddy w/center handle in rib- bon & flower design, two cov- ered jars w/spoons, Rodney Kent..**35.00**

Condiment server, hammered, Ferris-wheel style, three "baskets" holding dishes, Everlast **55.00**

Condiment server, hammered, revolving-type, cruets & covered jars in apple design, twisted center handle, Continental.............................**45.00**

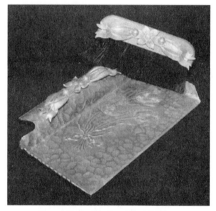

Crumber Set with Tulips

Crumber set: brush & rectangu- lar tray; the tray w/a rolled han- dle w/applied blossom & leaf sprig & an engraved tulip clus- ter in the tray, the brush w/a wooden handle applied w/a blossom & leaf sprig, Rodney Kent #444, tray 3¼ x 8½", 2 pcs. ....**25.00 to 35.00** (Illustration)

Crumber Set with Wild Roses

Crumber set: tray & scoop; the two pieces forming a disc, the larger tray section w/a tight curl handle, stamped wild rose sprig decoration, the scoop w/a long curved bar handle, Continental #725, 2 pcs. ....**25.00 to 35.00** (Illustration)

Crumber set: tray & brush; hammered, looped handles, Buenilum, the set **35.00**

Crumber set: tray w/hanging brush; hammered, rose decoration, Everlast, the set **35.00**

Crumber set, two-piece, hammered, scalloped edges, grape decoration on each piece, Everlast, the set **35.00**

Small Dish with Flamingo

Dish, shallow round sides with upturned rim, centered by a figural cast aluminum flamingo, Palmer-Smith #71, dish 6¼" d., flamingo 4" h. ....**70.00 to 90.00** (Illustration)

Dresser set: two covered glass dishes on tray, covers w/tulip finials, ribbon & flower design caddy handles extend to form feet; hammered, Rodney Kent #403, tray 6 x 12", the set **45.00**

Drink mixer, hammered, one-piece construction, large hole for long-handled stirring spoon, Everlast, 7" h. **60.00**

Gravy boat on attached undertray, hammered, wrapped handle w/decorative leaf, w/aluminum ladle, chrysanthemum decoration, Continental #610 ....**35.00**

Gravy boat on attached undertray, w/ladle, hammered, looped handles, Buenilum.......**35.00**

Ice bucket, cov., hammered, side handles, roses decoration, hammered ball cover knob, Everlast, 9½" h. **45.00**

Ice bucket, cov., hammered, handled, cover w/applied leaves under knob, Everlast Ice Cooler (with polar bear), #5008 ....**25.00**

Covered Ice Bucket with Loop Handles

Ice bucket, cov., wide slightly tapering cylindrical body w/decorative raised band around the rim, loop handles at sides, low domed cover w/wide ring finial, Keystone #115..........**35.00 to 45.00** (Illustration)

Ice bucket, cov., hammered, tulip cover finial, ribbon & flower handles, Rodney Kent.......................................**35.00**

Ice bucket, cov., polished, footed, large looped cover finial, Knight Kraft **28.00**

Ice bucket, cov., hammered, thin aluminum, handled, Nassco **10.00**

Ice bucket, open, hammered, chrysanthemum decoration, handles w/leaves, Continental #504 ....**55.00**

Open Ice Bucket with Willow Design

Ice bucket, open, cylindrical body w/curved rim tabs supporting a ring, embossed bands of willow leaves down the sides, Wendell August Forge, 7" d., 8" h. ....**100.00 to 150.00** (Illustration)

Jewelry, bracelet, hammered, zinnia link design, Wendell August....................................**55.00**

Jewelry, bracelet, stamped w/Western motif on each section, unmarked **55.00**

Jewelry, brooch, hammered, pine design, Wendell August, 1½ x 2" **45.00**

Jewelry, cuff bracelet, hammered, flowers & leaves, unmarked **25.00**

Lamp, hammered aluminum in zinnia design, silk shade, Wendell August....................**650.00**

Lamp, hammered aluminum w/walnut decoration, aluminum shade, Wendell August **650.00**

Magazine rack, hammered, thick aluminum, world map decoration, Arthur Armour.....**250.00**

Match box cover, hammered, kitchen size, Bali Bamboo patt., Everlast **35.00**

Match box cover, hammered, "penny box" size, Wendell August.....................................**35.00**

Match box cover, polished, kitchen-size, stylized fish & water design, Palmer-Smith....**55.00**

Match folder cover, polished, ducks decoration, unmarked.....**5.00**

Meat server, hammered, well & tree-type, curved band supports each end, floret & leaves decoration, Continental #544, 11 x 15½" **65.00**

Napkin holder, hammered, decorative ribbon & flower band forms feet, Rodney Kent **27.00**

Napkin holder, hammered, trefoil shape, roses decoration, Everlast **20.00**

Napkin holder, polished, machine-embossed roses, World....................................**15.00**

Napkin holder, polished, cactus decoration, Farber & Shlevin **12.00**

Nut bowl & picks, hammered, fruits & flowers decoration, looped handles, pedestal base, Cromwell, 10" d., the set........**27.00**

Nut Set with Fruit & Flower Design

Nut bowl & picks, wide flat-bottomed bowl w/low, incurved sides raised on a flaring domed pedestal foot, center post for nut picks, looped side handles, overall stamped fruit & flower decoration on bowl, Hand

Finished Aluminum,
the set........................**27.00 to 35.00**
(Illustration)

Nut Dish with Chrysanthemum

Nut dish, oblong two-section
type w/tapering scalloped &
fluted rim, stamped large
chrysanthemum decoration,
center arched leaf handle
w/blossom finial, Continental
#754, 5½ x 8"..........................**25.00**
(Illustration)

Patio cart, hammered, intaglio
leaves decoration, complete
w/serving pieces, wheels &
push handle, Everlast **650.00**

Pitcher, hammered, intaglio
band of stylized dogwood,
double twisted handle of large
rods, Everlast, 6" h..................**35.00**

Pitcher, w/ice guard spout,
hammered, Bali Bamboo patt.,
Everlast **55.00**

Pitcher, plain baluster-form
body w/angled shoulder tapering to a flaring rim w/curled
strap ice guard at the spout,
flaring domed foot, strap handle w/applied leaf at top &
base, Cromwell,
8½" h. ....**27.00 to 35.00**
(Illustration: top next column)

Pitcher w/ice guard spout, hammered, tulip decoration, tiny
tulips on ice guard, ribbon-
styled handle, Rodney Kent **45.00**

Pitcher w/ice guard spout,

Pitcher with Leaves on Handle

hammered, pine decoration,
Wendell August #760 ....**85.00**

Pitcher, hammered, flared at
top, Everlast **25.00**

Pitcher, hammered, mums decoration, handle w/leaf decora-
tion, Continental **45.00**

Pitcher, hammered, wild rose
decoration, Continental **35.00**

Pitcher, hammered, grooved
bulbous form, berry & leaf
decoration on handle, Cellini
Craft **75.00**

Pitcher, hammered, applied floret & leaves on body, World....**45.00**

Pitcher, polished, straight sides,
twisted handle, Buenilum **15.00**

Pitcher, hammered, looped &
twisted handle, Buenilum **35.00**

Pitcher, hammered, thin aluminum, grooved band around
center, Italy **10.00**

Punch bowl & ladle, hammered, grapes decoration,
Wendell August **350.00**

Punch bowl, tray & ladle, hammered w/blue crock liner, ring
handles, Keystone **125.00**

Punch bowl, tray & ladle, deep

Wendell August Punch Bowl & Ladle

rounded bowl on footring, stamped bar band around the rim, fleur-de-lis decoration in center of bowl & tray, Wendell August #517, bowl 14¼" d., tray 18" d., 3 pcs. ....**425.00** (Illustration)

Punch set: bowl, ladle & glass cups; hammered, pedestal base, hammered cup hooks, Everlast, the set **225.00**

Punch set: bowl, cups, tray & bottle opener; spun aluminum, bamboo rail on tray, Russel Wright, bowl 11½" d., 6¼" h., the set **1,250.00**

Two-part Relish Server

Relish server, two-part, shallow rectangular trays w/serrated flaring edges, each fitted w/a two-part fluted glass insert, trays joined by a wide arched flower-stamped pierced strap handle, unmarked Rodney Kent ....**30.00 to 35.00** (Illustration)

Server, cov., shallow base w/wide, flattened petal-form rim, domed cover w/arched handle flanked by leaves & a stamped design of bands of

Covered Server with Acorn Design

leaves & acorn clusters, Continental #512, 11" d.....**35.00 to 45.00** (Illustration)

Server with Baskets

Server, carrousel-type w/four baskets suspended on chains, disc foot, originally came w/four 10 oz. Fire King glass inserts w/scalloped edges, Everlast, 13½" w., 10½" h........**45.00 to 55.00** (Illustration)

Server, shallow rectangular tray w/forked overhead handle from end to end, fitted w/six squared pressed glass dishes w/a fruit design in the bottom, Keystone #606, 10 x 14½", the set ....**45.00** (Illustration: top next page)

Serving set: tray & utensils; the wide flattened rectangular tray w/curved edges & fluted corners centered by a rectangular

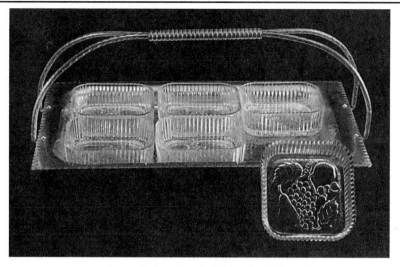

Long Server with Glass Inserts

blue pottery insert, tray decorated w/a pine decoration, w/a
matching spatula utensil &
salad serving fork, Wendell
August #525, tray 14 x 24",
the set..................**100.00 to 150.00**
(Illustration: below)

Serving utensil, gravy ladle,
polished, double looped han-
dle, unmarked Buenilum **15.00**

Serving utensil, pie or cake
server, hammered, twisted
double looped handle,
unmarked Buenilum **35.00**

Serving utensil, punch ladle,

polished, twisted, double
looped handle, unmarked
Buenilum **55.00**

Serving utensils, salad fork &
spoon, wooden w/decorative
aluminum inset on handle in an
Everlast pattern, unmarked.....**20.00**

Serving utensils, salad fork &
spoon, wooden w/bamboo
design section at each end,
unmarked **25.00**

Serving utensils, salad fork &
spoon, hammered, twisted
handles, unmarked Wendell
August....................................**45.00**

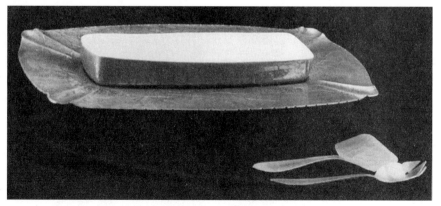

Server with Utensils

Silent Butler with Wild Rose

Silent butler, squared dish w/rounded corners, low domed hinged cover w/stamped wild rose decoration & curved thumb rest, strap side handle w/curled end, Crown Aluminum, 3¼" sq. plus handle ....**18.00 to 22.00** (Illustration)

Silent butler, oval, hammered, flower cluster decoration, Henry & Miller, 4½ x 6" **15.00**

Silent butler, oval, hammered, fruits decoration, Everlast, 7 x 9" **25.00**

Silent butler, round, hammered, bird on twig decoration, N. S. Co., 6" d. **18.00**

Silent butler, round, hammered, floral bouquet w/roses decoration, Canterbury Arts, 6" d. **25.00**

Silent butler, round, hammered, rose decoration, Everlast, 6" d. **15.00**

Silent butler, round, polished, intaglio design of roses, World, 6¼" d. **12.00**

Silent butler, round, hammered, apple blossoms decoration, thick handle, notched edge, Wendell August #95, 7" d. **45.00**

Silent butler, round, hammered, tulip decoration, Rodney Kent, 7½" d. **18.00**

Silent butler, round, hammered,

wooden handle, Corduroy patt., Continental #1505, 8" d. **18.00**

Silent butler, hammered, cattails decoration, unmarked, 5 x 6" **15.00**

Smoking set: hammered undertray, ashtrays & cov. cigarette box; blue pottery box, bittersweet decoration, Wendell August #75, the set **150.00**

Smoking stand, hammered, ducks pattern on ashtray, "bubble" protrusions on domed base, twisted stand & ring around top, Wendell August #926, 22¼" h. **275.00**

Sugar, creamer & tray, hammered, Bali Bamboo patt. on each piece, Everlast #B21 on tray, 3 pcs. **35.00**

Sugar, creamer & tray, hammered, chrysanthemum decoration on sugar & creamer, plain tray w/scalloped ends, Continental #515, 3 pcs. **35.00**

Sugar, creamer & tray, hammered, plain sugar & creamer, grape decoration on tray, Everlast, 3 pcs. **28.00**

Sugar, creamer & tray, plain, World, 3 pcs. **20.00**

Rare Wendell August Forge Table

Table, round removable tray top w/pine bough decoration, fitted in a twisted ring frame on square legs w/twisted sections joined by a cross-stretcher, Wendell August Forge #925......................**525.00 to 575.00**
(Illustration: bottom previous page)

Tidbit tray, polished, floral decoration, side handle, Hammercraft **7.00**

Tidbit tray, machine-embossed, tiered, unmarked **10.00**

Tidbit tray, hammered, tiered w/three trays, grape decoration, center stand w/ring handle, Everlast, 14" h. **22.00**

Toast rack, hammered, wheat decoration, Wendell August #709 ....**65.00**

Toast rack w/two each covered butter & jam jars, hammered, center toast rack, Rodney Kent.......................................**45.00**

Tray, hammered, coach & four decoration, Clayton Sheasley, 7½ x 17½" **65.00**

Tray, hammered, floral decoration, Clayton Sheasley, 7½ x 17½".......................................**30.00**

Tray, tab handle, hammered, heron & marsh scene, Leroy DeLoss, 8 x 13½".....................**25.00**

Tray, hammered, polo players decoration w/trophy inscribed with winners' names, dated "4-23-39", Wendell August, 8 x 23" **95.00**

Tray, flattened bullet-form w/slightly curved rim, notched at one end, embossed w/a large poppy blossom, Wendell August Forge #523, 8½ x 18"....................**75.00 to 85.00**
(Illustration: bottom previous column)

Tray, hammered, intaglio design of stylized dogwood, ribbed tab handles, Everlast, 9 x 11" **18.00**

Tray, grooved bar handles, hammered, scenic design of horse-back riders & lake, Arthur Armour, 9 x 13" **95.00**

Tray, handled, hammered, nautical motif, Lehman, 9 x 14".......**25.00**

Tray, tab handles, hammered, tropical fish decoration, Everlast, 9 x 14" **35.00**

Tray, tab handles, hammered, Bittersweet patt., Wendell August, 9½ x 14"....................**55.00**

Tray, hammered, small hand-stamped flowers, Palmer-Smith #33, 9½ x 20" **125.00**

Tray, rope pattern, ring handles w/small balls, hammered, Palmer-Smith #18, 10" d. **95.00**

Tray, handled, hammered, gold anodized, chessmen decoration, Arthur Armour, 10 x 16"...**45.00**

Tray, tab handles, hammered, oak leaves decoration, Wrought Farberware, 10½ x 13½" **14.00**

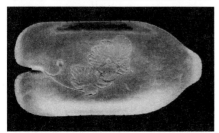

Tray with Poppy Decoration

Tray with Water Lilies

Handled Tray with Scene of Deer

Tray, oval, incised looping band of stylized water lilies around the rim, Palmer-Smith #82L, 10½ x 13½" ....**65.00 to 75.00** (Illustration: bottom previous page)

Tray, rectangular w/rounded corners & grooved end handles w/leaf ends, shallow heavily hammered interior w/scene of stag & doe, Continental Silver Co. #523, 10½ x 14½" ....**45.00 to 55.00** (Illustration: above)

Tray, handled, hammered, chrysanthemum decoration, handles w/decorative leaves, Continental #524, 11 x 22"......**45.00**

Tray, handled, hammered, bird & flowers decoration, N. S. Co., 11 x 16" **27.00**

Tray, looped handles, hammered, apple blossoms decoration, fluted sides, Federal Silver Co., 11½ x 15½" **25.00**

Tray, handled, machine-embossed hunt scene, crimped edges, Beautyline Designed Aluminum, 11½ x 16½" **15.00**

Tray, machine-embossed flowers, Wrought Aluminum, 12" d..**12.00**

Tray, square, hammered, rose bouquet decoration, Everlast, 12" w. **20.00**

Square Tray with Siesta Scene

Tray, square w/rounded corners, stamped scene of Mexican peasant asleep under a palm tree, wide border w/curved paneling, Everlast, 12" w........................**20.00 to 30.00** (Illustration)

Tray with Ornate Landscape Scene

Tray, oval, smooth, stamped wild roses decoration, fluted, unmarked, 12¼" l. **10.00**

Tray, looped handles, hammered, lake scene w/dock, fluted edge, Cromwell, 12½ x 14½" **18.00**

Tray, ribbed fanned end handles, rectangular w/cut corners, ornate detailed landscape scene w/mountains, a lake, trees & flying birds, Continental #555, 12½ x 18¼" ....**65.00** (Illustration: above)

Tray, bar handles, hammered, hunt scene, Keystone, 13 x 17" **45.00**

Tray, twisted handles, hammered, Wild Rose patt., fluted edge, Continental #703, 13½" d. **20.00**

Tray, tab handles, hammered, saguara cactus decoration, Wendell August, 13¼ x 21"...**195.00**

Tray, hammered, daisies or sunflowers decoration, DePonceau, 14" d. **35.00**

Tray, handled, hammered, tulip decoration, Rodney Kent, 14" d......................................**22.00**

Tray with Bowl of Fruit

Tray, round w/looped sides handles w/leaf terminals, center w/embossed fruit wreath framing a bowl of fruit, Cromwell, 14" d. ....**27.00 to 35.00** (Illustration)

Tray, flat handles w/flowers, simulated hammer marks, machine-embossed roses, World, 14 x 20".......................**20.00**

Tray, spun, raffia-wrapped hand grips, Russel Wright, 14½" d....................................**65.00**

Tray, grooved bar handles, hammered, hunt scene, Arthur Armour, 14¼ x 21½" **195.00**

Tray, handled, hammered, Bali

Bamboo patt., Everlast, 14½ x
20½".....................................**45.00**

Tray, anodized, highly polished,
compass design in brass,
Kensington, 15" d...................**37.00**

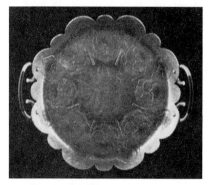

Tray with Ring of Pansies

Tray, wrapped handles, hammered, scalloped edge, ring of
large pansies, Continental
#852, 15" l..............................**65.00**
(Illustration)

Tray, looped handle w/leaf decoration, hammered, fruits decoration, Cromwell, 15½" d.......**25.00**

Tray, double handles curved to
side w/flower decoration, hammered frame w/berry stems,
American Limoges plate insert,

Wrought Farberware,
16½" d...................................**45.00**

Tray, loop end handles, oval
w/upturned scalloped rim, large
stamped oval wreath of leafy
branches, fern leaves, berries
& blossoms, signed "C.C.
Pflanz," Canterbury Arts,
17 x 22"....................**50.00 to 75.00**
(Illustration: below)

Tray, handled, hammered, oak
leaf & acorn decoration,
Continental #520, 17¼" l........**35.00**

Trivet, oval, hammered, cork
pads, leaves decoration,
Everlast, 5½ x 7".......................**8.00**

Trivet, hammered, cork pads,
ivy decoration, Everlast,
8 x 11"....................................**10.00**

Trivet, hammered, cork pads,
Tapestry patt., Arthur Armour,
8½ x 11"..................................**20.00**

Trivet, hammered, cork pads,
wildflowers decoration,
Everlast, 10" d.........................**12.00**

Tumbler, hammered, applied
floret & leaves, World, 20 oz...**10.00**

Tumbler, hammered, bamboo
joint design, Everlast.................**8.00**

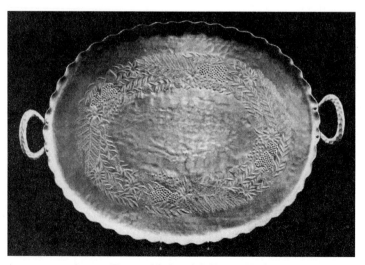

Large Tray with Leaf & Berry Wreath

Tumbler, hammered, beaded
base, Buenilum **6.00**

Tumbler, hammered, footed,
chrysanthemum decoration,
Continental **12.00**

Tumbler, stemmed base,
hammered, lightweight,
unmarked **6.00**

Tumbler, hammered, plain,
Buenilum **5.00**

Tumbler, hammered, plain,
Everlast **5.00**

Tumbler, hammered, plain,
flared, Leumas **4.00**

Tumbler, spun, wheat decora-
tion, West Bend.........................**4.00**

Vase, hammered, fluted top,
World, 8" h. **45.00**

Vase, hammered, chrysanthemum, Continental #630,
10" h.......................................**55.00**

Vase, hammered, hollyhock decoration, Wendell August #858,
12" h.....................................**150.00**

Vase, hammered, urn-shaped
w/handles, World #207,
12" h.....................................**125.00**

Vase in Aluminum Frame with Ducks

Vase, hammered, blue pottery in
aluminum holder w/flying ducks
& marsh scene, Wendell
August #840 ....**325.00**
(Illustration: bottom previous column)

Wastebasket, hammered, fluted
top, apple blossoms decora-
tion, Wendell August #900 ......**95.00**

**Wastebasket with Bittersweet
Decoration**

Wastebasket, hammered, oval,
Bittersweet patt., folded
grooved top rim, Wendell
August Forge **150.00**
(Illustration)

Wastebasket, hammered, oval,
dogwood & butterfly decora-
tion, Arthur Armour................**135.00**

Wastebasket, hammered, oval,
floral bouquet decoration,
Canterbury Arts.....................**195.00**

Wastebasket, hammered, hawthorne decoration, Everlast **75.00**

Wastebasket, hammered, lightweight, water lilies stamped
design, West Bend.................**25.00**

Wastebasket, hammered, wildflowers decoration, Everlast....**85.00**

Wine cooler & stand, a tapering
cylindrical container w/flared &
ruffled rim, angled side han-

Wine Cooler & Stand

dles, fitted in a ring support on a tall standard above a disc over four outswept supports on a ring foot, applied panels of grapes under the handles, sometimes marked "Everlast Ice Cooler," Everlast #5005, cooler 8½" d., 9½" h., overall 34" h., 2 pcs. ....**150.00** (Illustration)

BRASS

In the early days brass was referred to as a 'factitious' or artificial metal, meaning it was an alloy, not an element. Brass is an alloy of copper and zinc; each must be mined and refined before the alloy can be produced. Prior to 1871, brass was made by combining copper with calamine, which is the ore of zinc as metallurgists did not know how to extract the zinc from the ore. The refining process was patented in England in 1871. This discovery did much to aid in the production of brass as we know it.

Braziers and brassfounders were important members of the community as they were responsible for creating many of the utilitarian and decorative items used in daily living. Brassware was made of sheet metal or it was cast in a mold. Early brass ingots were hammered into sheets; however, with the inception of rolling mills in America in the eighteenth century, the work was made much simpler.

The work of the brassfounder was done on a small scale, perhaps in a 'smelting hut,' which suggests a rather unsubstantial set-up. It would probably consist of a furnace with a chimney to carry off the smoke, a pair of bellows and a hearth where the fire is made. It is this hearth that distinguishes the furnace from a forge. In the middle of the hearth is a small cavity about ten to twelve inches wide. It is divided in two by an iron grate; the upper part holds the crucible and fuel, the lower portion receives the ashes. Dry wood was used as the fuel, and when the maximum temperature was reached, the crucible full of metal was placed in the middle covered by an earthen lid. When the metal reached the molten state it would be poured into a mold. After the article was removed from the mold it would need finishing, such as the removal of rough edges. The final step would be the polishing. Some items were signed by the maker but, as a rule, they are unsigned.

Some items that were made in brass are andirons, fireplace tongs and shovels, pots, pans and kettles, various types of tools, bells, buttons and buckles, furniture hardware, door knockers, bed and foot warmers, candlesticks, candle sconces, teakettles and many, many other useful and ornamental items.

Price Listings:

Alms dish, circular w/deep well, the central embossed flowerhead surrounded by a verse, Flanders, 17th c., 16" d. (minor wear) **$1,150.00**

Alms dish, circular w/deep well, repoussé w/a central flower-head surrounded by calligraphy, Flanders, 17th c., 18" d. (worn) **805.00**

Andirons, acorn finial above ringed cylindrical stem, spurred arch supports, penny feet, 13½" h., pr...........................**275.00**

Andirons, ring- and ball-turned standard w/conical top ending in ringed finial, spurred arch supports ending in ball feet, 14¾" h., pr............................**137.50**

Andirons, belted ball w/crown & knob finial, spurred legs w/pad feet, dark patina, 17¾" h., pr...**385.00**

Andirons, reeded acorn finial above a reeded vasiform shaft over a faceted cylindrical plinth, on spurred arched legs w/ball feet, 18½" h., pr....................**288.00**

Andirons, Neoclassical-style, urn finial above goat's hoof feet, 18½" h., pr....................**546.50**

Brass Andirons Ca. 1800

Andirons, acorn finial above a ring-turned urn embellished w/bow-tied bellflower garlands above a rectangular molded plinth embossed w/a spread-wing eagle holding an olive branch & a bunch of arrows beneath an arch of fourteen stars, on arched spurred legs w/ball-and-claw feet, probably Philadelphia, Pennsylvania, ca. 1800, 19" h., pr.............**2,530.00** (Illustration)

Andirons, compressed ball & baluster finial above a spherical turned standard w/ring-turned mid-band, on arched legs w/ball feet, 19½" h., pr...**184.00**

Andirons, ovoid finial on a hexagonal shaft w/scrolled legs & ball feet, George III period, England, late 18th c., 25½" h., pr......................................**2,300.00**

Andirons, acorn finial above an urn on a square molded base over a tapering columnar shaft & molded rectangular plinth, on arched spurred legs w/penny feet, possibly Philadelphia, Pennsylvania, 1790-1815, 26⅜" h., pr.........................**1,495.00**

Ashtray, the central boss impressed w/the Russian Imperial Eagle & inscribed in Cyrillic "War, 1914" & "K. Fabergé," Fabergé, Russia, ca. 1914, 4¼" d. **805.00**

Ashtray, the central boss decorated w/the Imperial Russian Eagle & inscribed in Cyrillic "War, 1914" & "K. Fabergé," Fabergé, Moscow, Russia, ca. 1914, 4¾" d. **1,150.00**

Bed warmer, lid w/tooled & punched decoration, turned wood handle, 40" l.................**203.50**

Bed warmer, tooled bird design on lid, wooden handle, 42" l. (repair in pan at ferule & tab handle added to lid) **165.00**

Bedwarmer, the pan w/pierced & engraved lid, turned handle w/worn original graining, 42½" l. **440.00**

Bedwarmer, the lid centering an engraved bird surrounded by a

Early Fireplace Bellows

ring of pierced design, w/turned wood handle, overall 43½" l. **330.00**

Bellows, fireplace-type, the wheel-shaped handle w/fan mechanism below continuing to form a faceted cannon-form cylindrical air spout, mounted on a pine platform now painted brown, America or England, 1740-70, 30½" h.................**1,495.00** (Illustration: above)

Book ends, disc-form on rectangular base, decorated w/a hammered geometric design, original patina, impressed "Made By The Jarvie Shop," 5½" h., pr..............................**467.50**

Box, cov., honor box for dispensing tobacco, a coin is inserted to open the compartment allowing access to fill a pipe, indistinct inscription on lid "Red Lion Inn ...," England, 9¼" h. **1,100.00**

Brouillotte lamp, Louis XVI-style, two-light, the circular beaded base supporting a fluted standard w/two curved arms, w/adjustable red tole shade, France, late 19th c., 21" h. (electrified) **3,450.00**

Brouillotte lamp, Louis XVI-style, three-light, the circular basketwoven beaded base supporting a fluted standard w/three curved adjustable arms, w/a white painted tole adjustable shade, France, late 19th c., 24" h. (electrified, lacking finial)..............................**2,760.00**

Candlestick, round twelve-sided

base, knob stem, slender candle nozzle w/raised rings, 4½" h.......................................**550.00**

Candlestick, saucer base, bulbous standard & long slender candle nozzle, 5" h. **192.50**

Candlestick, square base on short heart-shaped feet, baluster stem, 5½" h. **577.50**

Candlestick, octagonal base, bulbous turned standard, slender candle nozzle, 5⅝" h.......**247.50**

Candlestick, square base & panelled stem, 6¼" h. **220.00**

Candlestick, octagonal base & baluster stem, tall slender candle nozzle, 6¼" h...................**247.50**

Candlestick, octagonal base w/bulbous turned matching standard, slender candle nozzle, 6⅞" h. **302.50**

Candlestick, flat scalloped base supporting knopped standard, w/scalloped lip, Queen Anne period **440.00**

Candlestick, Queen Anne style, scalloped base, ring-turned standard, base stamped "Geo. Grove," 7¼" h. **990.00**

Candlestick, dish base, ball-shaped connectors beneath-slender cylindrical stem w/push-up, 7½" h. **170.50**

Candlestick, pricket-type, stepped circular foot supporting a turned stem w/medial drip-pan, Holland, late 17th - early 18th c., 9½" h ....**431.00** (Illustration: center, top next page)

English & Dutch Brass Candlesticks

Candlestick, tripod base w/paw feet & baluster stem w/mid drip-pan, 11½" h....................**330.00**

Candlestick, triangular base w/paw feet, baluster stem w/mid drip-pan, 12½" h. **302.50**

Candlesticks, conical domed square base supporting a reeded & urn-turned cylindrical stem w/a shaped bobeche, England or America, 19th c., 6" h., pr..................................**115.00**

Candlesticks, disc base, cylindrical standard w/push-up, 6⅛" h., pr..............................**495.00**

Candlesticks, scalloped base, banded globular shaft, ring-turned nozzle, 6⅞" h., pr.......................................**2,310.00**

Candlesticks, square base w/cut out corners, knopped stem & scalloped lip, Queen Anne period, 7⅜" h., pr. **660.00**

Candlesticks, scalloped circular base supporting a cylindrical standard w/flaring center & ejector mechanism, Chippendale, late 18th c., 7½" h., pr.......................................**1,840.00**

Candlesticks, stepped domed base, ring-turned standard w/wide mid drip-pan, polished, 8¼" h., pr., (some damage & soldered repairs) **330.00**

Candlesticks, stepped square base below a tapering cylindrical stem, the flared bobeche

above an incised cylindrical candlecup, Scandinavian, ca. 1780, 9½" h., pr..............**288.00**

Candlesticks, circular foot supporting a tapered standard & baluster-form candlecup, Georgian period, England, late 18th c., 9⅞" h., pr. **517.00**

Candlesticks, gadrooned square foot supporting a baluster-turned & faceted stem, George III period, England, mid-18th c., 10" h., pr. **489.00**
(Illustration: left, above)

Candlesticks, Gothic Revival, ornate circular base supporting a cylindrical stem, cast w/Gothic tracery, w/prisms, Victorian, 19th c., 10" h., pr...**805.00**

Candlesticks, square base supporting a knopped baluster form stem, square drip-pan, gadrooned borders, George III period, England, late 18th c., 10¼" h., pr.........................**2,587.00**

Candlesticks, gadrooned square base supporting a tapered turned standard, George III period, England, mid-18th c., 10½" h., pr......**4,025.00**

Candlesticks, beaded square foot supporting a faceted & fluted square stem w/turned candle nozzle, George III period, England, late 18th c., 11" h., pr.......................................**374.00**
(Illustration: right, above)

Candlesticks, wide round base

supporting tall slender stem & ending in a bulging candle nozzle, script signature, Jarvie, early 20th c., 11" h., pr. **880.00**

Candlesticks, ring-turned beehive standard on an octagonal domed foot inscribed "The King of Diamonds," 19th c., 12½" h., pr. **632.00**

Tavern-type Brass Candlesticks

Candlesticks, tavern-type, saucer base supporting a shaped standard fitted w/a bell, early 19th c., 12¾" h., pr. ....**1,725.00** (Illustration)

Candlesticks, low domed base, ring- and baluster-turned standard w/slender candle nozzle, w/push-up, Victorian, 14" h., pr. **231.00**

Impressive Brass Candlesticks

Candlesticks, scalloped domed shell-form base supporting a turned standard & an elongated candle socket w/removable scalloped bobeche, England, ca. 1770, 19" h., pr. ....**52,900.00** (Illustration: bottom previous column)

Brass Pricket-type Candlesticks

Candlesticks, pricket-type, baluster-turned standard w/a dished cup on a circular base, repairs, Baroque, probably Holland, 18th c., 20½" h., pr. ....**2,300.00** (Illustration)

Candlesticks, circular spreading base w/a graduated spherical-turned standard supporting a dished drip-pan w/turned nozzle, Victorian, 19th c., 21" h., pr. (electrified) **1,610.00**

Candlesticks, cylindrical form raised on a stepped domed base, w/indistinct Cyrillic inscription on base, Russia, late 19th c., now fitted w/an etched hurricane shade, pr. **2,185.00**

Chamberstick, deep saucer base, slender cylindrical stem w/push-up, w/conical snuffer & scissor wick trimmers, 5⅜" h. **522.50**

Chambersticks, shallow saucer base w/spurred ring handle at

edge, cylindrical standard
w/pushup, flaring rim, 4¼" h.,
pr. **440.00**

Chambersticks, hand-hammered, cupped base w/tall
slender shaft w/riveted handle
rising from midsection to
beneath rim, w/original
bobeche, die-stamped mark,
Gustav Stickley, early 20th c.,
7" d., 9" h., pr. **935.00**

Chandelier, four-light, the ring &
baluster standard issuing four
scrolling supports, each w/a
molded candlecup above a
spherical pendant, probably
England, 19th c., 13½" h. **575.00**

Chandelier, eight-light, the scalloped corona w/chains supporting a gadrooned dish w/eight
scrolled candlearms ending in
drip-pans w/candle nozzles,
w/a pendant plume, George III
period, England, third quarter
18th c., 30½" d., 24" h. **21,850.00**

George II Brass Chandelier

Chandelier, twelve-light, the
gadrooned dish supporting
eight scrolled candlearms
w/dished drip-pans & colum-
nar-turned nozzles, the upper
tier w/four scrolled arms surmounted by an urn & hung
from chains, electrified, some
adaptations, George II period,
England, third quarter 18th c.,

36" d., 18½" h. **8,625.00**
(Illustration)

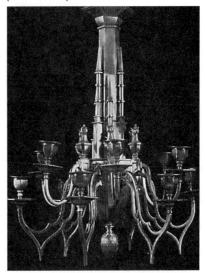

Gothic Revival Brass Chandelier

Chandelier, twelve-light, Gothic
Revival, formed as a cluster of
spires w/scrolled arms & flame
finials, England, second half
19th c., 27" d., 25" h. **3,737.00**
(Illustration)

"Sinclair Oils" Brass Clip

Clip, "Sinclair Oils," green &
white logo, minor tarnish, "Sinclair Cuba Oil Co. Havana,
Cuba," 2½" w., 2½" h. **330.00**
(Illustration)

Desk caddy, the shaped tripartite form on bracket feet
w/baluster-form grip centering
three circular reserves, each
containing a separate dome
top cylindrical castor, the caddy
also w/applied hanging hook

holding a bell, probably
England, 18th c., 7½" h.........**805.00**

Desk set: rectangular tray, pen
holder & paper clip holder; stylized Arts & Crafts design, polished, impressed "Carence
Crafters, Chicago," tray
8 x 12", 3 pcs. **357.50**

Dish, hand-hammered finish,
modeled in the form of a stylized duck raised on two
webbed feet, partly impressed
"GENAU WIEN," Hagenauer,
Vienna, Austria, 29" l.,
7¼" h................................**1,380.00**

Doorstop, cast, depicting a
race horse, inscribed "King's
Genius," "Copyright 1938, Rife
Loth Corp, Waynesboro, Va,"
12¼" h...................................**71.50**

Fireplace fender, the D-shaped
form embellished w/two
pierced leaf bands w/rounded
mid-rib above a molded base,
on paw feet, America or
England, first half 19th c.,
41¼" w., 11" deep, 9" h.........**575.00**

Brass Federal Furniture Pull

Furniture pulls, circular w/cen-
tral repoussé bust portrait of
Benjamin Franklin & inscribed
"BEN[N] (sic) FRANKLIN,
L.L.D.," Federal, ca. 1800,
1½" d., set of 8 ....**1,840.00**
(Illustration: one of eight)

Kettle, spun, cylindrical w/slight-
ly tapering sides, impressed
"The American Brass Kettle 2,"
w/iron bail handle, 7½" d.,
5" h......................................**88.00**

Kettle, spun, w/wire bail handle,
partial "Hayden Patent" label,
14½" d.................................**82.50**

Kettle, spun, w/iron bail handle,
marked "Miller & Co, Meriden,
Conn," 18" d. (minor dents).....**71.50**

Lamp, table model, modeled as
a stylized seated monkey
grasping a tree trunk, stamped
"MADE IN AUSTRIA," & w/the
firm's mark, Hagenauer,
Vienna, Austria, including finial
20" h................................**3,228.00**

Lamps, hanging-type, each
w/an oval wall mount centering
a cabriole-form arm w/circular
ring supporting a green glass
open baluster-form shade
w/cylindrical brass pendant
base, 13" h., pr..................**1,035.00**

Lantern, hanging-type, hexagonal surmounted by a ring finial,
the domed top pierced
w/hearts & ovals & the faceted
frame below surmounted by
lantern finials, the case fitted
w/a hinged door opening to
three baluster-form candle
cups, on flattened ball feet, the
upper section w/attached brass
chain, inscribed on the underside "Fait. A. Alost. Par 1751,"
w/clear glass insets, now fitted
for electricity, probably
Flemish, ca. 1751, 21" h. ...**5,462.00**

Lanterns, hanging-type, circular
glazed body w/an ornate brass
frame & four-light fixture, electrified, 14½" d., 28" h., pr....**4,887.00**
(Illustration: one of two,
top next page)

Letter racks, Gothic Revival, in
the form of a Gothic multi-
spired cathedral, each spire
labeled w/a day of the week in

Brass Hanging-type Lantern

French, on a stepped plinth, "B. Days, patent," w/the Royal Coat of Arms, Victorian, 19th c., 10" h., pr..................**402.00**

Mantel ornaments, urn form finial & columnar ring-turned base support on a square foot, Federal, first half 19th c., 12" h., pr..............................**287.00**

Matchholder, "Indian Motorcycle," detailed emboss-ing on both sides, J.E. Megott Co., Newark, N.J.,1½" w., 2¼" h. (minor tarnish)............**330.00**

Microscope, marked "J. Fentenmayer Philadelphia," early 19th c., includes lenses & glass slides, in case, 14¼" h..............................**1,380.00**

Mortar & pestle, cylindrical pes-tle w/flaring rim, squared han-dles at midsection, pestle w/flat disc finial, 4¾" h. **82.50**

Notary seal, "Recorder's Office of Forest County Penna," 1⅞" d. (some wear).................**27.50**

Pail, spun, tapering sides, "Hayden's Patent" label, w/bail handle, 10" d. (rim split) **38.50**

Pail, tapering cylindrical body w/a flared base, w/bail handle, Europe, late 19th c., 11" h.....**575.00**

Pail, spun, tapering cylinder, w/wrought-iron bail handle, "Hayden's Patent" label, 14" d.......................................**77.00**

Rare Cast Brass Posnet

Posnet, cast, the projecting tapered handle w/rounded lower end inscribed on the top "IN: TAYLOR . RICHMOND," the circular dished receptacle supported on three faceted tapering legs, John Taylor, Richmond, Virginia, ca. 1793, 18¾" l., 10¾" h..................**6,325.00** (Illustration)

Powder flask, embossed clasped hands, eagle & stand of flags, spout stamped "Ames, 1844," good patina **220.00**

Scale, countertop balance-type, two projecting arms supporting dished trays, the columnar standard mounted on an oak base, Victorian, mid- to late 19th c., 24" h. **345.00**

Seal of Philadelphia, Pennsylvania, cast in the half-round w/a central shield flanked by classical female fig-ures above cornucopias & a draped ribbon inscribed "Philadelphia" & "Manetoi," ca. 1876, 13" w., 15½" h ....**2,300.00** (Illustration: top next page)

Sextant, inscribed "E. & E. Emanuel...Portsea," case labeled "George Lee & Sons...Portsea," England, 19th c., w/lenses **517.50**

Sign, "Southwestern Bell

Brass Seal of Philadelphia

Brass Teapot by Josef Hoffmann

Telephone Company," rectangular, logo in circle above lettering, probably building-mounted, 16½" w., 21" h. (tarnished)............................**143.00**

Standish, the lozenge-shaped plate w/open scrolled feet, supporting two lidded canisters centering another w/a bell cover, probably Holland, 18th c.,10" l. **1,610.00**

Surveyor's compass, engraved dial inscribed "Knor & Shain Philadelphia," in case, 12¼" l. **632.50**

Surveyor's compass, engraved dial inscribed "R. Patten N. York," in case, 14" l. **805.00**

Surveyor's compass, engraved dial inscribed "Meneely & Oothout West Troy N.Y. 1837," in case **1,380.00**

Teapot, cov., shaped fluted body w/curved spout & large wooden handle, the cover w/bud finial, designed by Josef Hoffmann, impressed "JH - WIENER WERKSTATTE MADE IN AUSTRIA," ca. 1925, 6¾" h. ....**2,760.00** (Illustration: top next column)

Tobacco box, cov., circular w/hinged lid & spring catch, lid

& reverse side each engraved w/lengthy inscription dated "November the 20th No. Domini 1716," England, ca. 1716, 3¾" d., 1½" h...............................**11,500.00**

Tray, hand-hammered finish, mounted on an ebonized wood base, Middle Eastern, tray 22½" d..................................**172.00**

Trivet, spade-shaped, pierced w/four hearts & two diamonds, pierced handle, 8¾" l. **220.00**

Vases, bud, wide disc foot supporting a slender cylindrical body w/fluted rim, hammered finish, original greenish brown patina, impressed mark, Roycroft Shops, East Aurora, New York, early 20th c., 6½" h., pr. **330.00**

Rococo Two-light Brass Sconce

Wall sconce, two-light, Rococo, the back plate of asymmetrical

English Brass Two-light Sconces

design surmounted by three bellflower finials & various rocaille ornaments encompassing C-scrolls, shells, leafage & flowerheads, the two serpentine projecting candlearms ending in leaf-form chased drip plates w/shaped candle cups, signed John Gold, Birmingham, England, ca. 1765, overall 20¼" h.........................**1,955.00** (Illustration)

Wall sconces, pierced cartouche-shaped backplate above an oval drip pan, Continental, 19th c., pr........**1,495.00**

18th Century Brass Wall Sconces

Wall sconces, three-light, the circular body supporting three

removable scrolled arms, drilled for electricity, probably Holland, 18th c., 15" w., 15" h., pr............................**2,875.00** (Illustration)

Wall sconces, two-light, cast w/floral decoration, the baluster standard supporting scrolled arms & floral decoration, attributed to Christopher Dresser, third quarter 19th c., England, 23" h., pr. ....**2,875.00** (Illustration: one of two, above)

BRONZE

The era known as the Bronze Age occurred between the Neolithic Period, which was a phase of the Stone Age, and the Iron Age. The Bronze Age was a stage of cultural development when bronze, an alloy of copper and tin, was utilized in the production of many forms of tools, weapons and other articles.

Bronze is basically an alloy of copper and tin, but it can also contain small amounts of zinc and phosphorus. Alloys with up to 8 percent tin are used mainly for 'cold-worked' products such as sheets, wire and coins. Gears, bearings and marine hardware utilize the alloy with 8 to 12 percent tin. The principal product of the 20 to 25 percent alloy is bells, as this alloy is very hard and extremely brittle. From an engineering standpoint, the alloy containing less than 20 percent tin is the most useful. In modern usage some alloys containing no tin are considered bronze. These alloys consist of mixtures of copper and aluminum, silicon or beryllium.

As one of the oldest artificially produced alloys, bronze articles have been found in archaeological digs and have been instrumental in giving us some insight in life as it existed in early times. There are, of course, many bronze items, both decorative and utilitarian, that are easily found today. Some of these articles include vases, chalices, jardinieres, lamps, marine hardware, urns and, although not included in this survey, statuary. The early wares are rarely signed but the more recent pieces from the 17th century and onward are sometimes marked as to their manufacture.

Price Listings:

Andirons, each w/a putto seated on rockwork, one flanked by a kid, the other a dog, each flanked by pine cone finials, raised on a bow-fronted plinth base cast w/ribbon-tied grape vines, beading, fluting & paterae above *toupie* feet, the figures patinated, the remainder w/gilt finish, Louis XVI period, France, last quarter 18th c., 14¼" w., 13½" h., pr.......**$20,700.00**

Andirons, Louis XVI-style, modeled in the form of an *athenienne* w/flame finial, draped w/laurel swags, raised on a circular fluted pedestal encircled by laurel sprays continuing to the rectangular stretcher & circular fluted end surmounted by a pineapple finial, gilt finish, signed "Bouhon Frs.," France, 13½" w., 14" h., pr............**21,850.00** (Illustration: below)

Andirons, one w/a female figure w/a bird perched on her wrist, the other a male figure w/his

Louis XVI-style Bronze Andirons

Bronze Andirons with Reclining Lions

hands clasped to his chest, each dressed in chinoiserie costume & seated above voluted bases cast w/rockwork, scrolls & shells, gilt finish, Louis XV period, France, mid-18th c., 13½" w., 14½" h., pr. **26,450.00**

Louis XV-style Gilt-bronze Andiron

Andirons, Louis XV-style, the scrolled bracket surmounted by a putto, gilt finish, late 19th c., 14¾" l., pr. ....**1,725.00** (Illustration: one of two)

Andirons, Louis XV-style, modeled in the form of a cupid reclining on a swagged sphere, gilt finish, 15" h., pr. **1,150.00**

Andirons, Louis XV-style, modeled w/a cherub atop a scrolled bracket, gilt finish, late 19th c., 15" h., pr. ....**1,495.00** (Illustration: one of two, above right)

Figural Bronze Andiron

Andirons, Louis XVI-style, modeled as reclining lions on a foliate-cast rectangular base, the whole further raised on *toupie* feet, gilt & patinated finish, late 19th c., 16" l., pr. ....**5,750.00** (Illustration: above)

Gilt-bronze Figural Andiron

Andirons, formed as a recumbent roaring lion on a pierced bracket base, gilt finish, 17" l., pr. **18,400.00**
(Illustration: one of two, bottom previous page)

Andirons, designed in the rococo style w/elaborate curving columns & base, late 19th c., 17½" h., pr. **316.00**
(Illustration: below)

Andirons, Louis XVI-style, the bracket filled w/a female term holding a flaming torch, gilt finish, late 19th c., 18½" h., pr. **2,875.00**

Ashtray, floor-model, flaring trumpet-shaped base supporting a slender cylindrical standard & bowl-shaped ashtray w/center matchbook holder, decorated w/inlaid sterling silver stylized floral design, only ashtray portion cleaned, "HAMS" stamp, Heintz Art Metal Shop, Buffalo, New York, ashtray 8½" d., 31½" h. **522.50**
(Illustration: top next column)

Book ends, book-form, greenish brown patina, signed "C.A. Needham," stamped "B. Zoppo Foundry, New York," early 20th c., 6" h., pr. **259.00**

Box, cov., decorated w/two stylized sea horses among dense

Heintz Bronze & Silver Ashtray

branches of coral, in original green & brown patina, signed "ETH," E.T. Hurley, 2½ x 4½", 1½" h. **605.00**

Brazier stand, Empire style, three legs headed by winged beasts, on lion paw feet, mounted on a black & rouge marble base, late 19th c., 22⅝" h. (some damage) **1,380.00**

Cachepot, rococo style, shaped rectangular body, each corner set w/a lion, 10" l. **575.00**

Candelabra, two-light, each w/a central baluster-form standard supporting two scrolled candle branches w/eagle heads &

Rococo-style Bronze Andirons

Louis XVI Three-light Candelabra

hairy paw feet, w/ribbed drip-pans & candle nozzles centered by a flaming urn, raised on a circular domed leaf-tip carved base, gilt finish, Louis XVI period, last quarter 18th c., possibly Baltic region, 16" h., pr. **2,875.00**

Candelabra, three-light, Directoire, each w/a central urn supporting two downswept candle branches surmounted by a candle nozzle, the Egyptian term decorated w/anthemion mounts, raised on a circular stepped socle w/fly-ing swan mounts, mounted on a leaf-tip cast base, gilt & pati-nated finish, France, late 18th c., 16" h., pr. **4,600.00**

Candelabra, three-light, sur-mounted by a flaming urn fitted w/laurel swags above a circular tapered fluted shaft, the curved acanthus leaf-cast fluted can-dle branches issuing from leafy stylized masks linked by laurel swags, continuing to circular drip-pans cast w/*guilloche,* fit-ted w/leaf-cast nozzles, the cir-cular fluted foot cast w/a plume

of acanthus leaves, the slightly outset corners cast w/rosettes, gilt finish, Louis XVI period, France, last quarter 18th c., 17½" h., pr. ....**90,500.00** (Illustration: above)

Candelabra, three-light, Neoclassical-style, two-part construction: the upper section fitted w/two scrolled candle

Figural Egyptian Pharoah Candelabrum

branches centered by a tiered stem supporting a candle nozzle over a reeded stem w/a floral wreath capital, the whole raised on a circular domed base cast w/swans & fountains, gilt finish, Continental, 18¼" h., pr. **3,162.00**

Candelabra, three-light, the standard modeled in the form of a Pharoah, surmounted by three candle nozzles, 19th c., 24¼" h., pr.........................**6,900.00** (Illustration: one of two, bottom previous page)

Louis XVI-style Candelabrum

Candelabra, three-light, Louis XVI-style, circular fluted standard fitted w/three curved candle branches cast w/acanthus leaves linked by floral & foliate garlands, raised on hairy claw feet above a conforming base, gilt finish, ca. 1900, 34" h., pr. ....**3,737.00** (Illustration: one of two)

Candelabra, three-light, Louis XVI-style, the standard modeled as a female figure supporting a cornucopia issuing foliate candle branches, raised on an oval marble & gilt-bronze base, gilt & patinated finish, signed "Henry Dasson, 1875," 40" h., pr.........................**16,100.00** (Illustration: top next column)

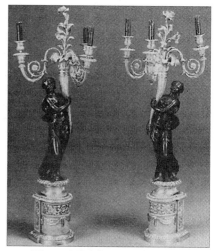

Figural Bronze Three-light Candelabra

Gilt-bronze Four-light Candelabrum

Candelabra, four-light, fluted standard supporting foliate scrolled branches, gilt finish, now electrified, late 19th c., 20" h., pr...........................**2,300.00** (Illustration: one of two)

Candelabra, four-light, Charles X-style, each w/a reeded stem & acanthus-cast capital supporting three scrolled candle branches & a central candle branch, raised on three hipped paw feet ending in a tripartite base, gilt & patinated finish,

now fitted for electricity,
21½" h., pr.........................**2,300.00**

**Empire Figural Bronze
Candelabrum**

Candelabra, four-light, the standard in the form of a 'Winged
Victory' female goddess raising
a pair of torcheres in each
hand, standing upon a gilt foliate dome & engine-turned
pedestal on a stepped base,
gilt & patinated finish, stamped
"Rabiat," Claude Francois
Rabiat, Empire period, France,
ca. 1810, 25" h. **15,400.00**
(Illustration: one of two)

Candelabra, four-light,
Neoclassical, each w/a winged
female figure holding aloft an
urn w/four scrolled candle
branches terminating in eagles'
heads supported by an orb
above a waisted rectangular
plinth fitted w/neoclassical dec-
orations ending in a stepped
base, gilt & patinated finish,
drilled for electricity, Russia,
first quarter 19th c., 27" h.,
pr. **13,800.00**

Candelabra, four-light, a female
figure raising four scrolled
branches aloft in her right
hand, raised on a marble base,
gilt & patinated finish, pr.....**7,475.00**
(Illustration: one of two,
top next column)

**Louis XVI-style Figural
Candelabrum**

Candelabra, five-light, one centrally cast w/a winged male figure, the other w/a winged
female figure, each holding
aloft a flower-filled cornucopia
supporting four scrolled candle
branches centered by a tapering candle branch & standing
on top of an orb raised on a
baluster-form standard cast
w/flowerheads over a domed
base ending in a stepped
plinth, gilt & patinated finish,
Charles X period, second quarter 19th c., 10½" w., 31½" h.,
pr. **5,462.00**

Candelabra, six-light, Charles
X-style, each w/an acanthus-
cast stem supporting five
scrolled candle branches surrounding a central candle
branch, raised on a stepped
rectangular plinth w/military tro-
phies, on four paw feet, mounted on a square base, gilt &
patinated finish, 27" h.,
pr. **5,175.00**

Candelabra, six-light, circular
standard cast w/leaf-tips &
flowerheads supporting foliate-
scrolled candle branches,
raised on a circular pedestal

decorated w/allegorical figures,
gilt finish, Charles X period,
France, second quarter 19th c.,
29¼" h., pr..........................**6,325.00**

**Empire-style Figural Bronze
Candelabra**

Candelabra, six-light, Empire-
style, the allegorical female figure supporting foliate-scrolled
candle branches, raised on a
circular pedestal fitted w/gilt
mounts, the figures w/a patinated finish, the candle branches
w/a gilt finish, late 19th c.,
34½" h., pr......................**20,700.00**
(Illustration)

**Bronze Mermaid & Merman
Candelabra**

Candelabra, six-light, one representing a mermaid, the other a
merman, each supporting a
foliate branch issuing six candle branches, figures in seated
position were formerly mounted
on a mantel, gilt & patinated
finish, late 19th c., 4' 7" h.,
pr.....................................**37,950.00**
(Illustration: bottom previous column)

Louis XVI-style Six-light Candelabra

Candelabra, six-light, Louis XVI-
style, one depicting a male
satyr, the other a female satyr,
each holding a cornucopia supporting foliate candle branches,
raised on a marble & gilt-
bronze circular base, the figures w/a patinated finish, the
remainder gilt, late 19th c.,
4' 11¼" h., pr...................**19,550.00**
(Illustration)

Candelabra, seven-light, Louis
XV-style, modeled in the form
of a putto lifting a cornucopia
issuing scrolling arms & ending
in wickerwork urn-form candle
nozzles, gilt & patinated finish,
28" h., pr............................**1,870.00**

Candelabra, seven-light, Louis
XVI-style, urn-shaped standard
supporting lily-form candle
branches, gilt finish, ca. 1900,
39½" h., pr.........................**3,162.00**
(Illustration: one of two,
top next page)

Bronze Candelabrum with Lily-form Branches

Candelabra, thirteen-light, the scrolling candlearms above a flaring standard on a foliate-cast base w/paw feet, on a concave-sided plinth, gilt & patinated finish, William IV period, England, ca. 1835, 20" d., 43½" h., pr.........................**34,500.00**

Figural Bronze Cherub Candelabrum

Candelabrum, cast in the rococo style w/a cherub on a shell-form & scrolled tripartite footed base, now electrified as a lamp, 23" h. **825.00**
(Illustration)

Bronze Candelabrum with Figural Putto

Candelabrum, eleven-light, Louis XV-style, modeled in the form of a seated putto holding a branch supporting foliate candle branches, raised on a foliate-scrolled base, gilt & patinated finish, third quarter 19th c. **3,450.00**
(Illustration)

Candlestick, octagonal base, baluster stem, 19th c., 5¼" h.....................................**192.50**

Candlestick, wide octagonal base & spiral stem, cylindrical candle nozzle, 6⅞" h..........**2,062.50**

Candlestick, the bulbous holder supporting by a sinuous vine forming a handle, terminating in a flattened lozenge-shaped leaf-form base, stamped "TIFFANY STUDIOS NEW YORK 1203" & inscribed w/the firm's monogram, 7¾" h. **518.00**

Candlestick, the shaped square base supporting a four-legged standard w/paw feet, issuing a socket w/detachable beaded bobeche, stamped "TIFFANY STUDIOS NEW YORK 5635," 10¾" h.................................**460.00**

Candlesticks, Empire-style, figural, modeled in the form of a

seated panther supporting the
candle socket, mounted on a
rouge marble base, 19th c.,
8³⁄₁₆" h., pr. **1,150.00**

Bronze Candlesticks by Tiffany

Candlesticks, low domed base
supporting a narrow turned
standard & urn-form socket,
impressed "Louis C. Tiffany
Furnaces, Inc., Favrile, 43,"
early 20th c., 8¼" h., pr. **330.00**
(Illustration)

Candlesticks, figural,
Neoclassical-style, modeled in
the form of a child balancing a
basket of fruit on his head,
9⅞" h., pr. **1,495.00**

Candlesticks, the shaped
scrolled base issuing a standard cast as a nude maiden
holding a shaped candlecup,
w/'alligator' finish, stamped
"TIFFANY STUDIOS NEW
YORK 1237," 10" h., pr. **5,750.00**

Candlesticks, Neoclassical,
domed base cast w/flower-
heads & arrows supporting a
spiral twisted stem, gilt finish,
Baltic region, second quarter
19th c., 10½" h., pr. **2,300.00**
(Illustration: top next column)

Candlesticks, each w/a leaf-tip
cast candle nozzle above a
reeded stem, raised on an
acanthus-cast domed base,

**Neoclassical Gilt-bronze
Candlesticks**

gilt finish, Charles X period,
France, second quarter
19th c., 12" h., pr. **5,175.00**

Candlesticks, Louis XVI-style,
circular gadrooned nozzle
raised on tripod supports headed by lions' masks above a
shaped support, the tapered
columnar shaft cast w/three
female terms decorated
w/satyrs' masks & linked by floral garlands, the base encircled
by a laurel wreath & raised on
a domed circular foot cast
w/acanthus leaves & beading,
gilt finish, France, first half
19th c., 13" h., pr. **40,250.00**

Candlesticks, each w/a waisted
candle nozzle above the reeded stem w/floral wreath capital,
raised on tripartite hipped paw
feet on a tripartite base, gilt finish, Charles X period, France,
second quarter 19th c.,
14½" h., pr. **5,462.00**

**Cassolettes (decorative
vases),** of typical form, the
upper section w/ram's head &
ring handles linked by laurel
garlands, the waisted cover
w/an acorn finial, on a fluted
cylindrical column & a square
base w/ball feet, 19th c.,
9" h., pr. **862.00**

Centerpiece, designed w/three putti holding aloft a pierced basket, now fitted w/a cut glass bowl, raised on a circular leaf-tip cast socle, gilt finish, Charles X period, France, second quarter 19th c., 21" h. **7,475.00**

Centerpiece, Louis XVI-style, the body cast w/scenes of putti at various pursuits, the paneled neck flanked by winged female busts, raised on a swirl-molded circular base ending in a red marble plinth, gilt finish, third quarter 19th c., 23" h. **7,475.00**

Chandelier, three-light, the elongated double gourd mount decorated w/openwork, issuing three curved arms each supporting a gold teardrop-shaped Favrile glass shade w/pulled feather design, Tiffany Studios, New York, New York, 18" d., 29" h. (hairline crack to one shade) **10,350.00**

Chandelier, four-light, Neoclassical-style, rococo leaf decoration, 19th c., 19¾" w..............**517.50**

Art Nouveau Gilt-Bronze Chandelier

Chandelier, five-light, Art Nouveau style, the openwork frame cast w/whiplash leafage & daffodil blossoms, gilt finish, unsigned, France, ca. 1900, lacks shades, 45" h. ....**2,300.00** (Illustration)

Chandelier, eight-light, the bulbous spiral-cast standard fitted w/scrolled arms, gilt & patinated finish, 19th c., 30" l. **5,750.00**

Louis XVI-style Gilt-Bronze Chandelier

Chandelier, eight-light, Louis XVI-style, the circular caged form composed of pairs of four columns hung w/foliate swags, supporting foliate candle branches, gilt finish, signed "Vian," ca. 1900, 35" h. ......**6,900.00** (Illustration)

Chandelier, ten-light, Charles X-style, the circular corona cast w/flower-filled baskets w/link chains supporting a central font w/flaming urn finial, fitted w/acanthus-cast candle branches, terminating in a pod drop, gilt & patinated finish, 24½" d., 32½" h..................**5,750.00**

Chandelier, fifteen-light, Regence-style, the baluster shaped standard fitted w/ram's heads, shells, leaf-tips & busts supporting two tiers of foliate-scrolled candle branches, sil-

Regence-style Silvered-bronze Chandelier

vered finish, 19th c.,
36" h. **6,900.00**
(Illustration)

Chandelier, sixteen-light, the corona fitted w/satyrs' masks & hung w/chains attached to the flared patinated bowl decorated w/gilt mythological figures, the rim surrounded by a leaf-tip border & fitted w/eight swan-shaped candle branches interspersed by eight candle branches cast w/anthemion, Empire period, France, first quarter 19th c., 37½" d., 38" h. **20,700.00**
(Illustration: bottom next column)

Console set: pair of candlesticks & bowl; the candlesticks on a stepped conical base supporting a swollen cylindrical standard beneath the slightly flaring candle nozzle, the flared bowl w/angular handles raised on a low stepped base, each decorated overall w/inlaid sterling silver thistles against an original dark brown patina, die-stamped diamond mark of Heintz Art Metal Shop, Buffalo, New York, bowl 11½" d., candlesticks 10½" h., the set **660.00**

Desk set: blotter ends, rocker blotter, letter opener, pencil tray, stamp box, paper rack & double inkwell; Venetian patt.,

gilt finish, stamped "TIFFANY STUDIOS" & w/model numbers, New York, New York, paper rack 4½" h., 8 pcs. **1,840.00**

Desk set: letter rack, cov. inkwell, paper clip, three cov. boxes, double inkstand, ashtray & two short blotter ends, American Indian patt., impressed "TIFFANY STUDIOS - NEW YORK" & numbered, 1909-18, 10 pcs. **2,300.00**

Desk set: letter tray, picture frame, table lamp, blotter, stamp box, ashtray, letter opener, calendar, match box & pen stand w/clock; Art Deco style design, ca. 1930, table lamp 18" h., 10 pcs. **575.00**

Desk set: two-slot letter rack, pen tray, blotter ends, inkwell w/glass insert, pen brush, letter opener, calendar holder, paper clip & divided stamp box; Zodiac patt., original dark brown patina, marked "Tiffany Studios, New York," 10 pcs. **2,310.00**

Fire fender, Neoclassical, modeled in the form of a pair of sea serpents supporting a link chain, the plinths decorated by foliate sprays, joined by an

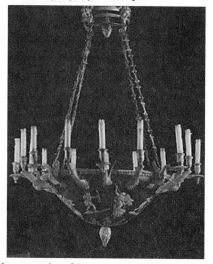

Impressive Sixteen-light Chandelier

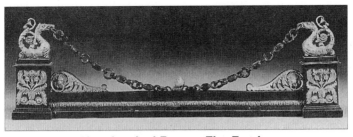

Neoclassical Bronze Fire Fender

egg-and-dart rail, gilt & patinated finish, Baltic region, second quarter 19th c., 33" w. ....**1,150.00** (Illustration: above)

Girandoles, six-light, Regence style, baluster-form, the scrolling arms fitted w/pendant drops, gilt finish, electrified, late 19th c., 30" h., pr...............**1,610.00**

Humidor, cov., Grapevine patt., oviform, the mottled green glass overlaid w/a grapevine openwork design, the cover cast w/grapevine decoration, w/interior lid under the cover, stamped "TIFFANY STUDIOS NEW YORK," 6¼" h. **1,380.00**

Humidor, cov., Arts & Crafts style, cylindrical body w/a high domed cover w/button finial, the base inlaid in sterling silver w/bands forming wide panels w/square loop upper corner brackets, dark patina, die-stamped "HAMS - patent," Heintz Art Metal Shop, Buffalo, New York, 5" d., 7½" h. **385.00**

Humidor, cov., rectangular w/molded base & overhanging top, the lid & sides molded in high-relief w/a shield & other devices, late 19th c. **275.00**

Incense burner, figural, modeled in the form of a crane-type bird perched on a lotus stem, Japan, late 19th c., 8¼" h. **489.00**

Inkstand, Renaissance style, the ink font flanked by griffins, raised on *toupie* feet, gilt finish, 19th c., 15" l. **575.00**

Jar, bulbous long-necked body supported by three exotic beasts, decorated overall w/a stylized floral design, Persia, 18th c., 16⅛" h. **460.00**

Jardiniere, figural, the ovoid body tapering out from the lip, on circular socle, cast in medum- and low-relief w/rippling water replete w/a lobster, a fish, a nautilus & conch, also cast w/the figure of a swimming maiden, w/upper torso & arms fully modeled, rising above the mouth of the vessel & resting against the lip, rich medium brown patina, signed "Rullier Paris," Noel Rullier, Paris, France, ca. 1896, 8" h. **690.00**

Jardiniere, squat bulbous form, Abilone patt., w/separate copper liner, impressed "TIFFANY STUDIOS - NEW YORK" &

Late 19th Century Bronze Jardiniere

"1729," 1899-1928, 9" d. (finish worn) **690.00**

Jardiniere, the bulbous body w/a central band centered on each side w/a Bacchus mask, the sides flanked by putti terms, raised on scrolled legs, gilt & patinated finish, late 19th c., 31½" h. ....**10,925.00** (Illustration: bottom previous page)

Lamp, table model, Arts & Crafts style, a domical mushroom-form metal shade swiveling between slender angled support arms above a cylindrical shaft w/a wide low-domed foot, the shade rim & foot rim decorated w/silver inlaid bands w/stylized geometric flowers, no visible mark, attributed to the Heintz Art Metal Shop, Buffalo, New York, 13¼" w., 14" h. (one mounting screw replaced) **1,100.00**

Figural Lamp with Arab Merchants

Lamp, figural, depicting two Arab merchants, one standing & the other seated, w/their wares beneath a canopy, cold painted finish, 19th c., 16¼" h. ....**3,162.00** (Illustration)

Lamp, the slender tapering fluted column w/Ionic capital, on a square base, 19th c., 17½" h. (electrified) **1,840.00**

Lamp base, the cushion base raised on four feet cast w/scrolls & tendrils, stamped "TIFFANY STUDIOS NEW YORK 25882" & w/theTiffany Glass & Decorating Company monogram, w/finial 20" h....**2,875.00**

Lamp base, the cushion-form lower portion cast w/stylized pods & raised on four curved feet, rich green-red patina, stamped "TIFFANY STUDIOS NEW YORK 395 S198," w/finial 25¼" h. **6,900.00**

Lamp base, the cushion base cast w/a pattern of overlapping leaves, the cylindrical standard applied w/scrolling vines, impressed "TIFFANY STUDIOS NEW YORK 6005," w/finial 26" h. **6,325.00**

Lamp base, table model, the shaped circular base supporting a faceted tapering cylindrical standard issuing four curved arms, w/gilt 'alligator' finish, stamped "TIFFANY STUDIOS NEW YORK 531," including finial 27" h. **2,875.00**

Lamps, one fitted w/a draped female figure reading a tablet, the other w/a male writing on a tablet, each seated on an oil lamp after the Antique cast w/gadrooning & fitted w/a flame nozzle, the oval socle raised on a square base above a later stepped marble plinth, gilt & patinated finish, Louis XVI period, France, last quarter 18th c., 14¼" w., 11¾" h., pr.........**10,925.00**

Lamps, table model, the base cast w/holly leaves, the shades in orange glass w/blue mottling, chips to shade rims & restoration to one base, bases inscribed "J. Leleu," shades enameled "A DELATTE - NANCY," France, ca. 1925,

Bronze Lamps by Leleu & Delatte

16¼" h., pr..........................**2,300.00**
(Illustration)

Lantern, hall-type, Regency
style, hexagonal w/glazed
sides, six beaded supports,
enclosing a six-light electric fixture, gilt finish, late 19th - early
20th c., 15¾" d., 33" h........**1,840.00**

Louis XVI-style Hanging Lantern

Lantern, hanging-type, Louis
XVI-style, twelve glazed sides
fitted on each angle w/four
faceted panels surrounded by
gilt finish borders, the upper
level fitted w/three bearded
male torsos interspaced by
shells & linked by scrolls, the

upper part surmounted by a
crown draped w/beads above
four leaf-cast cabochons linked
by foliate swags, the tapered
lower part fitted w/lion masks
flanked & separated by acanthus leaves & centered by an
acanthus leaf knob, gilt finish,
late 19th c., 43" h. **6,900.00**
(Illustration)

Paul Vera Silvered Bronze Mirror

Mirror, wall-type, oval frame
modeled w/flowerheads emerg-
ing from stylized elongated cor-
nucopiae enclosing the mirror
plate, silvered finish, Paul
Vera, ca. 1925, probably produced for La Compagnie Des
Arts Francais, 16" w.,
19½" h..............................**1,035.00**
(Illustration)

Mirror plateau, three-section,
Louis XV-style, each shaped &
scrolled section w/a pierced
trelliswork gallery w/a leaf-tip
reeded border framing a conforming inset mirror, gilt finish,
stamped "Boin Taburet a
Paris," France, ca. 1900,
overall 49½" **8,050.00**

Model of an elephant, the animal standing w/feet apart &
trunk raised, dark patina,
12½" **137.50**

Picture frame, Maple Leaf patt.,
rectangular w/beaded border,
the mottled green glass overlaid w/a maple leaf openwork
design, stamped "TIFFANY
STUDIOS NEW YORK 948,"
7½" h. **1,093.00**

Picture frame, Pine Needle
patt., rectangular w/a double
frame & beaded border, the
mottled green & white glass
overlaid w/a pine needle openwork design, stamped
"TIFFANY STUDIOS NEW
YORK," 8½" h. **1,955.00**

Picture frame, Pine Needle
patt., rectangular w/oval opening, the mottled amber & white
glass overlaid w/an openwork
pine needle design, gilt finish,
stamped "TIFFANY STUDIOS
NEW YORK 917," 14" h. **2,300.00**

Planter, flaring cylindrical form,
Art Deco style, molded in high-
relief w/a continuing row of
horses, light brown patina,
early 20th c., 10½" h. **1,610.00**

Plaque, circular, the center cast
in relief depicting an angel
before Adam & Eve in the
Garden of Eden, w/lush foliate
decoration, old gilt finish,
Continental, late 19th c.,
11" d. **220.00**

Plaque, oval, depicting a bac-
chanalian scene, brown patina,
within a brass frame, France,
late 19th - early 20th c., overall
14½" w., 11¾" h. **172.50**

Plaque, relief-molded bust portrait of Theodore Roosevelt
within a molded frame,
9½" w., 12½" h. **220.00**

Plaque, the symmetrically
shaped body decorated
w/pierced scrollwork suggest-
ing plant stems & tendrils, patinated finish, designed by
Hector Guimard for the Paris,
France Metro, ca. 1900,

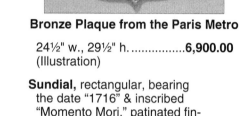

Bronze Plaque from the Paris Metro

24½" w., 29½" h. **6,900.00**
(Illustration)

Sundial, rectangular, bearing
the date "1716" & inscribed
"Momento Mori," patinated finish, Continental, 19th c.,
9" w. **230.00**

Tazza, holly decoration on base,
figural vulture stem, central fox
finial, decorated w/a hunting
theme, signed "J. Moigniez,"
France, 19th c., 10⅝" d.,
9½" h. **345.00**

Torcheres, figural, the standard modeled in the form of a
Nubian youth w/an elaborate
foliate cast costume & a
feathered turban, 62" h.,
pr. **3,450.00**

Torcheres on pedestals, Louis
XVI-style, each depicting an
allegorical female figure
w/arms upright, a foliate branch
from behind supporting a glass
globe, raised on a circular
pedestal w/a continuous figural
band, further raised on a marble plinth, late 19th c., 6' h.,
pr. **36,800.00**

Urn, cov., baluster-lorm w/ram's
head & swag decoration,
mounted on a black marble

base, France, late 19th c.,
14½" h. **200.00**

Urn, rounded sides decorated
w/relief bearded heads, intertwined handles, raised on a
flared fluted lower section,
mounted on a circular red
stone base, gilt finish, 9" d.,
10½" h. **770.00**

Regency-style Two-handled Urn

Urns, cov., Regency-style,
graceful body flanked by angular leaf-form handles, the cover
w/a fluted & lobed finial, raised
on a square base, black patinated finish, 19th c., 16" h.,
pr. **3,450.00**
(Illustration: one of two)

Urns, Louis XVI-style, the leaf-
decorated vessel supported by
triform legs headed by eagle
busts, gilt & patinated finish,
19th c., 17" h., pr. (lacking
lids) **4,025.00**

Urns, bulbous body raised on a
square base, flanked by double-headed angular handles,
patinated finish, late 19th c.,
17" h., pr. **5,462.00**
(Illustration: one of two,
top next column)

Urns, the vessel cast w/scrolls,
Greek key & leaf-tips flanked
by handles headed by female
busts, the hoof feet & legs centered by lion masks, gilt & patinated finish, raised on a con-

**Bronze Urn with Double-headed
Handles**

forming marble base, third
quarter 19th c., 20" h.,
pr. **3,737.00**

Vase, squat bulbous body
w/short neck & flaring rim, decorated on one side w/a sterling
silver inlay depicting a wild
rose & foliage on a dark brown
ground, die-stamped "HAMS -
Patent," Heintz Art Metal Shop,
Buffalo, New York, 5" d.,
5" h. **330.00**

Vase, two-handled, the upper
portion w/silvered finish cast
w/Celtic devices, the lower tex-
tured section w/green patina,
Gustave Gurschner, impressed
"MOD. B" twice, ca. 1900,
6" h. **1,840.00**

Art Nouveau Bronze Vase by Londe

Vase, cylindrical body w/low compressed globular base applied w/the stylized silver outline of a tree, patinated finish, Heintz Art Metal Shop, Buffalo, New York, ca. 1912, 8⅜" h. **302.50**

Vase, Art Nouveau-style, the rounded base tapering to a long slender neck w/narrow flared rim, the looping handles rising from the base to below the neck rim, decorated w/a detailed design of a blossom on a tall stem w/leaves, signed "Londe," 8½" h. **275.00**
(Illustration: bottom previous page)

Vase, the tapering oval body finely cast about the top w/four large beetles amid stylized overlapping leafage, the lower section gently ribbed & w/shaded olive green & reddish brown patina, stamped "CHRISTOFLE - FRANCE - 2475097," ca. 1925, 9¼" h. **3,565.00**

Vase, baluster-form body w/short wide neck, decorated w/inlaid sterling silver flowers & foliage on a dark ground, diestamped "HAMS - Patent," Heintz Art Metal Shop, Buffalo, New York, 4¼" d., 10" h. **495.00**

Vase, Art Deco-style, flowerpotform, cast w/a design of three-dimensional horses, 9" d., 10" h. **715.00**

Bronze & Silver Vase by Heintz

Vase, tall tapering body w/flaring rim, decorated w/a sterling silver overlay depicting freesia blossoms, original dark patina, die-stamped diamond mark of Heintz Art Metal Shop, Buffalo, New York, 3½" d., 11" h. **440.00**
(Illustration: bottom previous column)

Vase, oviform w/bulbous top, decorated w/iris blossoms in silver on a brown patinated ground, die-stamped "3627B - HAMS - Sterling on Bronze - Patent," Heinz Art Metal Shop, Buffalo, New York, 4¾" d., 11¾" h. **715.00**

Heintz Vase with Poppies

Vase, cylindrical w/flaring base, inlaid sterling silver decoration depicting poppies & leaves on a green & brown patinated ground, die-stamped diamond mark of Heintz Art Metal Shop, Buffalo, New York, 4¾" d., 12" h. **550.00**
(Illustration)

Vase, Arts & Crafts style, wide cylindrical form w/a widely flaring flattened rim, inlaid around the sides in sterling silver w/clusters of cattails near the base & flying birds above, dark patina, stamped Heintz Art Metal Shop mark & "3615E (?) Patent," Buffalo, New York, 5" d., 12" h. **440.00**

Vase, tapering body w/swollen rim, decorated w/sterling silver inlay depicting iris blossoms, dark patina, die-stamped "HAMS - Patent," Heintz Art Metal Shop, Buffalo, New York, 5" d., 12" h.............................**495.00**

Vase, two upward flaring open horn-shaped handles flanking the corseted body, decorated w/an inlaid sterling silver Moorish design at the neck & base, mottled green patina, die-stamped "HAMS - Patent," Heintz Art Metal Shop, Buffalo, New York, 6½" d.,12½" h. (small dimple on base).........**605.00**

Vase, flaring body w/rolled rim, decorated w/tall applied silver flowers on a brown patinated ground, die-stamped "379 4 - HAMS - Sterling on Bronze Patent," Heintz Art Metal Shop, Buffalo, New York, 5½" d., 12¾" h.................................**770.00**

Vase, ovoid base supporting a long slender neck, raised handles at the shoulder, decorated w/pine cones & needles, gilt finish, inscribed "A. Vibert" & impressed w/the Colin foundry seal, Alexandre Vibert, France, early 20th c., 13⅝" h. ....**1,380.00** (Illustration: top next column)

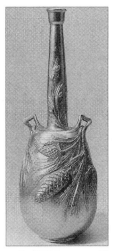

French Gilt-bronze Vase

Vases, Art Deco style, trumpet-shaped w/molded rings on lower section, verdigris finish, indistinct mark, 6½" h., pr......**187.00**

Vases, 'Warwick' style, the rounded base beneath a flaring rim, knotted bracket handles, raised on a circular foot, mounted on a marble plinth, gilt & patinated finish, late 19th c., 16½" h., pr.............**4,025.00** (Illustration: below)

Wall sconce, two-light, cast in the form of two intertwined dolphins, each holding in its

Bronze 'Warwick' Vases

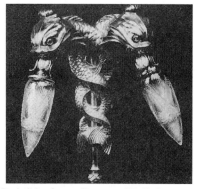

Dolphin-form Bronze Wall Sconce

mouth a foliate capped conical
cut crystal shade, w/a pineapple pendant, electrified, 17" w.,
24½" h..................................**880.00**
(Illustration)

Flaming Torch-form Wall Sconces

Wall sconces, Louis XVI-style,
in the form of a flaming torch,
mounted upon a ribbon-crested
& tasseled backplate, electrified, late 19th c., 15½" h.,
pr.......................................**1,760.00**
(Illustration)

Wall sconces, each formed as a
hand holding a torch, patinated
finish, 19th c., 20" h., pr. **6,900.00**
(Illustration: top next column)

Wall sconces, two-light, baluster-form w/two twisted upturned
branches each supporting
vase-shaped sockets, holding
bell-shaped Favrile glass
shades w/a gold iridescent

Hand with Torch Wall Sconces

pulled feather design on a
translucent iridescent ground,
gilt finish, each shade inscribed
"L.C.T.," Tiffany Studios, New
York, New York, shades
4¾" h., hardware 7" h.,
pr......................................**10,350.00**

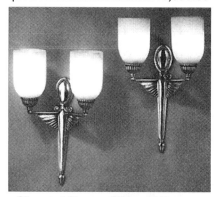

**Simonet Freres Silvered Bronze
Wall Sconces**

Wall sconces, two-light, reeded
dagger-form backplate conjoining two winged arms, each
supporting a reeded cup &
alabaster shade, silver finish,
alabaster replaced, Simonet
Freres, France, ca. 1925,
15¼" h., pr.........................**3,450.00**
(Illustration)

Wall sconces, two-light, Louis
XV-style, scrolling backplate &
arms w/foliate sockets & drip-

Louis XV-style Wall Sconces

pans, gilt finish, 19th c., 19" h.,
pr. **1,430.00**
(Illustration)

Ornate Louis XVI-style Wall Sconce

Wall sconces, two-light, Louis
XVI-style, the backplate in the
form of bow-knotted ribbons
centered by berried sprays, the
intertwined reeded candle
branches cast w/acanthus
leaves & berries, gilt finish,
late 19th c., 22½" h., pr. **8,050.00**
(Illustration: one of two)

Wall sconces, three-light, Louis
XVI-style, backplate centered
by a lion mask fitted w/foliate-
scrolled candle branches, gilt
finish, late 19th c., 17½" h.,
pr. **3,737.00**

Wall sconces, three-light, Louis
XV-style, foliate backplate supporting foliate-scrolled candle
branches, gilt finish, late

Bronze Foliate Design Wall Sconce

19th c., 29½" h., pr. **5,175.00**
(Illustration: one of two)

Wall sconces, two-light,
Empire-style, cornucopia arms
joined to a torch-form backplate, gilt finish, 13½" h.,
set of 4 ....**1,760.00**

Wall sconces, three-light, the
fluted & swag-draped standard
supporting foliate candle
branches & surmounted by
lovebirds, gilt finish, Napoleon
III period, France, mid-19th c.,
pr. **4,312.00**

Rococo Bronze Three-light Sconce

Wall sconces, three-light, Rococo style, the pierced scrolled backplate supporting foliate-scrolled candle branches hung w/pendants, surmounted w/a plumed fan, gilt finish, 19th c., pr................**8,625.00** (Illustration: one of two, bottom previous page)

Charles X Bronze Wall Sconces

Wall sconces, four-light, Charles X style, each central foliate scrolled backplate supporting four scrolled candle branches terminating in snake heads & fitted w/leaf-tip drip-pans, gilt & patinated finish, France, 17½" h., pr. ....**9,775.00** (Illustration)

Wall sconces, four-light, the circular reeded standard supporting scrolled candle branches,

Empire-style Figural Bronze Sconce

gilt & patinated finish, 19th c., 19½" h., pr........................**2,875.00**

Wall sconces, five-light, Empire-style, cast w/the winged female figure of Victory, holding wreaths in her outstretched hands, her head issuing an urn w/scrolling arms, poised upon a sphere, gilt & patinated finish, 19th c., 40" h., pr...........................**9,075.00** (Illustration: one of two, bottom previous column)

Louis XVI-style Bronze Sconce

Wall sconces, five-light, Louis XVI-style, the backplate fitted w/acorn leaves & a hoof supporting horn-form candle branches & upper scrolled branches, gilt & patinated finish, 40½" h. ....**9,200.00** (Illustration: one of two)

Wall sconces, three-light, Louis XVI-style, tapered foliate-decorated backplate supporting scrolled candle branches, gilt finish, 29½" h., set of 4.......**8,625.00**

Watch holders, Empire-style, modeled in the form of a winged cupid holding an ornate wreath aloft, mounted on a sienna marble & lapis plinth, late 19th c., some damage, 9½" h., pr...........................**1,495.00** (Illustration: top next page)

Empire-style Bronze Watch Holder

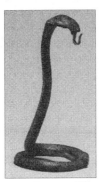

Edgar Brandt Bronze Watch Stand

Watch stand, modeled as a
cobra about to strike,
w/splayed hood & a hooked
tongue for hanging a watch,
black patina w/green accents,
traces of a gilt patina remaining, impressed "E - BRANDT,"
Edgar Brandt, ca. 1925,
9" h.....................................**2,185.00**
(Illustration)

Wine coasters, decorated w/a
pierced grapevine design, gilt
finish, 19th c., 5" d., pr. **460.00**

CHROME

The only ore mineral of chromium
is the mineral "chromite," a chromium
and iron oxide in the spinel group of
minerals. The chromium element is
relatively new, having been discovered by N.L. Vauquelin in 1798.
Chromium metal is prepared by
reducing the ore in a blast furnace
with carbon or silicon to form an alloy
of chromium and iron called fer-
rochrome. Chromium is difficult to
work with in its pure metal form as it
is brittle at low temperatures and its
high melting point makes it difficult to
cast. The most important use of
chromium is in chrome plating,
because it forms a hard, wear-resis-
tant and attractive surface.

One of the major companies in the
United States to utilize chrome plating in the manufacture of household
items began as the Waterbury
Manufacturing Company, which later
evolved into the Chase Brass and
Copper Company. This Waterbury,
Connecticut firm began setting sales
records in the 1930s.

Although the country was in the
midst of a financial depression, people still had a desire for the low-
priced but expensive-looking household items. Special departments
known as "Chase Shops," featuring a
plethora of exciting Art Deco pieces,
sprang up in stores across the country. Hostesses who could not afford to
use expensive silver were delighted
by the lovely chrome serving pieces.
Even Emily Post, the foremost
authority on etiquette at the time,
endorsed the use of chrome articles
when entertaining.

Because of the war effort, the
Chase Company discontinued its line
of decorative housewares during
World War II. By the time the war
ended, the Art Deco chrome, formerly
so popular, had lost its favor with the
consumers. Many other companies
produced chrome items at the same
time and suffered similar losses.

Today the Art Deco craze has
made the chrome items popular
again. Almost anything for entertaining and decoration can be found in
chrome from book ends to candleholders, electric casseroles and coffee makers to cocktail sets and ice
crushers to serving bowls.

Price Listings:

Glass & Chrome Basket

Basket, shallow incurved round purple glass bowl fitted in a pierced & arched chrome frame w/a rounded footring, arched & pointed chrome swing bail handle, Farber Bros. mark on base, 5⅜" d., 2" h. plus handle ....**$25.00 to 30.00** (Illustration)

Glass & Chrome Candlesticks

Candlesticks, thick clear glass candle socket w/flattened, flaring rim fitted in a pierced lacy chrome stem w/flaring, ringed foot, "Krome Kraft - Farber Bros." mark on base, 4¾" h., pr. ....**65.00 to 80.00** (Illustration)

Car mascot, Chevrolet eagle, zinc die cast w/chrome plating, designed by William Schnell & Fredrick Giun, patd. July 14, 1931, some pitting & minor age

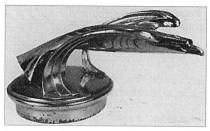

Chevrolet Chrome Car Mascot

crazing to chrome, 6¼" l., 3" h..................................**104.50** (Illustration)

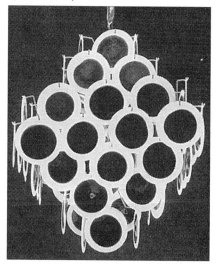

Intricate Chrome Chandelier

Chandelier, the squared metal framework composed of three tiers w/prong branches, each adorned w/an opaque white & aubergine glass disc, the middle tier centering eight lights, suspended from a link chain, Italy, largest tier 25" d., 31½" h.............................**1,150.00** (Illustration)

Cocktail glass, rounded cylindrical purple glass bowl fitted in a pierced chrome frame w/slender swelled stem & domed round foot, Farber Bros. mark on base, 5⅜" h. ....**10.00 to 12.00** (Illustration: top next page)

Cocktail shaker, cov., tall

Glass & Chrome Cocktail Glass

Chrome Cocktail Shaker

swelled cylindrical body on a
flaring foot, incised bands &
molded ring below the rounded
shoulder tapering to a short
cylindrical neck w/a screw-on
cover, short angled spout on
the shoulder, molded black
plastic scroll handle, "Krome
Kraft - Farber Bros." mark,
11" h. ....**20.00 to 30.00**
(Illustration)

Cocktail shaker, Art Deco style,
dumbbell-shaped, ca. 1930s,
4" d., 11" h. (minor dings)........**66.00**

Compote, open, shallow rounded amber glass bowl fitted in a
pierced chrome frame w/a fig-

Glass & Chrome Compote

ural nude lady stem & ringed,
domed round foot, Farber Bros.
mark on base, 5½" d.,
7½" h. ....**85.00 to 110.00**
(Illustration)

Glass & Chrome Decanter

Decanter w/stopper, tapering
teardrop-form purple glass
body set in a pierced lacy
chrome frame w/flaring foot,
clear glass tall pointed stopper,
Farber Bros. mark on
chrome, 12" h. ....**45.00 to 60.00**
(Illustration)

Ice bucket w/bail handle, deep
rounded cylindrical emerald
green glass bowl set in a
pierced & arched chrome base,
pointed & arched chrome bail
handle, Farber Bros. mark on

Glass & Chrome Ice Bucket

base, 4½" d., 6" h. plus
handle......................**50.00 to 75.00**
(Illustration)

Lamp, floor model, "Crane," the
six prong steel base supporting
a rectilinear chrome wire standard w/geometric counterbal-
ance, terminating in two light
sockets, w/paper label
"UNDERWRITERS LABORA-
TORIES" & molded "LEVI-
TON," America, ca. 1970, arm
45¾" l., standard 50" h.........**345.00**

**Glass & Chrome Salt & Pepper
Shakers**

Salt & pepper shakers w/origi-
nal lids, bulbous spherical
tapering green glass body
w/applied green glass handle,
fitted in a pierced & arched
chrome footed frame, mushroom-form chrome lid, "Farber
Bros." mark on base,
3½" h., pr. ....**15.00 to 20.00**
(Illustration)

Glass & Chrome Covered Server

Server, cov., ovoid paneled
green glass body w/applied
green handle, chrome neck,
rim & domed cover w/pointed
finial, 5" d., 10" h.....**75.00 to 100.00**
(Illustration)

Chrome & Glass Silent Butler

Silent butler, cov., shallow
rounded purple glass bowl fitted in a pierced & arched
chrome frame w/a thick rounded foot, hinged low domed
chrome sunburst-engraved
cover w/thumbrest & baluster-
turned wooden handle, "Farber
Bros." mark on base, 54" d.,
plus 4¾" l. handle,
2¾" h. ....**65.00 to 75.00**
(Illustration)

Table, the rectangular glass top
supported on U-shaped legs
joined together at the bottom
by a flattened horizontal
stretcher, resting on rectangular block feet, designed by
Donald Deskey for Deskey-
Vollmer, Inc., ca. 1927-31,
30 x 53¼", 23¾" h............**10,350.00**
(Illustration: top next page)

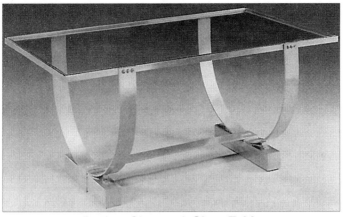

Deskey Chrome & Glass Table

Vase, cylindrical w/gently flaring lip, raised on a band of coils & spheres mounted on a square base, acid-etched monogram for La Compagnie General Trans-Atlantique, designed by Edgar Brandt & Georges Bastard for the liner Normandie, impressed "G. BASTARD" & "E. BRANDT," ca. 1935, 10½" h. **3,335.00**

Vase, cylindrical w/gently flaring lip, supported by a band of coils & spheres mounted on a square base, acid-etched monogram for Le Compagnie General Trans-Atlantique, designed by Edgar Brandt & Georges Bastard for the liner Normandie, impressed "G. BASTARD" & "E. BRANDT," ca. 1935, 13½" h. **4,312.00**

COPPER

Copper was the first metal used by man and it is second only to iron in its utility. In Roman times, much of the copper was mined on the island of Cyprus. In the 1700s, copper was found in large quantities in four sites in the United States: the Great Lakes region now known as Michigan;

another well-known mining area was located in Connecticut; Belleville, New Jersey was also the scene of heavy copper production; the fourth large mining site was in the state of Maryland.

Today, copper is mined in many parts of the world, and the largest producer is Chile, followed by the United States, Canada and the former U.S.S.R. Also known for their production of copper are Zaire, Zambia and Peru.

The coppersmith, as well as the brazier or brassfounder, was a very necessary member of early American communities and his products varied depending on where he was located. The coppersmith made the items needed for day-to-day living, such as pots, pans, kettles, coffeepots, chocolate pots, ladles, teakettles, and skimmers. A smith who plied his trade in an inland city made the utilitarian items as well as kettles for hatters, dyers, brewers and others. The smiths working in or near a seaport concentrated on making special items for use on ships.

Copper has also been used by artisans in creating decorative pieces for the home. Many impressive copper articles include vases, candle sconces, candleholders, desk sets, humidors, clock cases, ashtrays, boxes and trays. Because of the malleability of copper, some of these articles are enhanced by hammered or tooled decoration. Although copper was the first metal used by man, it still ranks high in popularity today.

Price Listings:

Ashtray, hand-hammered, deep round form w/flat rim, cleaned patina, impressed marks, Old Mission Kopperkraft, 4" d. **$33.00**

Ashtrays, hand-hammered, circular, shaped in the form of a hat, monogrammed in a medallion "AOS," open box mark, Dirk Van Erp, 5¼" d., pr. (typical use wear to patina) **275.00**

Book ends, hand-hammered finish, rounded-form decorated w/a circular leather medallion within a twisted metal frame, brass wash, impressed orb & cross mark, Roycroft Shops, East Aurora, New York, 4½ x 4¾", pr. **220.00**

Book ends, hand-hammered, arch-shaped w/a hammered floral design, excellent original dark brown patina, orb & cross mark, Roycroft Shops, East Aurora, New York, 3¾ x 5", pr. **275.00**

Book ends, hand-hammered finish, designed w/round hinged pulls on riveted straps, original dark patina, orb & cross mark, Roycroft Shops, East Aurora, New York, 4 x 5¼", pr. **330.00**

Book ends, hand-hammered, depicting a heavily-embossed poppy blossom, w/thin brass wash, fine original brass & copper patina, orb & cross mark, Roycroft Shops, East Aurora, New York, 5½ x 5½", pr. **522.50**

Book ends, hand-hammered, semi-circular w/cut back design of sailing ship at sea, original patina, signed "Harry Dixon San Francisco," 7" h., pr. **440.00**

Bowl, hand-hammered finish, three-footed, rounded sides, rolled rim, original patina, die-stamped orb & cross mark, Roycroft Shops, East Aurora, New York, 10" d., 4¼" h. **1,045.00**

Bowl, hand-hammered, delicately tooled Arts & Crafts design surrounding the rim above the rounded sides, original dark brown patina, impressed mark, Roycroft Shops, East Aurora, New York, 6½" d., 2½" h. **286.00**

Bowl, low w/rolled edge, new dark brown patina, impressed "Jarvie" in script, 7¾" d., 2½" h. **385.00**

Bowls, hand-hammered, sloping sides w/turned-in rim, applied silver monogram, rich recent dark brown patina, one marked "KALO," 7¾" d., 3" h., pr. **605.00**

Bowl-vase, hand-hammered, cylindrical w/slightly rounded sides & rolled rim, decorated w/stylized oak leaves on broad stems surrounding the body, lightly cleaned patina, impressed mark, Keswick, 6" w., 2½" h. **176.00**

Candleholders, three-light, hand-hammered finish, pair of scrolled feet supporting a narrow scrolled bar fitted w/candle nozzles, original patina, orb & cross mark, Roycroft Shops, East Aurora, New York, original patina, 8" l., 3" h., pr. **495.00**

Candlestick, hand-hammered, two heavy gauge square vertical supports riveted to square base & supporting classic candle holder, original brown patina, marked, Roycroft Shops, East Aurora, New York, 8" h. **220.00**

Candlesticks, hand-hammered finish, Princess patt., two four-sided riveted stems on a pyramidal base, original patina, orb & cross mark, Roycroft Shops,

East Aurora, New York, 7¾" h., pr. **715.00**

Candlesticks, hand-hammered finish, dish-form base, cylindrical standard w/applied riveted handle, stamped mark of Gustav Stickley, Model No. 74, 9" h., pr. **748.00**

Card tray, hand-hammered, circular w/wide rim decorated w/a design of overlapping petals, original patina, impressed mark, Peer Smed, 7" d. **187.00**

Chamberstick, hand-hammered, dished base w/riveted applied handle, low waisted candle holder, original dark brown patina, impressed mark, Roycroft Shops, East Aurora, New York, 5½" d., 1½" h. **242.00**

Chamberstick, hand-hammered, trumpet-shaped base w/wide base supporting candle nozzle in dished vessel, wide riveted handle rising from base to rim, rich original dark brown patina, impressed mark, Roycroft Shops, East Aurora, New York, 3" h. **231.00**

Gustav Stickley Copper Chandelier

Chandelier, hand-hammered, w/four long cylindrical lanterns w/overhanging tops & mica lin-

ers, suspended from an X-brace, original brown patina, original chains & ceiling plate, die-stamped mark, Gustav Stickley, 20" d., base of lanterns to ceiling plate 35" h. ....**770.00** (Illustration)

Charger, Arts & Crafts style, hand-hammered, the round center reserve w/a raised trefoil design, the wide flat flanged rim embossed w/large stylized hearts, center enameled in blue & green, original dark brown patina, in the style of Liberty & Co., England, unmarked, 12" d. **522.50**

Charger, Arts & Crafts style, hand-hammered, the dished middle centered by a round reserve w/large embossed swirling around a date "1894," the wide flanged rim embossed w/a band of pomegranates & leaves, cleaning to front patina, possibly English, unmarked, 13" d. **165.00**

Chargers, hand-hammered, circular, the wide border acid-etched w/a design of the nursery rhyme "Little Miss Muffet," fine new dark patina, marked "E.A. BROWN - 1912" & "E.A. BROWN - 1915," 11¾" d. & 10¾" d., pr. **550.00**

Cigarette box w/hinged lid, rectangular, decorated w/a small hammered band around edges, thin brass wash, orb & cross mark, Roycroft Shops, Fast Aurora, New York, 4 x 5¼", 2" h. **275.00**

Coffeepot, cov., modeled in the Turkish taste, of elongated baluster-form w/spot-hammered surface & die-rolled silver mid-band, rising to a silver reeded band at the rim, the handle w/ivory insulators, hinged ball cover w/ball finial, Gorham, Mfg. Co., Providence,

Rhode Island, 1883,
13" h.................................**2,300.00**

Coffee urn, cov., Classical-style,
the globular body raised on
four tall legs resting on a
shaped base, further raised on
ball feet, tall curved side handles, flattened domed cover
w/ornate finial, brass spigot,
17" h.....................................**220.00**

Crumber set, hand-hammered,
each piece w/lightly rolled
edges & handle grips, original
brown patina, impressed mark,
Dirk Van Erp, 4½ x 9" &
2½ x 8", the set **825.00**

Dish, hand-hammered, low
w/gently rolled rim, original
brown patina, impressed mark,
Roycroft Shops, East Aurora,
New York, 5" d. **198.00**

Dish, hand-hammered, circular
w/finely tooled Arts & Crafts
design around flaring border,
lightly cleaned patina,
impressed mark, Roycroft
Shops, East Aurora, New York,
6" d.......................................**275.00**

Door knocker, hand-hammered,
rectangular w/large square
faceted pull & a large hammered ring, fine new dark patina, impressed circular mark,
Gustav Stickley, 3" w.,
11" h..................................**1,210.00**

Double boiler on legs, dovetailed construction, outer pot
bulbous, interior pot cylindrical,
wrought-iron handles, raised
on three wrought-iron legs,
5½" d., 9¾" h.......................**302.50**

Ewer, hand-hammered, ovoid
base beneath a slender neck
w/narrow flaring rim, graceful
curved spout & high curved
handle, original brown patina,
large orb mark at waist, probably made for the Roycroft Inn,
Roycroft Shops, East Aurora,
New York, 6" h. **770.00**

Copper Ewer by Gorham

Ewer, cov., hand-hammered,
ovoid base tapering to a long
slender neck, curved spout, C-
form handle, ball stopper, decorated w/applied silver birds in
a landscape, Gorham Corp.,
Providence, Rhode
Island, 1888, 13" h. **2,760.00**
(Illustration)

Fire screen, decorated w/bul-
rushes & birds **80.00**

Incense burner, hand-hammered finish, semi-ovoid lower
section on three scrolled feet,
the pierced conical top w/a tall
finial, original patina, orb &
cross mark, Roycroft Shops,
East Aurora, New York, 3" d.,
3½" h..................................**385.00**

Jardiniere, Arts & Crafts style,
hand-hammered ground on the
wide swelled cylindrical body,
four embossed medallions of
large leafy trees around the
sides, original dark brown patina, impressed diamond W.M.F.
mark, Germany, early 20th c.,
14" d., 10" h..........................**715.00**

Kettle, round bottom, cast-iron
handles, 19th c., 16" d. (some
battering) **77.00**

Kettle, dovetailed construction,
brass spigot on bottom,

w/brass trim & swivel handle, 19th c., 17" h. plus handle.......**93.50**

Kettle, dovetailed construction, wrought-iron bail handle, 19th c., 19" d. **93.50**

Kettle, dovetailed construction, wrought-iron bail handle, 19th c., 36" d. (minor battering) **220.00**

Lamp, desk-type, Arts & Crafts style, the circular foot supporting a tapering standard, fitted w/two bowed arms supporting the domed hood shade w/slightly flaring rim, the lamp & shade each inlaid w/two silvered stylized geometric devices, in the manner of Frank Lloyd Wright, the shade monogramed, early 20th c., 10¼" h. (silvering worn, shade dented) **747.00**

Copper Lamp Base with Applied Decoration

Lamp base, kerosene-type, Anglo-Japanese style, rectangular body w/hammered finish applied w/silver & brass flowers, fruit, birds & insects, raised on four grotesque feet, brass burner, Gorham Corp., Providence, Rhode Island, 1881-85, 14" h...................**3,450.00** (Illustration)

Measure, "haystack"-form

w/large loop handle, marked "Quart," dovetailed construction, 19th c., 6½" h. **165.00**

Copper Planter by Karl Kipp

Planter, hand-hammered finish, circular, decorated w/four panels depicting embossed mushrooms, raised on four riveted legs continuing to rim, w/some of the original dark patina, much of the surface has been lightly cleaned, die-stamped "Karl Kipp - Hand Wrought - East Aurora - New York," 7" d., 4" h...........................**7,150.00** (Illustration)

Pot, cylindrical w/rolled slightly flaring lip, w/a rounded iron handle, 19th c., 18" h. **460.00**

Powder flask, side embossed w/scene of quail in tall grass, brass trim, 7" l. **82.50**

Powder flask, side embossed w/scene of stork within a foliate frame, brass trim, 7⅞" l. **148.50**

Powder flask, embossed hanging game & "James Dixon & Sons," brass trim, 7⅞" l. **82.50**

Powder flask, side embossed w/scene of treed bear, brass trim, 8⅜" l. **137.00**

Powder flask, embossed w/oak leaves, acorns & stag's head, brass trim, 8⅞" l. **126.50**

Radiator cover, Arts & Crafts style, hand-hammered finish, cast w/foliage, w/hinged upper section above a center door, (replaced) white marble top,

Arts & Crafts-style Radiator Cover

depatinated, ca. 1915, 14"
deep, 31½" w., 41¾" h. **2,530.00**
(Illustration)

Saucepans, cov., plain silvered
cylindrical body, w/slip-on
cover & loop handles, the base
inscribed in Cyrillic "K.
Faberge, War, 1914," Karl
Faberge, Moscow, Russia, ca.
1914, 5⅜" d., pr.................**7,475.00**

Skillet, dovetailed construction,
marked "S.B. Traub, Chicago,"
w/cast-iron handle, 17" d., 17"
handle **137.50**

Stamp box, cov., hand-hammered, decorated w/detailed
tooled design of leaves &
berries on twisting stems, original patina, impressed mark,
Bernh-M Linder, 2 x 5",
1½" h. **319.00**

Tankard, cov., Arts & Crafts
style, hand-hammered finish,
tapering cylindrical body
w/applied heart design & wide
bands at base & rim, riveted
applied handle, hinged cover
w/high thumbpiece & rounded
finial, rich original dark brown
patina, 13" h. **770.00**
(Illustration: bottom next column)

Tea caddy, cov., ginger jar-form,

decorated in the Japanese
taste, the spot-hammered surface applied w/branches bearing silver leaves & flowers, a
silver bird & moth, the slip-on
cover applied w/a silver lizard,
Gorham Mfg. Co., Providence,
Rhode Island, 1882,
4⅛" h. **6,325.00**

Teakettle, cov., the shaped
squat body w/dovetailed base,
the domed fitted lid w/brass
finial, gooseneck spout
w/scored latticework decoration
& snakehead terminal, the
swing handle inscribed "A.K.,
NY. 1827," New York, 1827,
13¼" l., 12½" h...................**3,450.00**
(Illustration: top next page)

Tray, hand-hammered, rectangular w/flat rim & reticulated
design of stylized blossoms at
ends, original patina, attributed
to Dirk Van Erp, 3½ x 8"........**121.00**

Tray, oval, decorated in the
Japanese taste, the surface
hammered into bark texture,
the sides raised & rolled over,
applied w/copper plum blossoms & twigs, silver pine
branches & a Japanese figure
riding the back of an ox & playing the flute, Gorham Mfg. Co.,
Providence, Rhode Island,
1883, 9¼" l. **4,025.00**

Copper Tankard with Heart Design

Copper Teakettle Dated "1827"

Tray, round floriform, impressed mark, W.A.S. Benson, 11½" d. **165.00**

Tray, hand-hammered, circular w/wide flat rim forming extended self-handles, original brown patina, impressed mark, Dirk Van Erp, 11 x 13", 1" h. **825.00**

Tray, hand-hammered, oval w/gently rolled edges & delicately hand-tooled linear design at edge, rich original dark brown patina, marked, Roycroft Shops, East Aurora, New York, 6 x 13½" **467.50**

Tray, hand-hammered finish, rectangular w/narrow open end handles, oval indentation in center, original patina, orb & cross mark, Roycroft Shops, East Aurora, New York, 6 x 13¾" **330.00**

Tray, hand-hammered, circular w/four broad impressions w/raised dot decoration surrounding a plain circular center, recent dark brown patina, Stickley Brothers, impressed "36," 14" d. **1,430.00**

Tray, hand-hammered, rectangular w/ornate cut-out heart-shaped handles flanked by protruding cut-out D-shaped devices, original dark brown patina, impressed "Benedict Studio 302," 8 x 15".............**297.00**

Tray, hand-hammered finish, rectangular w/rounded upturned edges & twisted handles, stamped mark of Gustav Stickley, 12" w., 15¾" l **690.00**

Tray, hand-hammered, circular w/tooled twisted rope design surrounding the edge, interior has lightly cleaned patina, the outer rim in original dark brown patina, marked, Roycroft Shops, East Aurora, New York, 16" d.....................................**412.50**

Tray, Arts & Crafts style, hand-hammered, rectangular w/rounded corners, double-braided loop end handles, excellent dark new patina, Gustav Stickley circular die-stamped mark, early 20th c., 12 x 18" **522.50**

Tray, rectangular center bordered w/an undulating rim incorporating cut-out handles, inscribed "Jarvie," Robert Jarvie, 12 x 18½" **1,840.00**

Tray, Arts & Crafts style, hand-hammered, round w/flanged rim & riveted loop side handles, rolled rim, original dark patina, die-stamped circular Gustav Stickley mark, early 20th c., 19½" d. at handles **1,045.00**

Tray, Arts & Crafts style, hand-hammered, round heavy gauge metal w/embossed tab handles on each side of the rolled rim, dished interior, recent dark patina, stamped open box mark of Dirk Van Erp, 17 x 21¼" **715.00**

Tray, Arts & Crafts style, hand-hammered, long oval form w/slightly dished sides, riveted loop end handles, impressed Gustav Stickley mark, Model No. 355, 11½ x 23" (cleaned) **431.00**

Tray, hand-hammered finish, rectangular w/undulating rim w/eared corners & rolled-in sides, rectangular center riveted border, unmarked, Benedict Studios, 11½ x 25" **1,100.00**

Vase, hand-hammered, Arts & Crafts style, tall bowl-form vessel w/tooled vertical panels rising to rim topped by a pattern of enameled blue diamonds & white dots, recessed rim in delicate design of tiny dots, original rich brown patina, illegible signature, 5½" d., 5" l. **357.50**

Vase, bud-type, hand-hammered woodgrain finish, the faceted base w/riveted angular handle to one side ending in a ring supporting a clear glass tube, original dark patina, die-stamped "KK," Karl Kipp, 8" h. **385.00**

Vase, hand-hammered, trumpet-form w/wide wavy rim, original dark brown patina, attributed to Benedict Studios, 10" h. **357.50**

Vase, rounded quadrangular form, spot-hammered surface, raised on four paw feet, one side applied w/an apple branch w/gilt leaves, one of which is being eaten by an applied silver bug, the other sides applied in silver w/a silver crane below two cranes in flight, a flower spray approached by two butterflies w/a frog below & a loosely-tied corn stalk below a butterfly & two swallows, Gorham Mfg. Co., Providence, Rhode Island, 1884, now mounted as a lamp, 10¾" h. plus lamp hardware..........**17,250.00**

Vase, hand-hammered, bulbous bottom rising to a wide bulging band & tapered neck beneath a wide fluted rim, rich original patina, Stickley Brothers, impressed "11," 11" h............**770.00**

Vase, Arts & Crafts style, hand-hammered, wide baluster-form body tapering to a short wide

neck w/rolled rim, original dark patina, die-stamped Dirk Van Erp 'open box' mark, early 20th c., 7" d., 11½" h.........**2,090.00**

Vase, hand-hammered finish, American Beauty-type, low foot supporting a squatty half-round base beneath a riveted band below a tall slender neck w/widely flaring rim, covered w/a brass wash, orb mark, Roycroft Shops, East Aurora, New York, 6" d., 12" h. **1,650.00**

Copper Vase by Harry Dixon

Vase, hand-hammered, deep hammered Arts & Crafts vertical leaf design, rolled rim, rich dark brown recent patina, marked "Harry Dixon San Francisco," 15" h. ....**1,650.00** (Illustration)

Vase, Arts & Crafts style, 'American Beauty' type, hand-hammered, footed wide squatty bulbous riveted base w/a wide flat shoulder centered by a tall ringed cylindrical neck w/a widely flaring rim, original dark brown patina, Roycroft Shops, East Aurora, New York, early orb & cross mark, early 20th c., 8" d., 19" h.........................**2,200.00**

Wall sconce, hand-hammered, narrow backplate w/applied disk, bending at right angle to support hanging electrical socket, hand-tooled geometric design, recent patina, impressed mark of Gustav Stickley, 3½" w., 8½" d., 10" h..................................**1,540.00**

Wall sconce, hand-hammered, rectangular backplate w/scrolled ends, nicely riveted, applied candleholder, original patina, impressed mark of Gustav Stickley, 3" w., 13" h.....................................**825.00**

Wall sconces, hand-hammered, rectangular backplate, the candleholder & bobeche held by an open wedge-shaped support, excellent original dark brown patina, unmarked, Karl Kipp, 2¾" w., 10" h., pr..........**440.00**

Wall sconces, hand-hammered, backplate w/scrolled ends, mounted w/single candleholder, original bobeche, original dark patina, unmarked, Gustav Stickley, 4" w.,12" h., pr. **935.00**

Wall sconces, hand-hammered, rectangular w/detailed hammering at edges & circular Arts & Crafts decoration near top, riveted applied candleholder, original dark brown patina, Old Mission Kopperkraft, 3½ x 12", pr..**605.00**

GOLD

Since before the days of the ancient pharaohs of Egypt, gold has been the most sought-after and fought-over natural mineral. Many great civilizations of the past were driven forward by their quest to accumulate priceless hoards of gold.

The search for new sources of gold and other riches of the Orient was the major force behind early European explorers. It wasn't long after Christopher Columbus' arrival in the New World that the Spanish Conquistadors were devastating the ancient cultures of Mexico, Central and South America with their insatiable hunger for their golden treasures.

Spain and its dominions continued to control the production of New World gold well into the 19th century, but following the discovery of gold in California in 1848 the United States joined the ranks of major gold producers. Then, in the 1890s, another huge lode of gold was uncovered in what had been considered the frozen wastelands of Alaska and the Yukon, spurring on another major Gold Rush. Russia, Australia and other points around the world have also contributed their share as sources of raw gold, but today the vast resources of the South African Transvaal surpass all other regions in production of raw gold for commercial and industrial use.

The purity of alloyed gold is indicated by the karat system in which the percent of gold by weight is given as a fraction of 24. Pure gold is 24 karat, 18 karat gold is 18/24 or 75 percent gold by weight. Very few items are made of 24 karat gold as it would be too soft; therefore, the gold is usually alloyed with some other metal to give it the needed strength.

Gold articles can be found in various colors. An alloy of gold, silver and copper, in which the amount of silver predominates, is called "green gold." An alloy of the same three elements, in which copper predominates, is called "red gold." An alloy of gold and nickel is called "white gold."

Gold, of course, has been used for ages to create jewelry and other articles of adornment. Another use for this precious metal is exquisite dinnerware, goblets and flatware which, although lovely, are astronomical in cost. At this time, gold is also in demand in industrial processes due to its relatively high electrical conductivity and extremely high resistance to corrosion. Finally, due to its lack of toxicity, it is indispensible in dentistry and medicine.

Price Listings:

18k Gold Two-light Candelabra

Candelabra, two-light, shaped square base raised on four floral bouquet feet, vasiform standard supporting two candlearms, pierced rims, engraved dedication under footrim, 18k, Tiffany & Co., New York, New York, 1902-07, 3¾" h., pr..................**$10,350.00** (Illustration)

Cigarette box w/hinged cover, rectangular, decorated w/bands of reeding, the cover inset w/a rock crystal plaque carved w/Buddha's feet, mounted w/a small tourmaline cabochon, 14k, Cartier, New York, New York, 4¾" l. (one cabochon missing) **2,875.00**

Cigarette box w/hinged cover, rectangular, the cover applied w/a carved jade plaque, the interior w/two compartments, 14k, 20th c., 5¾" l. **3,680.00**

Cigarette box w/hinged cover, rectangular, plain burnished finish, 18k, ca. 1930, 5¾" l. **4,025.00**

Gold & Jeweled Cigarette Case

Cigarette case, lady's, Somorodok-type, rectangular w/rounded corners, the cover corner inset w/a floriform spray

of diamonds & sapphires, w/cabochon sapphire thumbpiece, the interior surface w/erasure, Edward William Schramm, St. Petersburg, Russia, ca. 1900, in original retail box stamped "C.E. Bolin," 56 standard, 34¼" l. ....**2,875.00** (Illustration)

Russian Gold Cigarette Case

Cigarette case, rectangular, decorated w/panels of reeding, the cover applied w/a Russian Imperial Eagle set w/a diamond, w/cabochon sapphire thumbpiece, Morozov, St. Petersburg, Russia, ca. 1910, 3½" l. ....**2,070.00** (Illustration)

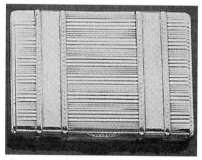

Gold Cigarette Case by Fabergé

Cigarette case, reeded & w/two engine-turned bands bordered by leaf-tips, w/diamond-set thumbpiece, marked w/initials of workmaster August Hollming, "Fabergé" in Cyrillic & 56 standard (14k), Fabergé, St.

Petersburg, Russia, ca. 1900, 3½" l. ....**13,800.00** (Illustration)

Cigarette case, bi-color, reeded w/alternating bands of green & red, w/cabochon sapphire thumbpiece, marked w/initials of workmaster A. Holmstrom, "Fabergé" in Cyrillic & 56 standard (14k), Fabergé, St. Petersburg, Russia, ca. 1910, 3¾" l. **4,600.00**

Gold Clasp ca. 1730

Clasp, oval w/applied panel w/three loop holes at either end for suspension, engraved w/a flowerhead within a reeded foliate band, maker's mark of William Cowell, Sr., Boston, Massachusetts, ca. 1730, overall 1" l. ....**3,450.00** (Illustration)

Clasp, oval w/bright-cut rim engraved w/contemporary initials "S.W." and attached to two (originally three) coral strands, the back engraved w/initials

"E.D.," Robert Fairchild, Connecticut, ca. 1790, 1½" l. **1,955.00**

Cuff links, in the form of a loosely tied knot, each set w/a cabochon sapphire & a ruby, marked w/Cyrillic initials of workmaster Andrei Gorianov & 56 standard (14k), Fabergé, St. Petersburg, Russia, ca. 1910, ¾" w. **8,050.00**

Cups & saucers, demitasse, the cups on a scrolled base w/scroll & floral handles, the rim w/beaded & applied *guilloche* band, the saucers w/matching rims, 18k, together w/Lenox porcelain liners w/gilt stylized floral band, Tiffany & Co., New York, New York, 1907-47, set of 12 ....**27,600.00** (Illustration: below, right)

Demitasse set: cov. coffeepot, cov. sugar bowl & creamer; tapering body w/molded domed base & double molded rim band, scroll handles, the coffeepot handle w/ivory insulators, the domed covers w/bud finials, 14k, Tiffany & Co., New York, New York, post-1947, coffeepot 10½" h., 3 pcs. ....**21,850.00** (Illustration: below, left)

Gold Demitasse Set and Cups & Saucers by Tiffany

Musical Gold Fob Seal

Fob seal, musical, in the form of two seahorses addorsed, their tails looped over their heads, the oval base w/a border of tendrils w/later carnelian base, wound by rotating the pendant ring & w/shut-off lever, Switzerland, ca. 1820, 1⅝" h. ....**1,265.00** (Illustration)

Locket-pendant, bi-color, irregular oval shape, decorated w/an Art Nouveau-style water lily, the interior w/two glazed compartments, Russia, ca. 1900, 1½" l. **805.00**

Picture frame, triple, each panel w/a plain gold border, 14k, Tiffany & Co., New York, New York, 1930, 6½" h. **3,450.00**

Picture frame, rectangular w/molded border, wooden back & strut, 14k, Tiffany & Co., New York, New York, ca. 1930, 7¾" h. **2,300.00**

Picture frame, rectangular, w/plain rim & wood back panel, engraved "FVG," 18k, Tiffany & Co., New York, New York, 1914-47, 12¼" h................**5,750.00**

Pin, formed as a circle & decorated w/a flower set w/three tiger's eye cabochons, marked w/initials of workmaster Erik Kollin & 56 standard (14k), Fabergé, St. Petersburg, Russia, ca. 1890, 1⅛" l. **3,162.00**

Plates, service, plain w/raised molded rim, Gorham Mfg. Co., Providence, Rhode Island, ca. 1920-30, 11⅛" d., set of 12 ....**61,900.00**

Snuff box, cov., oval, curved, engraved w/a border of leaves, the cover engraved w/crest & a motto, George III period, maker's mark "G.C.," London, England, 1801, 2⅞" l. **2,530.00**

Vari-colored Gold Snuff Box

Snuff box w/hinged cover, vari-colored, rectangular, the borders chased w/vari-colored shells & foliage on a matted ground, the cover mounted w/an enameled plaque painted w/a maiden at an altar of love, Continental, ca. 1830, 3¼" l. ....**3,450.00** (Illustration)

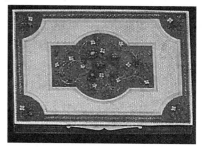

Swiss Gold Snuff Box

Snuff box w/hinged cover, vari-colored, rectangular, the cover engine-turned & chased w/a reserve of vari-colored flowers on a matted ground, the corners of the cover & base similarly chased, Switzerland, ca. 1815, 3⅜" l. ....**3,162.00** (Illustration)

Ornate Gold Snuff Box

Snuff box, cov., vari-colored, rectangular, the cover chased w/foliage on a matted ground, the base chased w/birds flanking a vase of vari-colored fruit & flowers, Switzerland, ca. 1820, 3½" l. ....**2,760.00** (Illustration)

Toilet set, traveling-type, eight glass jars or bottles w/gold covers, gold tubular container, three brushes, hand mirror, nail buffer, comb, shoehorn, two pairs of scissors, nail file & button hook, together w/a gold jar cover & three gold stoppers, in fitted leather case, 14k, Cartier, New York, New York, the set **4,485.00**

IRON

One of the most common elemental metals found in nature, raw iron, has been used by man since the dawn of history. Scientists believe early man may have extracted iron from meteorites, pounding it to form primitive tools and weapons. Eventually man learned to smelt the raw metal and by 1200 B.C., the beginning of the Iron Age, it was being widely used in many cultures.

Iron is utilized by two different methods. One is the casting of the molten ore in a mold to form the desired item. The other is the hand-wrought or forged method where the metal is heated to the red hot stage and formed by hammering the piece into the desired form.

Cast iron has been used for a multitude of purposes including the manufacture of many types of kitchenware, such as kettles, pots, muffin pans, griddles, skillets and teakettles. It has also been utilized in everything from children's banks to parlor stoves, building fronts to firebacks and fountains to doorstops.

Hand-wrought iron was used for many utilitarian and decorative articles including ornamental hardware, fireplace andirons and fireplace tools, kitchen tools and the decorative racks to hold the tools. Many farm implements were also made of hand-wrought iron such as plows, pitchforks, shovels and, of course, horse shoes. Because of its inherent strength and durability, iron work is commonly found at antiques shops and auctions and can form the nucleus of a very interesting collection.

In recent years, reproductions of both cast and wrought iron have flooded to the market, so care is needed when buying. Newer cast pieces tend to be coarser and cruder than their original counterparts, and items such as banks and toys often have ill-fitting joints and rough edges. New iron wares also tend to rust much more quickly than early examples, so be suspicious if a piece has a thin, even, rusty red surface.

Price Listings:

Andirons, cast, cast in the half-round as a female figure continuing to shaped supports, America, early 20th c., 12½" h., pr. ....**$460.00** (Illustration: top next page)

Andirons, cast, modeled in the form of a lady wearing a cap & V-neck dress, raised w/arched legs terminating in claw-and-ball feet, Shenandoah Valley,

Cast-Iron Figural Andirons

Virginia, 1810-20, 9¾" l., 12" w., 14⅞" h., pr. (restoration to rear of one log support) **4,887.00**

Cast-Iron Figural Owl Andirons

Andirons, cast, modeled in the half-round as an owl w/inset yellow glass eyes, log supports marked "918-1 Made in U.S.A.," 20th c., 15" h., pr. ....**2,012.00** (Illustration)

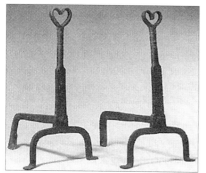

Iron Heart-form Andirons

Andirons, hand-wrought, heart-

form top above spurred arched supports ending in pad feet, probably Pennsylvania, early 19th c., 15¼" h., pr. ....**4,025.00** (Illustration)

Andirons with Smiling Faces

Andirons, cast, the finial in the form of a smiling man's face within a sunflower, the serpentine stem raised on an arched base, impressed "PAT'D AUG 24 1886," America, ca. 1890, 16½" h., pr. ....**2,587.00** (Illustration)

Andirons, cast, surmounted by a sunburst, Bradley & Hubbard, Meriden, Connecticut, 17" h., pr. **575.00**

Andirons, cast, modeled in the half-round as the figure of a man w/his hands on his knees, painted black, America, 20th c., 17" h., pr. **690.00**

Cast-Iron Figural Cat Andirons

Andirons, cast, modeled in the half-round as a seated cat w/tail wrapped around its legs, w/yellow glass eyes, on scrolling base, stamped "P.S.W. & Co." on body & log arm, America, 20th c., 17½" h., pr.......................................**2,012.00** (Illustration)

Andirons, cast, in the form of a Hessian soldier wearing a British Revolutionary uniform & carrying a sword, gilt finish, America, 19th c., 19" h., pr....**368.00**

Andirons, cast, modeled in the full round as a castle turret, painted black, America, 20th c., 22¼" h..................................**575.00**

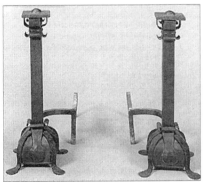

Cast- and Wrought-Iron Andirons

Andirons, cast & hand-wrought, the cushion-form base applied

w/wrought scrolls, raised on four spade-shaped feet, w/rectangular standards terminating in square tops w/scrolls below, 26¼" h., pr.........................**1,380.00** (Illustration)

Andirons, hand-wrought, scroll form w/large scroll at base filled in w/smaller scrolls continuing to a further small scroll beneath an openwork section beneath a curling top, black finish, Roycroft Shops, East Aurora, New York, 14" w., 27" h., pr. (some wear to finish).........**2,860.00**

Andirons, hand-wrought, coiled body in the form of a stylized pineapple shape w/ornate scrolled & coiled top, on elaborate scrolled feet, possibly Roycroft, early 20th c., 37" h., pr...............................**575.00** (Illustration: below)

Apple peeler, cast, mechanical-type, w/table clamp, marked "Sinclair, Scott & Co., Baltimore"...............................**82.50**

Baking mold, cast, figure of Santa Claus w/"Hello Kiddies" at base, two-part, "Griswold," 12¼" h.................................**522.50**

Coiled Wrought-Iron Andirons

Cast-Iron Decorative Baluster

Baluster, cast, the central shield within an ellipse bordered by ornate scrollwork & surmounted by stylized foliage, designed by Adler & Sullivan, executed by the Yale and Towne Manufacturing Co. for the Guaranty Building, Buffalo, New York, 1894-95, 34¾" h................**2,300.00** (Illustration)

Betty lamp (early grease lamp), hand-wrought, lid w/bird silhouette finial, w/hanger, 3½" h. plus hanger (pick missing) **302.50**

Betty lamp, hand-wrought, heart shaped finial on font lid, brass hanger finial w/stamped crossed hammers, 4" h. plus hanger.................................**220.00**

Betty lamp, hand-wrought, the pot-form burner swiveling between scrolled supports above a turned standard & X-form base, probably Pennsylvania, early 19th c., 8½" h...............................**1,840.00**

Book ends, cast, depicting an elephant walking w/trunk down, figure w/old red paint, old polychrome ground, marked "112," 4" h., pr.................................**82.50**

Book ends, cast, modeled in the form of a saddled horse w/head down grazing, old polychrome paint, marked "110," 4⅝" h., pr...............................**60.50**

Book ends, cast, model of an Airedale on a grassy base, polychrome paint, worn "Hubley" label, 5¼" h., pr. **121.00**

Book ends, cast, modeled in the form of a camel in kneeling position, old polychrome paint, marked "1153," 5¼" h., pr. **93.50**

Book ends, cast, modeled as two quail on a leafy base, old polychrome paint, 5½" h., pr. (wear) **137.50**

Bootjack, cast, "American Bull Dog," pistol shape opens to bootjack, debossed lettering, 8¼" l. (very minor rust)...........**49.50**

Boot scraper, cast, two full-bodied horses mounted on rectangular blocks which hold wooden-backed brushes w/space between to accommodate a boot or shoe, old repaint in black, brown & white, 12 x 10", 14½" h. (light rust, brushes are worn & weathered)...............**275.00**

Cast-Iron Bracket with Cow & Bell

Bell & bracket, cast, the standing figure of a full bodied horned cow standing on a black painted scrolling bracket continuing to a bell suspended from a triangle, America, late 19th c., 24" w., 29" h. ....**3,220.00** (Illustration)

Broad axe, hand-wrought, ash handle, blade 9" w.,11" h. (pitted) **71.50**

Candelabra, five-light, hand-wrought, the domed circular foot supporting a scallop-edged panel enclosing a stylized floral openwork design & issuing four arms, each supporting a candleholder, surmounted at top w/a finial candleholder, one stamped "COBERG GERMANY," the other "GERMANY," 13¼" h., pr. **805.00**

Candlestick, Arts & Crafts style, hand-wrought, an arched tripod base w/'penny' feet supports a ropetwist stem w/central ring below a wide dished drip pan & cylindrical candle socket, original mellow patina, Samuel Yellin, impressed "YELLIN," early 20th c., 7½" w., 13" h. **1,540.00**

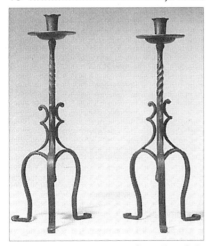

19th c. Hand-wrought Candlesticks

Candlesticks, hand-wrought, three scrolling legs supporting a twisted standard & tulip-shaped candle socket, probably Highland County, Virginia, 19th c., 15¼" h., pr. ....**3,737.00** (Illustration)

Chandelier, hand-wrought, three-light, twisted detail, three curved arms w/conical candle nozzles, 12¾" h. plus link......**357.50**

Arts & Crafts-style Chandelier

Chandelier, cast, Arts & Crafts style, five-light, designed w/four conical hanging lanterns w/white & yellow slag glass & an inset center dome lamp, w/heavy chains & conical ceiling plate, 22" d., overall 40" h. ....**880.00** (Illustration)

Coffee grinder, cast, painted decoration, "Enterprise Mfg. Co. Philadelphia pat'd 1873," 11" h. **431.00**

Coffee grinder, cast, countertop model, single wheel w/wooden handle & filigree star design, marked "Swift Mill, Lane Brothers, Poughkeepsie, N.Y.," worn old red paint w/black & gold trim, 14" h. **385.00**

Coffee grinder, cast, countertop model w/large side wheels, square base, ovoid center section & covered bowl top, marked "Enterprise Mfg. Co. Philadelphia," wooden drawer front in base w/faded label "No. 2," 21" h. (wooden bottom board & finial missing)...........**170.50**

Cookie mold, cast, oval w/cor-

nucopia center surrounded by
frame of dots, 4 x 5¼" **165.00**

Doorstop, cast, full-bodied figure of Aunt Jemima, worn original polychrome paint, 9" h.....**275.00**

Doorstop, cast, modeled in the
form of a cockatoo, worn old
polychrome paint, 12" h. **137.50**

Doorstop, cast, nodding-type,
full-bodied model of a donkey,
old black patina, 11" l. **187.00**

Doorstop, cast, waisted basketweave base filled w/flowers
& surmounted by a tall overhead handle topped by a ribbon, old polychrome paint
w/some touchup, 15½" h.......**110.00**

Doorstop, cast, seated German
Shepherd on shaped base, flat
back, old gold paint, 9½" h......**55.00**

Cast-Iron Pekingese Dog Doorstop

Doorstop, cast, full-bodied
model of a Pekingese, worn
original polychrome paint,
14" l. **1,320.00**
(Illustration)

Doorstop, cast, modeled in the
form of a squirrel in seated
position w/tail up, holding a nut
in its paws, gold w/black de-
tails, 6½" h. (some wear) **170.50**

Doorstop, cast, modeled in the
form of a pair of swallows on a
berried branch, worn original
polychrome paint, 8¼" h. **220.00**

Doorstop-bank, cast, full-bodied figure of a black minstrel
player, worn original poly-
chrome paint, 10" h. **165.00**

Dough scraper, hand-wrought,
heart cut-out in blade, 5" l. **412.50**

Cast-Iron Elevator Door Medallion

Elevator door medallion, cast,
pierced circular form w/Celtic
interlace & scrolling foliate
design, designed by George
Elmslie for Louis Sullivan's
Carson Pirie Scott store,
Chicago, Illiois, 1904,
22⅝" d. **6,900.00**
(Illustration)

Sheet-Iron Silhouette of an Indian

Figure of an Indian, sheet-iron,
the silhouette figure of an
archer painted w/an ochre face
& upper body, black hair &
ochre moccasins, mounted on
a red, ochre & brown mottled
rectangular plinth, originally
used as a directional on an
early locomotive engine,
America, 19th c., figure
16" h. **2,070.00**
(Illustration)

Sheet-iron Figure of a Rooster

Figure of a rooster, sheet, modeled in silhouette form w/stylized features, w/stand, possibly America, early 19th c., 8¼" h.............................**1,380.00** (Illustration)

Fireback, cast, depicting a man astride a horse, inscribed "Louis XV. Roy de France et de Navarre," France, 17½" w., 22½" h................................**143.00**

Cast-Iron Decorative Fireback

Fireback, cast, square, cast in three registers, the top w/relief double-arch centering flower-and-heart & urn-and-flower designs over a band w/raised lettering "George Ross George Steven" above a lozenge enclosing the year "1762," probably Pennsylvania, 1762, 26" w., 24" h.......................**1,035.00** (Illustration)

Unique Cast Iron Fireback

Fireback, cast, arched oblong, the crest centering a shell flanked by leafage, the tombstone panel below centering the pedestaled bust portrait of a lady wearing a crown w/drapery swags & a fleur-de-lis above, the whole w/a surround decorated w/flowers & leafage, Virginia, ca. 1730, 20⅜" w., 30¼" h.............................**72,900.00** (Illustration)

Fireback, cast, three-part, decorated in bas-relief w/a floral & oak design, T. Harris, Chicago, Illinois, Victorian, late 19th c., center 26" w., 31¼" h., sides 14⅞" w., the set **632.50**

Fire mark, cast, oval w/central spread-winged eagle flanked by "U" & "F," raised stud decoration at rim,11" l. (pitted w/rust) **71.50**

Fire mark, cast, oval, depicting a hydrant w/hose flanked at the top by "F" & "A," 11" h. (pitted, w/black repaint) **104.50**

Fireplace set: pair of andirons, shovel, tongs & poker w/stand; cast, the andirons modeled in the form of an owl perched on a branch, w/glass eyes, the

Cast-Iron Figural Owl Fireplace Set

tools w/matching owl handles, America, 19th c., andirons 20" l., 14½" h., the set........**2,070.00** (Illustration)

Fireplace set: pair of andirons, tongs, shovel & rack; hand-wrought, the andirons w/scrolled arched feet supporting a squared column w/three hooks surmounted by a foliate finial, the rack w/a domed circular base w/pierced scroll & scallop design supporting a squared column surmounted by foliate finial & issuing two applied scrolled & arched brackets fitted w/fire tools decorated w/scrolled & knopped handles, all stamped "E. BRANDT," andirons 28" h., rack 37¾" h., the set **12,650.00**

Wrought-Iron Fire Screen by Brandt

Fireplace tools: poker, shovel & pair of tongs in holder; cast, squared handle topped by a ball finial, brass wash, raised lettering "Bradley and Hubbard Manufacturing Co." stand 10½ x 30½", the set **660.00**

Fire screen, hand-wrought, Art Deco style, the frame of hammered square form set w/scrolls & foliate devices, raised on trestle feet, France, ca. 1925, 24" w., 23¾" h. ...**5,175.00**

Fire screen, hand-wrought, square, the center w/a stylized fountain flanked by curving flowered branches, raised on four scrolled feet, by Edgar Brandt, ca. 1924, 29¼" w., 36" h.................................**20,700.00** (Illustration: bottom previous column)

Wrought-Iron Fire Screen with Deer

Fire screen, hand-wrought, rectangular, depicting a deer amid stylized flowers & branches, all above a stylized floral frieze, raised on scrolled legs, by Edgar Brandt, ca. 1925 ....**29,900.00** (Illustration)

Fork, roasting-type, hand-wrought, the blade inlaid w/a brass panel inscribed "Philadelphia" & the date "1815," w/loop handle, Philadelphia, ca. 1815.......**2,875.00**

Fork, roasting-type, hand-wrought, the blade handle decorated w/a heart, w/rattail hook, probably Pennsylvania, ca. 1800, 13¾" l. **172.00**

Fork, hand-wrought, three-tine, the center tine formed as a heart w/long point, found in Pennsylvania, 17¼" l..........**1,155.00**

Fork, roasting-type, hand-wrought, the heart-pierced handle w/hook terminal & punch-work-decorated top continuing to form a diamond-decorated notched support terminating in a pair of tapered tines, probably Pennsylvania, 1750-1810, 19" l. **1,265.00**

Fork, hand-wrought, rattail hanger above a blade w/inset brass panel bearing the initials "LT" above a heart, probably Pennsylvania, early 19th c., 21½" l. **2,300.00**

Garden figure, cast, modeled in the form of a full bodied rabbit, worn old white repaint, 10½" h..................................**220.00**

Garden urns, cast, modeled in the form of a cherub standing on a plinth & holding an oval basketweave bowl on his head, worn old white repaint, 45" h., pr............................**5,940.00**
(Illustration: one of two, top next column)

Cast-Iron Figural Garden Urn

Gate, cast, rectangular, centered w/a Revolutionary War cap painted w/an American eagle & powder horn, flanked by a U.S. Mail bag, crossed swords & flintlock rifles all within foliage, within borders of darts & circles, surmounted by five stars flanked by two spearheads, old repaint in green, black, red & white, manufactured by the Old Union Forge Company, Highbridge, New Jersey, third quarter 19th c., 77" w., 45¼" h...............................**6,900.00**
(Illustration: below)

Gates, hand-wrought, the scalloped top enclosing stylized florettes & scrolls above vertical

Cast-Iron Gate with Revolutionary War Theme

Wrought-Iron Gates by Paul Kiss

bars centered by a panel featuring elongated leaves, scrolls & flowers, stamped "P. KISS PARIS," ca. 1928, each gate 4" deep, 30" w., 62½" h., pr.....................................**17,250.00** (Illustration)

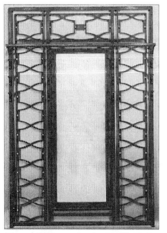

Art Deco Wrought-Iron Hall Stand

Hall stand, hand-wrought, Art Deco style, the central scalloped frame w/upper shelf enclosing a mirror plate, the surround wrought w/X-devices & gold-painted spheres, the upper section set w/coat hooks, France, ca. 1925, 4' 7" w., 6' 8" h....................**1,380.00** (Illustration)

Conestoga Wagon Hatchet Holder

Hatchet holder for Conestoga wagon, hand-wrought, modeled in the form of a fish w/scales & punched eye w/two prongs behind, Pennsylvania, late 18th - early 19th c., 8" l., 3" h..................................**6,900.00** (Illustration)

Hearth game broiler, hand-wrought, w/drip pan, raised on penny feet, 16" l. **550.00**

Hearth toaster, hand-wrought, twisted detail, well shaped handle, 14 x 19" **247.50**

Jardiniere, hand-wrought, rectangular w/shaped ends, raised on eight ball feet, the arched sides decorated w/a stylized fountain surrounded by scrolls & beading, w/removable liner, stamped "E. BRANDT," 6¼ x 11½", 6¼" h........................**5,750.00** (Illustration: below)

Kettle stand, hand-wrought, rotating-type, tripod base w/penny feet & round top, brass trim, 8½" d., 12" h........**302.50** (Illustration: top next page)

Wrought-Iron Jardiniere by Brandt

Wrought-Iron Rotating Kettle Stand

Ladle, hand-wrought, the blade handle pierced w/a heart, w/rattail hanger, probably Pennsylvania, early 19th c., 14½" l. **345.00**

Ladle, hand-wrought, the blade engraved w/geometric designs & the initials "AM" above a shaped standard, probably Pennsylvania, early 19th c., 21½" l. **2,300.00**

Ladle, hand-wrought, the tapered handhold w/hook terminal & handhold inlaid w/the initials "P.F." continuing to a tapered bar w/three horizontal inlaid bars of copper & brass, the slightly flared support continuing to a circular bowl, probably Pennsylvania, 1760-1800, 21⅞" l. **805.00**

Lancet, hand-wrought, rectangular, the top w/the initials "P.D." & the date "1846," attributed to Peter Derr, Tulpehocken Township, Berkshire County, Pennsylvania, ca. 1846, 3¾" l. **1,035.00**

Lantern, cast, Arts & Crafts style, hanging-type, three-sided, linear design w/pyramidal screws, white slag glass liner, w/original chain & ceiling plate, unmarked, 7½" w., w/chain 16" h..........................**82.50**
(Illustration: top next column)

Lighting fixture, hand-wrought, ceiling-type, the square frame

Arts & Crafts-Style Hanging Lantern

w/a pierced cross-shaped design, enclosing four sprigs of foliage, applied w/a C-scroll border, brown patina, stamped "E Brandt," 16" sq..................**460.00**

Lock, hand-wrought, w/"Y"-shaped keeper, w/key **104.50**

Meat hook, hanging-type, hand-wrought, open domed top holding four short hooks & one long central hook, late 19th - early 20th c., 21" l. **467.50**

Mirror, wall-type, hand-wrought, shaped rectangular form w/two projecting tabs on either side, surmounted by a cascade of stylized foliage, Raymond Subes, 25" w., 43" h...........**8,050.00**

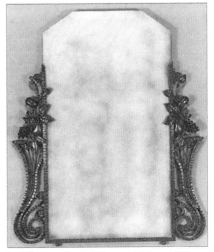

Art Deco-Style Wrought-Iron Mirror

Mirror, wall-type, hand-wrought, Art Deco style, the beveled mirror plate w/lower surround wrought w/clusters of fruit & scrolling devices, France, ca. 1910, 36½" w., 46" h. ...**2,300.00** (Illustration: bottom previous page)

Mirror, wall-type, hand-wrought, the rectangular mirror plate flanked by decorative side panels featuring a diamond & chevron design, the panels hinged to allow cleaning of the mirror behind, in the style of Paul Kiss, France, 24 x 56" **6,325.00**

Model of an American eagle, cast, the full-bodied figure depicted w/its body thrusting forward, perched on an acanthus-molded scroll, retains much of the original gilding, now mounted on a pine base, 19th c., 11½" l., 4½" h. **1,495.00**

Model of a turtle, cast, four legs, head & tail extended, traces of old red paint, 7½" l. **165.00**

Moto meter, cast, "Boyce," junior model, The Moto Meter Co., Inc., Long Island City, N.Y., 8" w., 4¾" h. (overall wear, glass missing) **44.00**

Nutcracker, cast, model of a dog on an openwork base, lift tail, put nut in dog's mouth & lower tail to crack, black, 4½" deep, 9" w., 5¼" h. (very minor rust & soiling) **33.00**

Oven peel, hand-wrought, long handle w/ram's horn end, 41½" l. **82.50**

Plant stands, cast, everted foliate rim, raised on a standard decorated w/elaborate foliate & scrolling pierced designs, painted finial, Victorian, 35" h., pr. **2,185.00**

Porringer, cast, circular w/rounded sides & tab handle w/radiating ribs, marked "Kenrick one pint," 5½" d.........**33.00**

Rush light holder, hand-wrought, plain standard w/candle socket counterweight, on tripod base w/scrolling ends, late 19th - early 20th c., 42¼" h. **165.00**

Scale, countertop balance-type, cast, old black, green, red & gold paint, w/brass hopper & fittings, w/three weights, 18" l. **137.50**

Scale, grocer's balance-type,

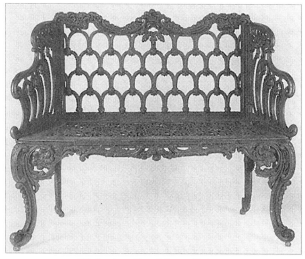

Victorian Cast-Iron Settee

cast, w/ceramic tray & three weights, gilt decoration, labeled "Cooperative Wholesale Society Limited," Victorian, 18½" l. **165.00**

Scale, balance-type, hand-wrought, twisted detail on end hooks, 24½" l. **93.50**

Settee, cast, the swagged crest-rail above a back composed of an openwork horseshoe design, flanked by scrolling arms, the seat w/a pierced scroll design, raised on ornate scrolling legs, painted blue, Victorian, late 19th c., 44" l., 36½" h. **862.50**
(Illustration: bottom previous page)

Shooting gallery figure, cast, rooster **88.00**

Sign bracket, hand-wrought, w/conestoga wagon, tree, oxen, people & other figures across the top, polychrome paint, 20th c., 67" l. **275.00**

Skewer, hand-wrought, the twisted & blade skewer flanked by scrolls, the blade w/the punched initials "TC," w/loop hanger, Continental, 19th c., 30¾" l. **690.00**

Skewer holder & skewers, hand-wrought, heart-shape surmounted by a pierced circle above a bar w/coiled ends,

Wrought-Iron Skewers & Hanger

holding twelve skewers, found in New Hampshire, the set **715.00**

Skewers & hanger, hand-wrought, the hanger w/a shaped body above a terminal w/scrolled ends, ten skewers of varying sizes ending in ring hanging holes, overall 13½" l., 11 pcs. **1,840.00**
(Illustration: bottom previous column)

Skimmer, hand-wrought, large circular dished pierced pan, wooden handle, 23" l. **99.00**

Cast-Iron Snow Bird

Snow birds, cast, modeled in the form of a spread-winged eagle w/head turned to right, 6½" h., set of 3 ....**49.50**
(Illustration: one of three)

'Socony' Cast-Iron Soap Dispenser

Soap dispenser, cast, "Socony," spherical w/handle at one side, pull handle to dispense soap, mounted on a wooden back, scratches & soiling, 6" w., 5½" h..............**165.00**
(Illustration)

Spatula, hand-wrought, the blade w/three brass bands, the larger w/the initials "J.G." &

dated "1819," the others engraved w/scrolls, probably Pennsylvania, ca. 1819, 14½" l. **1,265.00**

Spatula, hand-wrought, handle w/two brass inlays, one w/initials & the other w/heart & "1823," 15¼" l. (bottom inlay glued in place, blade has edge wear, hanger incomplete) **357.50**

Spatula, hand-wrought, the handle crested w/a heart, w/rattail hanger, probably Pennsylvania, early 19th c., 16" l. **345.00**

Spatula, hand-wrought, the blade crested w/an inset brass panel engraved w/a spreadwing American eagle & shield beneath the inscription "Liberty," further decorated w/incised stars, the shaped blade pierced, w/rattail hanger, probably Pennsylvania, early 19th c., 16¼" l. **1,840.00**

Spatula, hand-wrought, the blade w/two brass panels, one w/initials "BJ" above a heart, the second panel w/the date "1822," w/rattail hanger, probably Pennsylvania, ca. 1822, 17¼" l. **920.00**

Spatula, hand-wrought, the elongated handle w/hook terminal continuing to a diamond-

shaped medial section & terminating in a heart-pierced blade, probably Pennsylvania, 1750-1810, 22⅜" l. **690.00**

Stove, cast, kerosene-type, w/two burners, marked "Fireplace Heater, Dietz Noz," complete w/font & burners, 18" h. (mica panels in top part have minor damage & small holes, some rust & pitting) **192.50**

Stove, parlor-type, cast, curving legs supporting a rectangular fire box w/ornate decoration, two pipes issuing from top & joined by an ornately decorated arch, marked "Stanley's Patent No 2," 33½" h. ....**440.00** (Illustration: bottom previous column)

Egyptian Revival Parlor Stove

Stove, parlor-type, cast, Egyptian Revival style, the central feather plume finial above a double-arched double-serpentine & relief-decorated crest over two decorated squared columns-on-urns on egg-and-dart embellished plinths above a decorated base impressed w/the name "E.N. PRATT & CO. ALBANY" surrounding the central stovepipe hole, over a shaped & molded skirt, on embellished scroll feet, E.N. Pratt & Co., Albany, New York,

Stanley's Patent No. 2 Stove

'Yale' Cast-Iron Tire Rack

ca. 1837-44, 15¼" deep,
34½" w., 58½" h. **2,300.00**
(Illustration)

Table, hand-wrought, the flat
rectangular top w/a single
rounded corner, supported by a
slender cylindrical column &
terminating in a flattened circular base, painted black, Pierre
Chareau, France, ca. 1930, 22"
deep, 15½" w., 25¾" h. **13,800.00**

Table, console-type, hand-
wrought, the scrolled support
w/a branch design, supporting
a demilune marble top, all resting on a conforming marble
base, Raymond Subes, 14"
deep, 34" w., 32" h. **14,950.00**

Table, console-type, hand-
wrought, the four scrolled legs

Silver-mounted Iron Tea Caddy

supporting a scalloped apron
decorated w/stylized roses,
leaves & stems, surmounted by
a demilune marble top,
stamped "E. BRANDT," Edgar
Brandt, ca. 1920s, 17" deep,
61" w., 35" h. **24,150.00**

Tea caddy, hand-wrought, of
oval form w/fluted base, the
sides applied w/a silver dragon,
fan & the initials "A.R.," further
inset w/a panel depicting a
sculptor carving a demon
mask, the slip-on cover surmounted by an applied silver
crab & carved w/stylized
scrolls, Gorham Mfg. Co.,
Providence, Rhode Island,
1883, 6¼" h. **6,900.00**
(Illustration: bottom previous column)

Tire rack, cast, "Yale," yellow &
green, folds down, repainted,
13½" w., 7" h. **66.00**
(Illustration: above)

Torcheres, hand-wrought, twisted standard on curving tripod
legs & pad feet, terminating
into six curved arms & straight-
ened central arm, connected
by an openwork horizontal
band, w/animal head & loose
ring terminals below the candle
cups & bobeches, stamped "W.
Barton Benson - Wyncote -
Pa." on the legs, late 19th -
early 20th c., 71" h., pr. **2,990.00**
(Illustration: top next page)

Wrought-Iron Seven-light Torcheres

Toy, cast, "Contractor's Dump Wagon," pulled by single horse, traces of old paint, 14½" l. (lacking driver) **247.50**

Toy, cast, "Hansom Cab," vehicle w/driver, pulled by a white horse, Kenton Hardware Co., Kenton, Ohio,16" l. **550.00**

Toy, cast, motorcycle w/driver, blue w/original rubber tires, 6½" l. (small piece off front, paint chips)...........................**132.00**

Toy, cast, motorcycle w/driver, orange Harley Davidson w/civil-ian driver, original paint & tires, "2064," Hubley ....**550.00** (Illustration: below)

Toy, cast, "Overland Circus," polar bear cage wagon, pulled by a pair of white horses w/riders, driver seated at top of cage, Kenton Hardware Co., Kenton, Ohio, unused condition in original box, 14" l..............**495.00**

Toy, cast, truck, "Champion Gas & Motor Oil," red w/metal wheels, Champion, Geneva, Wisconsin, ca. 1930s, 8" l. (paint chipping) **660.00**

Trivet, cast, the top pierced w/a tulip, supported on four feet, Pennsylvania, mid-19th c., 5¾" d....................................**345.00**

Umbrella stand, cast, cast in the Liberty style as a stylized artichoke w/a stellate opening, on an octagonal base, ca. 1900, 20¼" h. ....**1,552.00** (Illustration: bottom next page)

Urns, cast, circular w/rounded bottom & rolled rim, ornate side handles, raised on square foot, 10½" d., 10½" h., pr. **385.00**

Utensil rack, hand-wrought, the back w/three hearts above straight bar, probably Pennsylvania, early 19th c.,

Iron Toy Harley Davidson Motorcycle

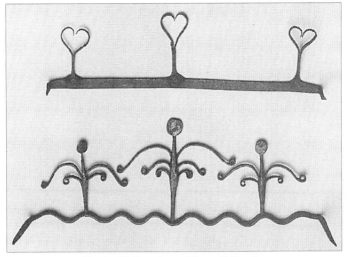

Early 19th c. Iron Utensil Racks

15¼" l. **920.00**
(Illustration: above, top)

Utensil rack, hand-wrought, the
back w/three 'tree of life'
uprights on a wavy base, probably Pennsylvania, early
19th c., 16¾" l. **1,380.00**
(Illustration: above, bottom)

Wafer iron, cast, the circular
mold w/floral decoration surrounded by a band of acorns &
oak leaves, probably Pennsylvania, 19th c., overall
26" l. **172.00**

Liberty-style Iron Umbrella Stand

Wafer iron, cast & hand-
wrought, cast w/starflower
design, long hand-wrought
handles, 4 x 7¾", handles
27" l. **27.50**

Wafer iron, cast & hand-
wrought, cast waffle design
w/Masonic pyramid in sunrays,
wrought handles, 29" l. **165.00**

Wall sconces, hand-wrought,
two-light, slender bar supporting two facing roosters, each
w/a candle socket, flanking a
short stem pierced for hanging,
12" l., pr. **132.50**

Weathervane, cast, the full-bodied & statuesque figure of a
horse w/left front leg raised,
molded forelock, incised mane
& wavy-cut applied sheet metal
tail, Rochester Ironworks,
Rochester, New Hampshire,
late 19th c., now mounted on a
rectangular black metal base,
24½" l., 19¼" h. **9,200.00**

Weathervane, modeled in silhouette form depicting an
Indian mounted on a rearing
horse & thrusting a spear,
painted grey, America, 19th c.,
29¼" w., 23" h. (lacking stan-
dard & directionals) **403.00**

Weathervane, sheet, the silhouetted figure of a pig painted white w/brown spots, probably Pennsylvania, ca. 1880, now mounted on a rod in a stepped black painted wood base, 34½" l., overall 25" h. **7,475.00**

Cast-Iron Stagecoach Weathervane

Weathervane, cast, modeled in silhouette form depicting a stagecoach, painted red w/black detail, America, late 19th c., 48" l., 46½" h. ....**2,587.00** (Illustration)

Weathervane, the stylized rooster silhouette painted in yellow & red, mounted on a rod & a rectangular wooden base, America, 19th c., 24" l. (losses to paint) **1,035.00**

Windmill weight, cast, crescent shape, "Eclipse A13," Fairbanks, Morse and Company, Chicago, Illinois, 10½" l. **93.50**

Windmill weight, cast, crescent shape, "Eclipse B13," Fairbanks, Morse & Company, Chicago, Illinois, 10½" l. **93.50**

Windmill weight, cast, rooster, "10 FT No 2," Elgin Wind Power and Pump Company, Elgin, Illinois, old white repaint w/polychrome, 16" h.............**528.00**

Windmill weight, cast, rooster, "A20," attributed to Elgin Wind Power and Pump Company, Elgin, Illniois, old worn surface

w/traces of paint, on wooden base, 20" h. **1,265.00**

LEAD

One of the oldest metals known to man, this heavy bluish-grey element has been used for thousands of years as a building material, to produce decorative objects and as a base for a glaze on inexpensive pottery.

It has been known for centuries that lead is toxic to humans, so few household objects were made using the raw metal. It could be combined with other metals, such as tin and antimony, to form more durable pieces, but contrary to popular myth, very little or no lead was used in the best antique pewter. The English, in particular, had stringent regulations controlling the quality of pewterwares, and pewterers in the American colonies followed those standards.

Since lead alloys are easily worked and produce objects which resist water corrosion, many pieces of garden statuary and ornaments have been made using lead. Early examples of these decorative artworks can bring high prices in today's antiques market, and we list a selection below.

Price Listings:

Fountain, garden-type, modeled in the form of a putto holding a dolphin, 31" h. plus base **$1,725.00**

Figure of Santa Claus on low disc base, worn polychromed finish, 4⅛" h. **165.00**

Fountain, model of a dolphin w/an oversized head, water issues from the mouth, 48" l. ....**3,737.00** (Illustration: top next page)

Lead Dolphin Fountain

Garden plaque, continuous scene of frolicking cherubs, very heavy & soft, 54½" w., 12¾" h. **605.00**

Plaque, figural, the shaped oval w/molded rim cast in low- and medium-relief w/a nude maiden w/flowing hair lying in the frothing surf, inscribed "Ledru, SUSSE Fres. Paris Edt.," August Ledru, France, ca. 1890, 31¾" l., 22¼" h. **1,725.00**

Models of whippets, reclining dogs w/front legs extended, designed for garden display, 48" l., pr. ....**4,887.00** (Illustration: below)

Wall sconces, two-light, the scrolled shield-shaped backplate centered by a satyr's mask supporting two acanthus-

Gilt-Lead Two-light Wall Sconce

cast candle branches fitted w/gadrooned drip pans & baluster-shaped nozzles, gilt

Lead Whippets

finish, Régence period, France, early 18th c., 18" w., 24½" h., pr. **28,750.00**
(Illustration: one of two)

PEWTER

Pewter is a silver-grey alloy of tin with various amounts of antimony, copper and lead. Early pewter used bismuth rather than antimony but this produced a lowered melting point and made the metal brittle. The proportions of each metal was, to a large measure, based on what was available, the purpose for which the metal would be used and the preference of the worker. Incidentally, brittania metal utilizes the same ingredients but without lead.

Pewter goes back to the Bronze Age. Examples of pewter wares have been found in various parts of the Roman Empire and there have been excavations of pewter in Britain. Pewtering was a well-established craft in England by the mid-1300s as indicated by the presence of the 'Craft of Pewterers' which regulated quality and workmanship.

The manufacture of pewter items in America began in Colonial times. The English, trying to control the American production of pewter, imposed stiff regulations and taxes on tin. After the Revolutionary War, Americans were free to trade with whomever they chose.

Early pieces were made by the casting technique using molds and articles requiring multiple castings were soldered or fused. About 1827 the stamping technique was adopted in America. Stamping consisted of shaping a flat sheet of metal between a male and a female die. In 1834 another technique was introduced in America. This was a spinning process that produced the various sections of the article, which were then soldered in the same fashion as the cast pieces. After all of the above processes the pieces were "skimmed," which entailed holding a sharp steel tool on a wooden handle against the article as it rotated on a lathe. This removed small amounts of metal in a spiral pattern. After this the piece was burnished while it was still on the lathe. This was done with a tool that had a polished stone or steel face that smoothed out small areas of roughness. Next the piece was buffed using a disk made of pieces of hide or cloth treated with a ground abrasive polishing powder.

All varieties of housewares were made of pewter, including candlesticks, basins, plates, goblets, porringers, coffeepots, teapots, chocolate pots, cruet sets and creamers and sugar bowls. Also included in the pewter production were church-related items such as flagons, chalices, beakers, church cups and baptismal basins. It is interesting to note that, while most pewter articles are marked in some way, ecclesiastical pewter pieces are rarely found with a maker's mark. Many examples that were listed in early inventories are now very rare. It is thought that as they became obsolete they were melted down. Some such items are nursing bottles, buttons, buckles, picture frames, various types of boxes and chamber pots.

By the mid-19th century, pewter was out of style as an everyday houseware product and was superseded by inexpensive silver-plated wares, which often used pewter as the base metal to be highlighted with the silver plating.

It was not until the revival of interest in "early American" antiques in the 1920s that pewter once again attracted the public's fancy. During this revival period, many pewter objects were made which closely resembled their 18th and 19th century ancestors. Fortunately for today's collectors, these later copies often carry a manufacturer's marking and the words "Genuine Pewter," a phrase never used on antique originals.

Price Listings:

Baptism bowl, footed, unmarked, America, mid-19th c., top 6½" d., 3¾" h....**$259.00**

New England Baptismal Bowl

Baptismal bowl, deep wide rounded bowl tapering to a pedestal on a wide domed & ringed foot, probably New England, early, 6" d., 4¾" h...**715.00** (Illustration)

Basin, eagle touch mark of Gershom Jones, Providence, Rhode Island, 7¾" d. (minor pitting) **467.50**

Basin, Gershom Jones, marked, 7⅞" d.....................................**431.00**

Basin, low sloping sides w/narrow everted rim, touch mark of Samuel Pierce, Greenfield, Massachusetts, 1792-1830, 8" d.....................................**1,035.00**

Basin, rounded sides & narrow everted rim, touch mark of Thomas Danforth III, Philadelphia, Pennsylvania,1806-12,10¼" d........**1,265.00**

Basin, hammered finish, deep w/molded rim, touch mark of Peter Young, Albany, New York, 1775-95, 10⅞" d. **2,300.00**

Beaker, handled, cylindrical w/narrow molded base & flaring rim, scrolled strap handle w/thumbrest, touch mark of Boardman & Hart, New York, 1828-53, 3⅛" h......................**345.00**

Beaker, tapering cylindrical body w/slightly domed foot beneath a narrow band, gently flaring lip, touch mark of John Will, New York, 1750-74, base 4" d., 4¾" h................................**16,100.00**

Beaker, tall cylindrical body w/molded base & flaring rim, touch mark of Timothy Boardman & Co., New York & Hartford, Connecticut, 1822-25, 5¼" h...................................**920.00**

Candle mold, twelve-tube, in pine frame w/old patina, 18" l., 12¾" h..............................**715.00**

Candle mold, twenty-four tube, in pine frame w/old worn finish, 7 x 18¾", 14" h. (minor edge damage)................................**825.00**

Candlesticks, low domed foot slender ring-turned standard, flaring candle nozzle, unmarked, possibly Meriden, Connecticut, 5½" h., pr..........**187.00**

Candlesticks, domed base beneath a wide disc drip-pan, cylindrical ringed standard, flaring candle nozzle, fleur-de-lis mark w/"H.E.," Continental, 6½" h., pr.............................**440.00**

Candlesticks, baluster-form w/removable bobeches, unmarked, 7¾" h., pr.............**172.50**

Candlesticks, flat disc base supporting a baluster-turned stem, w/push-up, 8⅞" h., pr..**253.00**

Candlesticks, the slightly domed foot cast w/a swirling design & issuing three flattened supports, topped by an oblong candlecup w/wide everted rim, one impressed "MADE BY LIBERTY & CO ENGLISH PEWTER MADE IN ENGLAND 0223 P.," the other "5 ENGLISH PEWTER MADE IN ENGLAND," Liberty & Co., England, 9" h., pr...................................**978.00**

Candlesticks, baluster-form w/removable bobeche, Henry Hopper, New York, New York, 19th c., marked, 10" h., pr.....**690.00**

Candlesticks, low domed base, ring-turned standard, reeded detail w/matching bobeche, 10¾" h., pr.............................**165.00**

Cann, tulip shape, "IF" mark of John Fryers, Newport, Rhode Island, 1705-76, 4⅞" h.........**632.50**

Castor, typical of Meriden Britannia, Meriden, Connecticut, mid-19th c., 5¾" h.........**259.00**

Chalice, w/engraved presentation inscription "The Gift of Mr. Benj Luce to ye church of Christ of Edgartown, 1750," 6¼" h.....................................**862.50**

Charger, deep, eagle touch mark of Samuel Danforth, Hartford, Connecticut, 11" d.....................................**660.00**

Engraved Pewter Charger

Charger, circular dished form, the rim engraved w/acanthus leaves & shells within arched bands, engraved on the edge w/the inscription "Hanna Feeshel In Shepherds Town Anno Domine 1782," the inscribed name centering an engraved prancing deer, touch mark of Townsend, London, England, ca. 1782, 12" d.......**575.00** (Illustration)

Charger, partial "London" touch mark, 12" d.............................**115.50**

Charger, deep, eagle touch mark of Thomas D. Boardman, Hartford, Connecticut, 13" d. (wear & pitting)......................**605.00**

Charger, Thomas Danforth II, Middletown Connecticut, 1755-82, 13¼" d..................**690.00**

Charger, molded brim, touch mark of Nathaniel Austin, Boston, Massachusetts, 15" d.....................................**517.50**

Charger, circular, the rim cast in low-relief w/luna moths, impressed factory mark, Kayserzinn, Germany, ca. 1900, 15⅝" d. **460.00**

Chess set, w/robed kings & queens, he w/sword, the bishops as gowned ladies, the knights as rampant horses, the rooks as elephants w/hexagonal towers, the pawns as hunched figures, all stylized, 16 pieces w/plain finish & 16 pieces w/gilt finish, designed by Marie Bloomberg, Sweden, 1½" to 3" h., the set............**2,875.00**

Coffeepot, cov., tall 'lighthouse' style, gooseneck spout, scroll handle, unmarked, America, 10¼" h. (soldered repairs).....**220.00**

Coffeepot, cov., tall 'lighthouse' style, wooden handle, ivory finial, Hiram Yale, Wallingford, Connecticut, 1822-25, 10⅜" h. **747.50**

Coffeepot, cov., tall 'lighthouse' style, gooseneck spout, scroll handle, domed cover, America, 10⅜" h. (minor repair) **220.00**

Coffeepot, cov., tall 'lighthouse' style, bright-cut band around body, wooden handle & finial, Eben Smith, Beverly, Massachusetts, 1841-56, marked, 10½" h. **489.00**

Coffeepot, cov., tapered pear-shaped body, wooden handle & finial, partially struck mark of George Richardson, Boston, Massachusetts, early 19th c., 10⅝" h. **632.50**

Coffeepot, cov., low stepped foot, tapering cylindrical body w/rounded base, gooseneck spout, eagle touch mark of Roswell Gleason, Dorchester, Massachusetts, 11" h. (cleaned, minor pitting) **247.50**

Coffeepot, cov., cylindrical w/rounded lower section raised on a low flared foot, gooseneck spout, ornate scrolled handle, rounded cover w/cast flower finial, H. Homan, Cincinnati, Ohio, 11" h. **220.00**

Coffeepot, cov., cylindrical, rounded at shoulder & base, on low foot, scroll handle, goose-neck spout, flaring conical cover, unmarked, America, 11¼" h. **412.50**

Coffeepot, cov., globular melon-ribbed body raised on a domed foot, slender waisted neck, gooseneck spout, domed cover w/wooden finial, wooden scroll handle, Dixon & Son, England, 11½" h. **137.50**

Coffeepot, cov., double bellied form, w/wooden handle & finial, Sellew & Co., Cincinnati, Ohio, 1830-60, marked, 11½" h. (dents) **287.50**

Coffeepot, cov., triple-belly form decorated w/bright-cut design, touch mark of Boardman & Hart, New York & Hartford, Connecticut, ca. 1830s, 11¾" h. (minor etching inside) **517.50**

Coffeepot, cov., tall 'lighthouse' style, bright-cut decoration, Oliver Trask, Beverly, Massachusetts, 1825-30, 12" h. (minor dent) **460.00**

Coffeepot, cov., tall 'lighthouse' style, high domed cover, wood-en handle, bright-cut decora-tion, attributed to the Trasks, Beverly, Massachusetts, sec-ond quarter 19th c., 12½" h. **517.50**

Coffeepot, cov., semi-ovoid lower section beneath a waist-

Exceptional 18th c. Coffeepot

ed upper section, gooseneck spout, waisted cover w/tall finial, on square base, probably Philadelphia, Pennsylvania, 18th c., minor imperfections, base 4⅜" sq., 14¾" h. ....**36,800.00** (Illustration)

Coffeepot, cov., bulbous body tapering to a waisted neck, raised on a low flaring foot, gooseneck spout, angular han-dle, domed cover w/turned finial, touch mark of Roswell Gleason, Dorchester, Massachusetts, 1822-71 ....**287.50**

Communion flagon, cov., cylin-drical w/flaring base, ornate scroll handle, stepped domed cover w/tall finial, flaring lip, unmarked, America, 12⅜" h. **935.00**

Creamer, three-footed, touch mark of Edward Quick, London, England, 1735-60, 3½" h. **1,840.00**

Creamer, bulbous body on low stepped foot, flaring rim & lip, cast ear handle, unmarked, possibly Meriden, Connecticut, 5½" h. **181.50**

Flagon, cov., tall cylindrical body w/molded base, lower body

w/narrow raised band, ornate
scrolled handle w/thumbpiece,
curved spout, stepped domed
cover w/three-tier finial, touch
mark of Boardman & Com-
pany, Hartford, Connecticut &
New York, two-quart,
12¾" h. **1,725.00**

German Pewter Masonic Goblet

Goblets, domed foot tapering to
a ball connector supporting a
cup w/slightly flaring rim, each
w/incised name, date &
Masonic symbols, Germany,
18th c., 7" h., pr. **690.00**
(Illustration: one of two)

Inkwell, tapering cylinder on a
wide flat base, tooled rings at
midsection, 7" d. (ceramic
insert stained) **82.50**

Jar, cov., cylindrical body flaring
slightly at base & rim, cover
w/figural finial, 5" d. **192.50**

Ladle, rounded bowl & arched
handle, Thomas Danforth
Boardman, Hartford, Con-
necticut, 1804-73, 13½" l. **259.00**

Lamp, cylindrical on a flat
stepped base, marked "Capen
& Molineux, N.Y.," single spout
burner w/brass snuffer, 2¾" h.
plus burner **110.00**

Lamp, table model, camphene-
type, touch mark of Capen &
Molineaux, New York, 1848-54,
7½" h. **287.50**

Pewter 'Lozenge-top' Lamp

Lamp, table model, 'lozenge-top'
style, stepped domed foot &
turned standard, touch mark of
Roswell Gleason, Dorchester,
Massachusetts, 1822-60,
8" h. **230.00**
(Illustration)

Lamp, table model, double
bull's-eye type, unmarked,
attributed to Roswell Gleason,
Dorchester, Massachusetts,
1821-71, one bull's eye marked
"patent," 8½" h. **977.50**

Lavabo, *bombé*-form covered
cistern, w/maker's mark,
Continental, 19th - 20th c.,
14" h. **115.00**

Model of a horse & hound, the
full-bodied figure of a saddled
horse standing beside the full-
bodied figure of a hound holding the horse's reins in its
mouth, on a naturalistic base
marked "Emile Loiseau,"
9½" h. **690.00**

Mug, tapering cylinder w/flared
base, scrolled handle, touch
mark of Boardman & Hart, New
York, 1828-53, pint, 4" h. ...**1,495.00**

Mug, tapering cylinder w/gently
flaring molded base & rolled
rim, scrolling handle, marked
on handle, probably Joseph
Danforth, Sr., Middletown,
Connecticut, 1780-88, pint,

4½" h. (some pitting inside bottom) **1,092.00**

Mug, tapering cylindrical body w/narrow raised band near base, stepped molded base, flared lip, scrolling strap handle, touch mark of Samuel Hamlin, Providence, Rhode Island, 1771-1801, 1 qt., 6" h. **1,380.00**

Pitcher, cov., water, globular lower section w/low flaring foot, high scrolled handle & flaring spout, hinged stepped cover w/tall turned finial, touch mark of the Boardman group, mid-19th c., gallon, 11¼" h. (minor dents to body) **632.50**

Kayserzinn Pewter Pitcher

Pitcher, broad-based body w/fluted rim, decorated w/a tooled design of a grinning bearded devil w/prominent eyebrows & long curling horns among large iris blossoms & leaves, handle in the form of a twisted stem, original grey patina, impressed "Kayserzinn, 54," Germany, 12½" h. ....**495.00** (Illustration)

Plate, Thomas D. & Sherman Boardman, Hartford, Connecticut, 1810-30, marked, 6½" d. **690.00**

Blakeskee Barns Pewter Plate

Plate, eagle touch & "B.Barns, Phila.," Blak(e)slee Barn(e)s, Philadelphia, 1812-17, wear & scratches, 7⅞" d. ....**220.00** (Illustration)

Plate, touch mark of Thomas D. Boardman, Hartford, Connecticut, ca. 1810-35, 7⅞" d. **115.00**

Plate, touch mark of William Danforth, Middletown, Connecticut, 7⅞" d. **287.50**

Plate, lamb & dove touch mark of Richard Austin, Boston, Massachusetts, 1793-1817, 8" d. **489.00**

Plate, wide brim, touch mark of Parkes Boyd, Philadelphia, Pennsylvania, 1795-1819, 8" d. **632.50**

Plate, marked three times w/the touch mark of William Billings, Providence, Rhode Island, 1791-1806, 8¼" d..................**402.00**

Plate, touch marks of Gershom Jones, Providence, Rhode Island, 1774-1809, 8¼" d. **546.00**

Plate, lion touch mark of the Boardman group, Hartford, Connecticut, 9⅜" d. **259.00**

Plate, shaped rim, marked "Reed & Barton," Taunton, Massachusetts, 10" d. (dents) **71.50**

Plate, chop, London touch mark & "S.E.," Samuel Ellis, 12" d. (wear & scratches) **181.50**

Platter, touch mark of Samuel Danforth, Hartford, Connecticut, 1795-1816, 7⅞" d. **201.00**

Porringer, miniature, pierced scrolling tab handle, unmarked, attributed to Richard Lee, Springfield, Vermont, ca. 1795-1815, 2¼" d..................**431.00**

Porringer, modified 'Old English' style pierced tab handle, touch mark of Thomas Danforth Boardman & Sherman Boardman, 3¼" d. **690.00**

Porringer, shallow rounded bowl w/cast crown handle, faint "S.G." mark, Boston, Massachusetts, 4¼" d. **275.00**

Porringer, pierced 'flower' tab handle, touch mark of Samuel E. Hamlin, Jr., Providence, Rhode Island, 1801-56, 4½" d. **862.50**

Porringer, shallow bowl w/rounded sides, cast flower handle, attributed to Gershom Jones, 5" d. **247.50**

Porringer, shallow circular form w/cast crown handle, marked "S.G.," 5½" d. **220.00**

Porringer, pierced 'flower' tab handle, marked "TD and SB" in a rectangle, T.D. & S. Boardman, Hartford, Connecticut, ca. 1810-30, 5½" d. **747.50**

Porringer, circular w/flowered tab handle marked on back, Samuel Hamlin Sr., Hartford, Connecticut & Providence, Rhode Island, 5½" d. **805.00**

Porringer, tab handle pierced w/single hole, probably by Simon Pennock, Lancaster County, Pennsylvania, 1817-45, 5½" d. **747.50**

English Sauceboat by Joseph

Sauceboat, scalloped rim, elon-

gated lip, low foot, scrolled handle, marked "HI," Henry Joseph, London, England, 1736-80, 7¼" l., 4" h.............**920.00** (Illustration)

Seder plate, the center engraved w/a crowned double eagle displaying a shield engraved in Hebrew "A Night of Watching," the rim engraved in Hebrew "Pour out thy wrath on the Nations....," & in a scroll "we were slaves to the Pharaoh....," Germany or Austria, late 18th c., 16½" d. (repairs to rim)...................**1,150.00**

Spoon, Thomas Danforth Boardman, Hartford, Connecticut, 1804-73, 8" l. **287.50**

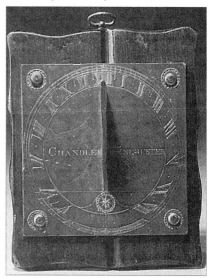

American Pewter Sundial

Sundial, square face centering a triangular sun directional, the dial engraved w/Roman numerals w/a stellar device decoration at the lower section, the center of the dial w/the raised inscription "CHANDLEE WINCHESTER," now mounted on a mahogany platform, signed by Goldsmith Chandlee, Winchester, Virginia, ca. 1775, sundial 5¼" sq...................**6,900.00** (Illustration)

Syrup jug w/hinged lid, cylindrical w/flaring base & lip, eared-handle, polished, unmarked, America, 6¼" h. (some battering & repairs)........................**165.00**

Tankard, cov., tulip-shaped body on low flared foot, scrolled handle, flattened dome cover w/thumbpiece, marked "SM" within a circle, England, mid-18th c., 6" h.................**1,035.00**

Tankard, cov., straight-sided body flaring slightly at the molded base, raised band on lower body, scrolling strap handle, hinged flattened dome cover w/thumbpiece, touch mark of William Eddon, England, ca. 1720, 7¼" h. (some pits to interior).........**1,495.00**

Teapot, cov., globular form, ornate scrolled handle, touch mark of Boardman & Hart, New York & Hartford, Connecticut, 1825-27, one-cup size, 5" h....................................**1,840.00**

Teapot, cov., pigeon-breasted form, possibly by Roswell Gleason, Dorchester, Massachusetts, one-cup size, 5¼" h. (minor dents).........................**431.00**

Teapot, cov., low stepped foot, gooseneck spout, unmarked, attributed to the Boardman group, one-cup size, 5½" h. (minor dents).........................**546.00**

Teapot, cov., elongated oval raised on a footed base, curved spout, wooden scroll handle, W.W. Allis, England, 6⅜" h......................................**93.50**

Teapot, cov., pear-shaped body raised on three feet, wooden handle, Samuel Ellis, London, England, ca. 1750, 6¾" h...**4,600.00**

Teapot, cov., cylindrical w/flaring base, gooseneck spout, scroll handle, domed cover, unmarked, America, 7¼" h........**220.00**

Teapot, cov., ovoid body, interi-

or marked, Robert Bush, Jr., Bristol, England, late 18th c., 7¼" h. (minor dents)............**489.00**

Teapot, cov., cylindrical w/flaring base, gooseneck spout & scroll handle, the cover w/cast flower finial, marked "H. Homan," Cincinnati, Ohio, 7½" h. (dents)...................................**110.00**

Teapot, cov., flaring stepped foot, compressed globular body, gooseneck spout, domed cover w/high finial, bright-cut decoration, touch mark of Eben Smith, Beverly, Massachusetts, 1813-56, 7½" h......................**460.00**

Teapot, cov., spherical body w/bright-cut thistle design, Boardman & Hart, New York, New York, 1830-50, marked, 7⅞" h. (lid repair)...................**517.50**

Teapot, cov., tapering stepped base, globular, gooseneck spout, scrolled handle, domed cover w/high finial, touch mark of Boardman & Co., New York, 1825-27, 8" h........................**345.00**

Teapot, cov., compressed globular body w/short neck, gooseneck spout, ornate scrolled handle, domed cover w/turned finial, touch mark of Ashbil Griswold, Meriden, Connecticut, 1808-1830s, 8" h..........**374.00**

Teapot, cov., pear-shaped body w/an extended base, touch mark of Thomas D. Boardman, Hartford, Connecticut, ca. 1810-20, 9" h................**2,300.00**

Teapot, cov., globular body raised on a low foot, gooseneck spout, wooden scroll handle, domed cover w/turned finial, Leonard, Reed & Barton, Taunton, Massachusetts, 9½" h......................................**82.50**

Teapot, cov., pigeon-breasted body on a pedestal base w/paneled foot, swan's-neck spout, scrolled wooden handle,

Courtesy Garth's Auctions

Three Pigeon-Breasted Pewter Teapots

Leonard, Reed & Barton, Taunton, Massachusetts, 1835-40, wear & some battering, 9½" h. **137.50**
(Illustration: above, left)

Teapot, cov., pigeon-breasted body on a pedestal base w/paneled foot, swan's-neck spout, scrolled wooden handle, Leonard, Reed & Barton, Taunton, Massachusetts, 1835-40, wear & battering, 10" h. **137.50**
(Illustration: above, right)

Teapot, cov., pigeon-breasted body on a pedestal base w/paneled foot, swan's-neck spout, scrolled wooden handle, Leonard, Reed & Barton, Taunton, Massachusetts, 1835-40, wear & battering, 12½" h. **165.00**
(Illustration: above, center)

Arts & Crafts-style Pewter Vase

Tray, oval w/wide handle decorated w/a design of stylized leaves, stems & berries, enameled aqua & green rectangle in center, impressed "English Pewter, Made By Liberty & Co., 0357, RD 440032, 3," 9 x 12" **660.00**

Tray, oval w/wide rim, original patina, impressed mark, Karl Kipp, 9 x 19" (some scratches to patina) **330.00**

Vase, Arts & Crafts style, tapering cylindrical body, w/hand-hammered Queen Anne's lace & butterflies in heavy relief, the wings of the butterflies mounted w/glass cabochons of red & purple, against a hammered ground, signed "AN" hammered into side at base, probably England, 4½" d., 12" h. **715.00**
(Illustration: bottom previous column)

Chalices, tall bell-form bowl on a short pedestal foot, unmarked, America, 19th c., 5¼" h., pr..............................**121.00**
(Illustration: No. 2, top next page)

Communion flagon, cov., tall slightly tapering cylindrical body w/a swelled ringed center band & flaring ringed foot, rim spout, domed cover, C-scroll metal handle, unmarked, America, 19th c., some battering, 10½" h. **115.50**
(Illustration: No. 3, top next page)

Courtesy Garth's Auctions

Pewter Teapots, Chalices & Flagon

| 1   2   3   2   4 |

Teapot, cov., bulbous body on a short flaring foot, cylindrical short neck & stepped domed cover, swan's-neck spout, angled scroll metal handle, Reed & Barton, Taunton, Massachusetts, mid-19th c., cover hinge resoldered, 8¼" h......................................**181.50** (Illustration: No. 4)

Teapot, cov., banded spherical body raised on a short wide pedestal base, flaring rim & domed cover, swan's-neck spout & S-scroll metal handle, Roswell Gleason, Dorchester, Massachusetts, 1821-71, old soldered repairs on bottom, cover finial incomplete, 9" h. .**192.50** (Illustration: No. 1)

Courtesy Garth's Auctions

Pewter Candlesticks, Chargers & Pitcher

| 1   2   3   4   1 |

Candlesticks, tall bell-form socket above a shouldered tapering cylindrical shaft on a flaring foot, w/removable bobeches, America, 19th c., 8¾" h. pr..............................**198.00** (Illustration: No. 1)

Charger, lion touch mark of Joseph Danforth, Middletown, Connecticut, 1780-88, wear & scratches, 13¼" d. ....**550.00** (Illustration: No. 2)

Charger, shield touch mark of Richard Austin, Boston,

Massachusetts, 1793-1817, wear & scratches, split in rim, 13½" d..................................**357.50** (Illustration: No. 4)

Pitcher w/hinged cover, footed ovoid body w/a long rim spout, C-form handle, domed cover w/button finial, lion touch mark of Thomas Danforth Board-man, Hartford, Connecticut, 1830-60, wear, corrosion & minor old soldered repair, 10½" h.................................**660.00** (Illustration: No. 3)

Various Pewter Lamps & Candlesticks

1	2	3	4	3	5	1
6		7	8	9	10	6

Candlesticks, cylindrical socket w/flattened flaring rim above the slender waisted shaft on a domed flaring foot, w/push-ups, unmarked, America, 19th c., 8" h., pr.................................**220.00** (Illustration: No. 1)

Candlesticks, tall flaring waisted socket above a trumpet-form stem above a disc ring over the stepped domed foot, w/push-up, unmarked, America, 19th c., 9" h., pr...............................**330.00** (Illustration: No. 6)

Chamberstick, cylindrical shaft w/flat rim & push-up tab handle, on a dished foot w/ring side handle, unmarked, 19th c., 4¼" h.....................................**247.50** (Illustration: No. 10)

Lamp, whale oil, bell-form font w/domed top fitted w/burner, on a ringed pedestal in a wide dished base w/a ring handle at the side, touch mark of Roswell Gleason, Dorchester, Massachusetts, 1821-71, 5¼" h. .....**495.00** (Illustration: No. 2)

Lamp, whale oil, tapering cylindrical font w/a domed top fitted w/a burner, on a baluster-form pedestal w/ring handle above the wide, flat dished base, cast floral decoration, 19th c., brass & tin burner somewhat battered, 5½" h. plus burner.......**375.00** (Illustration: No. 5)

Lamp, camphene-type, large inverted pear-shaped font fitted w/a camphene fluid burner, on a knobbed turned pedestal above the flaring disc foot, touch mark of Capen & Molineux, New York, New York, 1848-54, 7¾" h. plus burner.................................**440.00** (Illustration: No. 8)

Lamp w/two glass bull's-eye lenses, whale oil, the round disc lenses above the flattened round font on a ringed pedestal above the ringed domed foot, weighted base, unmarked, America, 19th c., w/brass burner, overall 8½" h.............**990.00** (Illustration: No. 4)

Lamp w/one glass lens, flattened disc font w/attached lens & whale oil burner, on a swelled turned pedestal on a stepped & ringed disc foot, weighted base, unmarked, America, 19th c., tab holding lens needs resoldering, brass

burner, overall 8⅞" h.............**550.00** (Illustration: No.9)

Lamps, whale oil, small cylindrical font fitted w/a burner, on a slender swelled pedestal on a flaring disc foot, unmarked, America, 19th c., 5¼" h., pr...**385.00** (Illustration: No. 3)

Lamps, whale oil, cylindrical font w/burner raised on a tapering cylindrical shaft on the stepped & domed foot, touch mark of Rufus Dunham, Westbrook, Maine, 1837-60, 5¾" h. plus burner, pr. ....**550.00** (Illustration: No. 7)

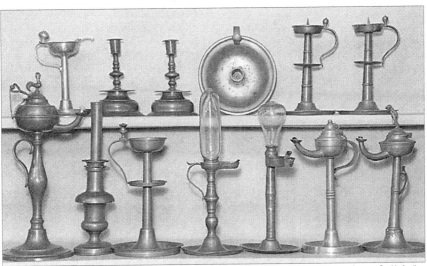

Courtesy Garth's Auctions

Foreign Pewter Candlesticks & Lamps

	1	2		3		4	
5	6	7	8	9	10		11

Candlesticks, cylindrical candle socket w/flattened rim raised on a ring- and knob-turned shaft above a wide flat disc above the high stepped, domed base, faint touch mark, Europe, 19th c., 6¼" h., pr. ...**297.00** (Illustration: No. 2)

Candlesticks, pricket-type, a

wide dished socket w/a center 'pricket' above the slender & slightly tapering ringed shaft w/a central flat disc, raised on a flaring disc foot, a thin strap handle w/knob thumbrest extends from socket rim to center disc, Holland, possibly 19th c., 8" h., pr......................**22.00** (Illustration: No. 4)

Chamberstick, deep round dished base w/short cylindrical socket & ring rim handle, marked "England," 20th c., 7" d..**38.50**
(Illustration: No. 3)

Lamp, fluid-type, a round dished cup w/wick spout raised on a slender cylindrical shaft on a disc foot, a strap handle fitted w/a knob w/a hole for a wick pick, the handle from the rim of the cup to the center of the shaft, Holland, 7¼" h..............**49.50**
(Illustration: No. 1)

Lamp, fluid-type, a round dished cup w/slightly flaring rim raised on a slender cylindrical shaft w/a central dished tray above the wide, flat dished foot, a strap handle w/knob for wick pick from the rim to the center tray, Holland, base engraved "AW 1849," 10½" h..................**93.50**
(Illustration: No. 7)

Lamp, spout-type, a half-round font w/domed top & small cap, an upturned wick spout extending from the font bottom, raised on a slender ringed stem on a wide dished foot, a wide strap handle from the side of the font to the stem, marked "N. Regensburg," Germany, probably 19th c., replaced wick pick, 10½" h.................................**104.50**
(Illustration: No. 10)

Lamp, spout-type, the half-round font w/domed top fitted w/a hinged cap w/a naked lady finial, a long upturned wick spout extending from base of the font, raised on a tall slender cylindrical shaft w/a small C-scroll handle, on a wide slightly dished foot, Europe, possibly 19th c., some battering, poorly soldered repair on base of shaft, 11¾" h.........................**27.50**
(Illustration: No. 11)

Lamp, pump-type, a tall slender cylindrical column above a

flared ring on a cyindrical section above the urn-form font on a disc foot, France, partial marks, some damage, 12" h. ..**27.50**
(Illustration: No. 6)

Lamp, time-type, a clear inverted pear-shaped blown glass fluid bulb raised atop a swelled cylindri cal shaft w/a wide angled wick spout, on a wide dished foot, Germany, probably 19th c., pewter band w/Roman numerals around the bulb missing, 12" h.......................**220.00**
(Illustration: No. 9)

Lamp, time-type, a tall slender clear blown glass top bulb for fluid above a baluster- and ring-turned shaft w/a long top rim wick spout & C-scroll handle, on a wide dished foot, Germany, probably 19th c., 13¼" h.................................**385.00**
(Illustration: No. 8)

Lamp, spout-type, squatty bulbous ringed font w/long curved spout extending from the lower rim, the domed top fitted w/a rooster finial & wick pick on a chain, the font raised on a tall swelled shaft w/a C-scroll handle above the flaring ringed base, Holland, 19th - 20th c., 14½" h.................................**165.00**
(Illustration: No. 5)

SHEFFIELD PLATE

The term "Sheffield Plate" refers to a very specific variety of silver plated ware produced in England during the 18th and early 19th century.

Beginning in the 1740s, manufacturers in the city of Sheffield developed a technique of bonding together thin ingots of copper and pure silver using tremendous heat and pressure. These ingots could then be rolled out into very thin sheets of metal which would be used to fashion decorative objects. These pieces appeared identical to sterling silver pieces but could be sold at a fraction of the cost. Any fashionable silver object could be copied in Sheffield plate, including epergnes, coffee and teapots, candlesticks, serving dishes and trays.

For nearly a century, true Sheffield plate was widely popular with the British and American buying public; however, in the mid-1840s, the development of the process of silver plating through electrolysis soon killed off the Sheffield plate trade. The new form of plating was faster, cheaper and required less pure silver to obtain the same effect.

True Sheffield plate wares were only produced in England and never in the American colonies or the United States. The earliest English Sheffield was not often marked by the manufacturer because the authorities were afraid such markings might mislead the buying public. By the late 18th century, however, some Sheffield platers were allowed to use simple markings which would not be confused with the strictly controlled sterling silver hallmarks.

Because the layer of silver used in Sheffield plate was quite thin, the copper base metal may begin to show through after years of polishing. Serious wear can affect the market value of Sheffield plate pieces, but they should never be replated since this destroys their value as antiques. Also, in the late 19th and early 20th centuries, many silver plating companies began to use the term "Sheffield Plate" as a part of their markings. This silver plate ware has no relationship to the original hand-crafted English wares, which were never marked with this phrase.

Price Listings:

Candelabra, three-light, baluster-form shaft w/gadroon & shell borders, fitted w/pairs of two-arm, three-light branches of complementary design which can be arranged in a single five-light candelabrum, ca. 1820, 20½" h., pr........**$1,725.00** (Illustration: below)

Candelabra, three-light, baluster-form w/gadrooned edges, England, 19th c., 19" h., pr. (rosing)............................**747.50**

Candelabra, three-light, baluster-form candlestick base w/gadroon borders, fitted w/application having pair of reeded upward scrolling arms w/urn-form sconce terminals encircling the central urn-form sconce, Matthew Boulton &

Sheffield Plate Three-light Candelabra

Co., Sheffield, England,
ca. 1800, 19½" h., pr.........**1,150.00**

Large Sheffield Plate Candelabrum

Candelabra, four-light, stepped
circular base w/gadroon bands,
half-fluted tapering baluster
stem to half fluted urn-form
sconce, the branches w/a low
center light w/finial & three
identical reeded upward
scrolling arms fitted w/urn-form
sconces w/waxpans & nozzles,
Matthew Boulton & Co.,
Sheffield, England, ca. 1810,
26" h., pr...........................**4,312.50**
(Illustration: one of two)

Candelabra, five-light, circular
w/plain columnar stem rising

from & headed by bands of
vertical lobes, detachable arms
& screw-on central light, vase-
shaped sconces w/detachable
nozzles, gadroon borders,
ca. 1800, 27½" h., pr.........**3,737.00**
(Illustration: below)

Candlesticks, square scalloped
base, ring-turned stem ending
in gadrooned trumpet-form
section, tall slender candle
nozzle, 5" h., pr. (minor
wear) **137.50**

Candlesticks, baluster-form
w/applied shell & scroll borders, England, 19th c., 8" h.,
pr. (rosing)...........................**230.00**

Candlesticks, oval base rising
to a conforming baluster stem
& urn-form sconce, w/nozzle,
wavy band decoration & reeded borders, England, ca. 1790,
11½" h., pr...........................**575.00**

Candlesticks, baluster-form
standard w/scroll & leaf decoration, w/bobeche, England,
19th c., 12" h., set of 4
(rosing) **172.50**

Dinner plates, gadrooned border, engraved w/an earl's coronet, marked "RG-SG" w/
pseudo hallmarks, 9½" d.,
set of 8 ....**805.00**

Ca. 1800 Sheffield Plate Candelabra

Sheffield Plate Covered Platter

Dish cross, good detail **93.50**

Epergne, oval frame on four
tapering tall supports w/paw
feet, joined w/a shaped
lozenge-form stretcher centered w/a bud finial anchoring
the reeded scrolled arms, w/
later glass fittings, ca. 1800,
12⅜" h...............................**1,495.00**

Sheffield Plate Four-arm Epergne

Epergne, shaped square base
on four paw supports from
which rises a knob supporting
four detachable scrolling arms
w/frame terminals & four S-
curve brackets holding the
upper central ring frame, the
whole fitted w/matching set of
one large & four smaller circular glass bowls w/stepped
bases, diamond-cut sides &
fan-cut rims, ca. 1820, overall

22" w., 13½" h. **2,587.50**
(Illustration)

Hot water urn, *bombé* oval
form, half-fluted, w/lion mask &
loose ring handles, raised on
four curved supports w/goat's
head terminals, set on a conforming stand centered w/a
lamp, Regency period,
England, 16" h......................**977.50**

Hot water urn, *bombé* oblong
urn form, domed lid w/bud
finial, bracket handles w/lion
mask terminals, raised on four
curved supports, on a conforming base, centered w/detach-
able lamp, engraved w/a period
crest framed in oak & acorn
wreath, ca. 1800, 16½" h. **805.00**

Inkstand, modeled in the form of
a globe raised on a flared
base, applied w/drapery swags
between lion masks & opening
to reveal sander, inkwell & two
bottles, the base inscribed
"This Inkstand belonged to
Dante Gabriel Rossetti Poet &
Painter," England, ca. 1800,
10¼" h..............................**1,725.00**

Meat platters, oval rococo rim,
engraved twice w/contempo-
rary arms, England, ca. 1835,
27¼" l., pr. **1,552.00**

Platter, cov., shaped oval platter

w/a scroll, shell & floral rim molding, w/a conforming lid w/complementary border, full armorial engraved on both sides of the cover, Regency period, England, platter 21" l. ....**1,380.00** (Illustration: top previous page)

Soup tureen, cov., plain oval form, the base raised on four scrolled supports, bracket handles w/foliate terminals, fitted w/a stepped domed lid w/foliate handle, engraved w/crest on base & lid, Roberts, Cadman & Co., Sheffield, England, ca. 1810, 16½" l. across handles, 10½" h. **1,380.00**

Sheffield Covered Soup Tureen

Soup tureen, cov., of *bombé* oval form w/fluted lower section, engraved w/contemporary arms, raised on four paw feet headed by floral cartouches, similar ring finial, detachable liner, England, ca. 1820, across handles 17½" l........**2,185.00** (Illustration)

Soup tureen, cov., of boat-form w/tall loop handles, chased w/a collar of Vitruvian scrolls, the domed cover & pedestal foot chased w/stiff leaves, engraved w/contemporary crest & monogram, detachable liner w/ring grips, England, ca. 1780, across handles 19" l..........**2,587.00**

Table, circular top chased w/rococo ornament, w/oak backing, knopped columnar stem, domed base & three paw

Unusual Sheffield Plate Table

feet, England, ca. 1835, 24" d., 31" h. ....**7,475.00** (Illustration)

Tea caddy, tall rectangular body w/low circular top, marked "Sheffield," 4½" h. (some wear) **77.00**

Tea caddy, cov., ovoid, engraved w/a swag design, the cover w/wooden finial, George III period, England, 6" h........**316.00**

Teakettle, cover & lamp stand, ribbed ovoid-form, monogrammed, England, 19th c., overall 11½" h. (some wear) **144.00**

Teapot, cov., elongated oval body w/molded edge beneath shoulder, curved spout, domed cover w/fruit finial, angular wooden handle, 6¼" h. (minor wear) **60.50**

Tea urn, cov., lobed vase-form w/lion mask & ring side handles, raised on a square base w/ball feet, the interior fitted w/a heating rod holder & cap, ca. 1800, 18½" h. ....**1,150.00** (Illustration: top next page)

Tray, circular, the beaded rim alternating w/flowers at intervals, the center engraved w/an

Ca. 1800 Sheffield Plate Tea Urn

armorial, on three pierced scroll feet, England, ca. 1780, 14⅛" d. **862.00**

Tureen, cov., compressed globular body w/upright side handles, raised on a low circular base, the domed lid w/open ring finial, w/engraved crest dated 1749 - 1806, 9¾" d. plus handles, 11¼" h. **935.00**

Urns & covers, oval w/lion mask & loose ring handles, stepped domed cover w/foliate finial, gadrooned borders, on a conforming pedestal base, engraved w/a period crest, ca. 1805, 9¾" h., pr. **920.00**

Vegetable dish, cov., rectangu-

lar w/gadrooned edge, cover w/ scrolling leaf finial, England, 19th c., 7 x 10" **172.50**

Wine coasters, of ship's decanter size, w/beaded rim, pierced & engraved w/paterae, swags & running leaves, turned mahogany base, England, ca. 1785, 7¾" d., pr. **3,737.00**

Sheffield Plate Wine Cooler

Wine cooler, campana-form, reeded bracket handles w/foliate terminals at the sides, applied molded leaf-tip rim, ca. 1810, 9¾" h. ....**460.00** (Illustration)

Wine coolers, half fluted campana-form, the sides engraved w/a coat of arms, the crest on the reverse, marked on bases

Sheffield Plate Wine Coolers

w/single sun mark, first quarter
19th c., 8½" h., pr..............**1,380.00**

Wine coolers, partly fluted campana-form decorated w/applied
shells, engraved w/arms, crest
& motto, detachable rim & liner,
England, ca. 1820, 9⅜" h.,
pr......................................**2,875.00**

Wine coolers, tapered cylindrical form w/reeded handles rising from flowerheads above a
band of Vitruvian scrolls, lobed
border, detachable rim, later
liner, England, 1805-10,
9¾" h., pr...........................**4,025.00**

Wine coolers, of fluted campana-form on domed foot, the
leaf-scroll handles spreading
into floral sprays, detachable
rim & liner, Roberts, Smith &
Co., England, ca. 1830,
11¼" h., pr.........................**1,035.00**

Wine coolers, campana-form
w/shellwork rims & bases, bodies crested & applied
w/grapevine spreading from
forked branch handles, detachable liners, England, ca. 1830,
12½" h., pr.........................**3,450.00**
(Illustration: bottom previous page)

SILVER

AMERICAN - STERLING & COIN

The search for silver was one of
the enticements that lured Europeans
to the New World. The Spanish
Conquistadors, of course, discovered
fabulous amounts of silver in Mexico
and South America, but the early
English settlers along the Eastern
Seaboard were frustrated not to find
similar riches in that region. As the
English colonies grew and prospered,
however, there soon was a demand
for the services of trained goldsmiths
and silversmiths. By the late 17th
century, several smiths were working
in the New England region. Their custom-made wares mirrored the styles
popular in England and the
Continent.

The various styles consisted of the
Renaissance tradition from 1650 to
1690; the Baroque from 1690 to
1720; and to the lighter lines of
Hogarth from 1720 to 1750. This was
followed by the Rococo style from
1750 to 1775, with a return to the
Classical style, which received its
major thrust from England and the
talent of Robert Adam, from 1775 to
1810. The period from 1810 to 1840
was taken over by the heavier forms
influenced by Egyptian, Greek and
Roman antiquities.

The actual mass manufacture of
silver objects in America began in the
early 1840s. Prior to that time, most
items were custom-made. Early
American silver pieces had no official
stamps or letter dates to identify
them, as was common in England
and many other countries. Only the
maker's name or initials were to mark
most objects before the mid-19th
century. With the advent of factory-
made silver items, many of the
wholesalers and retailers started
marking their wares.

It should be noted that the word
"coin" can be found on silver articles
made during the period from about
1830 to 1860. This indicated that the
silver used was of the same quality
as was used for coinage although,
since the silversmith could now buy
sheet silver, the objects usually did
not contain melted coins as they had
previously. "Sterling," the English
standard, referred to a metal which
was .925 or 925/1000 parts silver
with 75/1000 parts of an added metal,
usually copper, to give it strength and
stiffness. This term appeared on
Baltimore silver from the 1800 to
1814 period and elsewhere after
around 1860.

Connecticut, Pennsylvania, New
York and New Jersey became the
heart of the silver industry in America,
and many well-known companies
continue in business today producing
fine wares.

Price Listings:

Asparagus serving dish, shaped oblong raised on four acanthus & paw supports, the undulating rim chased w/fluted leaf pattern, w/pierced removable foliate scroll liner chased w/rocaille & trelliswork, w/bracket handles, engraved under base "1899," Tiffany & Co., New York, New York, ca. 1899, 12½" l. **$2,990.00**

Asparagus dish, shell & scroll rim, the center monogrammed "MJO," on four leaf-headed paw feet, w/a liner pierced & engraved w/diaper, Tiffany & Co., New York, New York, 1891-1902, 12⅝" l. **3,450.00**

Basket, oval fluted body raised on a fluted domed foot, openwork overhead handle, goldwashed interior, William Gale & Son, New York, New York, 1850-60, 5½" l., 6½" h. **230.00**

Basket, ovoid vasiform body w/reticulated strapwork & trelliswork sides, the oval base applied w/a foliate rim, swing handle, monogrammed, w/liner, Gorham Mfg. Co., Providence, Rhode Island, 1910, 11" h. **1,725.00**

Basket, oval, reticulated sides, monogrammed, Whiting Mfg. Co., Providence, Rhode Island, late 19th c., 13½" l. **517.50**

Basket, oval, the sides pierced in a scrolling floral & foliate design, Whiting Mfg. Co., Providence, Rhode Island, late 19th c., 13½" l. **345.00**

Basting spoon, plain rounded terminal, engraved w/a monogram, maker's mark of Daniel Dupuy, Sr., Philadelphia, Pennsylvania, ca. 1780, 12⅜" l. **2,185.00**

Beaker, realistically formed as a bucket chased w/barrel staves & hoops, woodgrained surface, Ball, Black & Co., New York, New York, 1851-76, 4¾" h. **863.00**

Bell, domed floral chased bell finished w/a die-rolled lower rim, the handle a baluster stem flanked by female half-figures, No. 4793, Tiffany & Co., New York, New York, 1873-91, 4" h. **460.00**

Bonbonniere, cast openwork bowl, the S-curve handle w/mask terminal, No. A291, Gorham Mfg. Co., Providence, Rhode Island, retailed by Montgomery Bros., 9" l. **690.00**

Bonbonniere, cast openwork bowl of scrolls & flowers, S-curve handle w/cartouche-form finial, No. A292, Gorham Mfg. Co., Providence, Rhode Island, 1898, 10" l. **805.00**

Bouillon cups, rounded bowl on low spreading foot, the rim applied w/trailing leaves, *repoussé* & chased w/foliage on matted ground, w/shaped handles, engraved w/monogram, fitted w/ivory Lenox porcelain liners w/gold trim, Samuel Kirk & Sons, Baltimore, Maryland, 1903-07, across handles 5⅛" l., set of 18.....**2,530.00**

Bowl, child's, the sides worked in relief depicting Noah's Ark, Gorham Mfg. Co., Providence, Rhode Island, 4½" d.............**488.00**

Bowl, hemispherical w/flared molded rim & raised pedestal foot, the base engraved w/contemporary initials "MME," Elias Boudinot, Philadelphia, Pennsylvania, ca. 1750-60, 5¾" d. **5,175.00**

Bowl, decorated w/a chased spiral pattern, Gorham Mfg. Co., Providence, Rhode Island, ca. 1902, 6¼" d. **144.00**

Bowl, decorated in the Japanese taste, circular w/spot-hammered surface, on spreading base, the sides applied w/copper grapevines suspending copper grapes & gilt leaves, also applied w/a copper butterfly, swallows in flight & shore birds by a marsh, Gorham Mfg. Co., Providence, Rhode Island, 1882, 6⅝" d. **8,050.00**

Bowl, spot-hammered *bombé* body applied in copper & silver w/a branch of olives, a prunus spray, an exotic bird in flight, two butterflies & a bug, raised on three trunk feet, Gorham Mfg. Co., Providence, Rhode Island, 1883, rim 8½" d. **2,070.00**

Bowl, circular body w/applied & chased poppy blossom decoration, George W. Shiebler & Co., New York, New York, ca. 1900, 8⅝" d. **517.50**

Bowl, lotus-form, International Silver Co., Meriden, Connecticut, 9⅛" d. **137.50**

Bowl, low cylindrical body w/rolled rim, the rim decorated w/chased florals, monogram, S. Kirk & Son, 19th c., 9¾" d. **345.00**

Bowl, *Martelé,* circular lobate body, the undulating rim w/chased floral & leaf decoration, raised on four cast scroll supports, monogrammed "M"

on side, stamped "H - EC," Gorham Mfg. Co., Providence, Rhode Island, 1905, .950 standard, 10" d., 4" h. **5,175.00**

Bowl, applied & reticulated clover design border, monogrammed, Tiffany & Co., New York, New York, 1891-1902, 10⅛" d. **632.50**

Bowl, circular, the everted rim w/applied strawberry design, Mauser Manufacturing Company, New York, New York, early 20th c., 10½" d. **345.00**

Bowl, berry, in the Japanese taste, of circular form w/spot-hammered surface, w/raised bronze loop handles continuing around the footrim & bound by silver wire, the body applied w/water lilies w/gold-sheathed buds, w/applied die-rolled border around the rim, gilt interior, Gorham Mfg. Co., Providence, Rhode Island, 1879, across handles 11" l. ....**5,750.00** (Illustration: below)

Bowl, the lobed rim chased w/hibiscus blossoms, the center engraved w/a monogram & inscription, Whiting Mfg. Co., Providence, Rhode Island, early 20th c., 12½" l. **632.00**

Bowl, salad, finely & deeply embossed & chased w/a scene of bearded demi-tritons riding

Silver Berry Bowl with Applied Decoration by Gorham

Ornate Silver Salad Bowl by Tiffany

sea horses, all surrounded by applied seaweed, the shaped domed base w/hammered surface, similarly applied, further seaweed applied to the inside of the undulating rim, hammered & gilt interior, the base engraved w/a contemporary inscription dated "April 21 1888," Tiffany & Co., New York, New York ....**21,850.00** (Illustration: above)

Bowl, salad, round base w/shallow fluted sides rising to a shaped octagonal rim, the sides chased as panels w/cornucopias & baskets of fruit framing diaper panels, No. 667, Tuttle Silversmiths, Boston, Massachusetts, 15" d............**575.00**

Bowls, hand-wrought, Revere-type, monogrammed "C.W.L." on sides & "November 15, 1927" on underside, Herbert Taylor for Arthur Stone, Gardner, Massachusetts, ca. 1927, 4" d., 2" h., set of 12....**862.50**

Bowl & underplate, child's, decorated in relief w/scenes from nursery rhymes divided by Art Nouveau leafy tendrils, the bowl w/gilt interior, engraved inscription dated "January 29, 1914," Tiffany & Co., New York, New York, ca. 1914, underplate 7" d., 2 pcs. **1,955.00**

Bowls & underplates, circular w/beaded border, *repoussé* & chased w/architectural landscapes amid foliage on a matted ground, the underplates w/similar decoration & centrally engraved w/script initials, the bowls engraved w/the same under the base, Samuel Kirk & Sons, Baltimore, Maryland, 1903-24, bowl 4⅝" d., plate 7⅛" d., 12 sets **6,325.00**

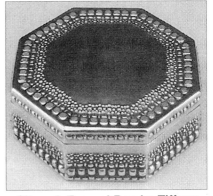

Silver & Enamel Box by Tiffany

Box, cov., octagonal, the slip-on cover w/turquoise enamel border w/bubbled *repoussé* bands on body & cover, Tiffany Furnaces, Corona, New York, ca. 1905, designed by Louis Comfort Tiffany, 4¾" d. ....**18,400.00** (Illustration)

Box w/hinged cover, rectangular, the cover w/a dome of wire & vari-colored floral enamel centering a purple cabochon, the cover & sides w/applied wire & silver balls forming geometric foliate decoration, designed & made by Elizabeth Copeland, Boston, Massachusetts, 1920-37, 6⅛" l. ...**8,050.00**

Bracelet, bangle-type, w/tooled stylized four-petal blossoms, on a planished ground, "Dedicated to Nina Downing Beak 12/25/19," die-stamped "KK-Sterling," Karl Kipp, 2¾" w. **715.00**

Brandy warmer, cov., bulbous form w/chased flowerhead border & upswept turned wood handle, the removable cover w/an acorn finial, the side engraved w/initials "EMB," maker's mark of John & Peter Mood, Charleston, South Carolina, ca. 1834-41, 7⅛" h. **5,520.00**

Bread & butter plates, circular w/hand-chased panel border depicting urns of flowers & ribbon-tied fruit garlands, w/applied ribbon-tied laurel leaf & berry border band, Hayes & McFarland, Mount Vernon, New York, ca. 1910, retailed by Daniel Marot, 7⅛"d., set of 12 ....**2,070.00**

Bread basket, *trompe l'oeil* style, shaped oblong body w/canted corners & basketweave decoration, w/tied branch-form handles, the field *repoussé* & chased w/a sheaf of wheat, maker's mark of Kennard & Jenks, Boston, Massachusetts, ca. 1880, 12¾" l. **4,370.00**

Bread tray, elongated quatrefoil form, the border hand-hammered & floral chased in the *Martelé* style, inscribed on back "Handwrought W C," possibly William Codman, Bixby Silver Co., Providence, Rhode

Silver Bread Tray by Bixby Silver Co.

Island, late 19th - early 20th c., 12" l. ....**402.00** (Illustration)

Bread tray, *Martelé,* shaped oblong w/undulating rim, the borders *repoussé* & chased w/wheat & leaves, Gorham Mfg. Co., Providence, Rhode Island, ca. 1900, 14⅝" l......**3,450.00**

Bread trays, oval w/shaped rim, Alvin Corp., Providence, Rhode Island, 20th c., 11¾" l., pr. **259.00**

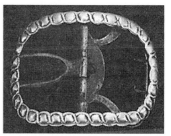

Ca. 1770 Silver Shoe Buckle

Buckles, shoe, shaped oval form chased w/guilloche, w/iron clips, maker's mark of Philip Syng, Jr., Philadelphia, Pennsylvania, ca. 1770, 2⅜" l., pr. ....**3,450.00** (Illustration: one of two)

Butter dish, cover & drain, in the Aesthetic taste, of shaped square form w/matte finish, the base w/a die-rolled fluted band, applied w/stylied flowerheads, w/cast part-fluted handles, the drain grille pierced w/stylized flowers, w/plain high-domed cover & plain baluster finial, the cover engraved w/a monogram "APT," Gorham Mfg. Co., Provi-

dence, Rhode Island, 1877,
4½" h. **1,380.00**

Butter dish, liner & cover, flat
base, squat urn-form w/bracket
handles, raised on four claw-
and-ball feet, fitted w/pierced
platform liner, high domed
cover w/berry finial, chased
overall w/flowers & foliage,
monogrammed "A.A.McL." on
underside, S. Kirk & Son,
Baltimore, Maryland, 1880-90,
6¾" h. **805.00**

**Silver Butter Pats with Copper
Decoration**

Butter pats, circular, the spot-
hammered borders engraved
w/seagrass & applied w/copper
crabs, silver gilt starfish, copper fish, turtles, frogs & various
sealife, the spot-hammered
centers gilt, Tiffany & Co., New
York, New York, ca. 1880,
3⅛" d., set of 12 ....**9,775.00**
(Illustration: two of twelve)

Cake plate, shaped edge
w/chased fruit design, Watson
Company, Attleboro,
Massachusetts, early 20th c.,
10¾" d. **172.50**

Candlesticks, circular beaded
base supporting a simple column, Gorham Mfg. Co.,
Providence, Rhode Island,
7½" h., set of 4 ....**862.00**

Candlesticks, oval base supporting a hexagonal baluster-
form stem, monogrammed "M,"
No. 17659, Tiffany & Co., New
York, New York, 1907-47,
9¼" h., set of 4 ....**2,587.00**

Candlesticks, reticulated
domed base, baluster-form

stem, reticulated flaring
bobeche, J. E. Caldwell & Co.,
Philadelphia, Pennsylvania,
late 19th - early 20th c.,
10⅝" h., set of 4 ....**2,990.00**

Candlesticks, domed lobed foot
supporting a waisted cylindrical
standard, w/pierced floral &
foliate decoration, Black, Starr
& Frost, Ltd., New York, New
York, 11" h., pr. **2,990.00**

Candlesticks, Colonial Revival
style, weighted, Gorham Corp.,
Providence, Rhode Island,
ca. 1926, 11¾" h., pr. **747.50**

Candlesticks, silver-gilt, in the
Rococo taste, on a shaped
spreading base, cast & chased
w/foliate scrolls, rising to a
knopped twisting baluster stem
w/shaped twisting socket &
removable drip pan chased
w/ovolo & flutes, Howard &
Co., New York, New York,
1898, 13⅜" h., set of 4 ....**7,820.00**

Cann, cylindrical, inlaid in vari-
colored gold & copper w/a
scene of vines w/columbine-
like flowers & a butterfly in
flight, C-scroll handle, Dominick
& Haff, New York, New York,
1879, 3¾" h. **2,415.00**

Cann, baluster-form on molded
circular base, w/molded rim &
scroll handle w/thumbrest, the
front engraved w/a contemporary crest, one side later
engraved w/a crest above the

18th c. Silver Cann from Boston

monogram "C.W.V.R.," maker's
mark of Simeon Soumaine,
New York, New York, 1740-50,
4⅞" h. **6,900.00**

Cann, baluster-form on spreading molded foot, w/leaf-clad
scroll handle, molded rim, maker's mark of Samuel Minot,
Boston, Massachusetts, 1760-
80, 5¼" h. **5,060.00**
(Illustration: bottom previous page)

Center bowl, circular on spreading foot, the body & foot
repoussé & chased w/a frieze
of architecture in a landscape,
the center engraved w/a monogram, Samuel Kirk & Sons,
Baltimore, Maryland, 1903-07,
8¾" d. **1,380.00**

Silver Center Bowl by Kirk & Sons

Center bowl, low-sided bowl,
raised on a spreading foot
chased w/rocaille & foliage,
w/similar trailing foliage on
body on a matted ground,
enclosing cartouches engraved
w/two monograms, w/rocaille
rim, Samuel Kirk & Sons, 1846-
61, 9¼" d., 7⅝" h. **1,150.00**
(Illustration)

Center bowl, vasiform w/a rolled
rim, on a single spreading foot,
overall reticulated scrolling
design, slight dents, Shreve,
Criump & Low, Boston,
Massachusetts, 8" h. **920.00**
(Illustration: top next column)

Center bowl, shaped rounded
bowl raised on a spreading foot

Ornate Reticulated Center Bowl

w/lobed gadrooned rim, chased
w/strapwork, shells & flowers,
the body *repoussé* & chased
w/foliate scrolls & stiff leaves
enclosing vacant cartouches
below an everted gadrooned
rim, maker's mark of Grosjean
& Woodward for Tiffany & Co.,
New York, New York, 1854-65,
8⅝" d. **2,300.00**
(Illustration: bottom this column)

Center bowl, simple form, the
rim applied w/foliate scrollwork,
Gorham Mfg. Co., Providence,
Rhode Island, 9½"d...............**460.00**

Center bowl, presentation-type,
paneled baluster-form body
decorated w/a chased &
engraved floral design,
engraved inscription, Black,
Starr & Frost, New York, New
York, early 20th c., 10" h. **805.00**

Center bowl, circular on spreading foot, the borders *repoussé*
& chased w/figures amid
Vitruvian scrolls, Tiffany & Co.,

Repoussé & Chased Center Bowl

Graceful Center Bowl by Tiffany

New York, New York, 1882-
1902, 10¼" d.....................**4,600.00**
(Illustration)

Center bowl, undulating circular
body, the reticulated border
decorated w/oak leaves &
acorns, Gorham Mfg. Co.,
Providence, Rhode Island,
12" d...............................**1,092.00**

Center bowl, flaring oval form,
the sides pierced w/scrollwork,
Howard & Co., New York, New
York,15" l.............................**920.00**

Center bowl, shaped oval
raised on four acanthus-clad
paw supports, rising to an
everted undulating rim elabo-
rately chased w/foliage &
scrolls, Tiffany & Co., New
York, New York, 1886-91,
16¼" l. **4,600.00**

Centerpiece w/undertray, the
shaped oval bowl raised on
four scroll supports, the undu-
late collar border chased &
embossed w/clusters of roses
& finished w/an applied cast
scroll & rose edge, the platter-
form conformingly shaped
undertray w/matching decoration, both pieces engraved
w/elaborate three letter monogram, the bases engraved
"July 5, 1900" & w/various pre-
sentations, Nos. A6823 &
A7474, Gorham Mfg. Co.,
Providence, Rhode Island, ca.
1900, retailed by Theodore B.
Starr, New York, New York,
undertray 21" l., centerpiece
16" l., 5" h., the set.............**8,050.00**

Centerpiece, oval body w/undu-
lating rim, applied cast scroll
rim & bracket handles, resting
on four scroll supports, continuous embossed & chased fruit &
floral decoration against a matted ground, No. 4045, Tiffany &
Co., New York, New York,
1873-91, 13½" l., 5" h.........**3,737.00**
(Illustration: below)

Centerpiece, basket-form,
shaped oval body w/shallow
bowl & wide borders,
engraved, pierced & applied
w/hollow molded scrollwork
decoration, fixed overhead
handle pierced & applied
w/molded scrollwork, w/plated
liner & wire frog fittings, Shreve
& Co., San Francisco,
California, 1909-22, 13¼" w.,
15¾" l., overall 10" h. 2,587.00
(Illustration: top next page)

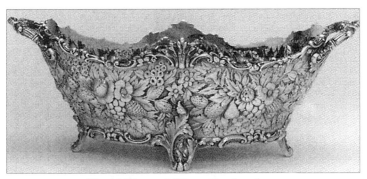

Floral Chased Silver Centerpiece

Basket-form Silver Centerpiece

Centerpiece, Classical Revival style, the elongated oval bowl mounted w/mythical beasts at each end, raised on an ornate stem & foot, the interior chased w/a scrolling design, Gorham Corp., Providence, Rhode Island, late 19th c., retailed by Matson & Hoes, 11½" h. **1,610.00**
(Illustration: bottom next column)

Centerpiece, circular, the domed rim embossed w/ogee arches above openwork acanthus, on rim foot, monogrammed, Tiffany & Co., New York, New York, ca. 1915, 16" d. **6,325.00**

Centerpiece, Classical Revival style, in the form of a shallow bowl pierced w/panels of scrolling foliage between applied flowerheads, the raised center mounted w/a classical figure, the whole raised on a pedestal foot w/a border of festoons on matted ground, Gorham Mfg. Co., Providence, Rhode Island, 1871, 17" h. **4,025.00**

Centerpiece, rectangular, embossed w/rococo ornament below the applied foliate scroll rim, raised on a spreading pedestal foot w/scroll supports, gilt interior, Bailey, Banks & Biddle, Philadelphia, Pennsylvania, ca. 1890, 18¼" l **6,325.00**
(Illustration: top next page)

Centerpiece, circular, the everted domed sides embossed & applied in the form of a rose trellis, Redlich & Co., New York, New York, ca. 1900, 19½" d. **4,600.00**

Centerpiece bowl, oval, everted sides chased w/rococo ornament below an applied leafy rim, the center monogrammed, on four winged paw supports, Tiffany & Co., New York, New York, ca. 1885, 13½" l. **2,587.00**

Chafing dish on lampstand, circular, the stand on four paw-like supports w/chased Art Nouveau-style waves, w/central circular burner, the dish lifting out of a hot water pan, w/a band of similar wave-like design at the rim, w/shaped ivory handle, the domed cover w/wavy band below the urn-form finial chased w/similar waves, Tiffany & Co., New York, New York, 1891-1902, 9" d., 10⅜" h **6,325.00**

Chafing dish on lampstand, waved scrolled borders w/leaves at intervals, straight ivory handle, the stand w/four splayed supports, triple wick lamp & detachable underdish, Tiffany & Co., New York, New York, 1902-07, 10½" h. **4,025.00**

Chalice & paten, hand-wrought,

Classical Revival-style Silver Centerpiece

Silver Centerpiece with Rococo Decoration

hemispherical bowl w/peened exterior raised on a stem of four strapwork struts, centered w/a hexagonal rosewood node, on a peened domed base w/applied cross, the matching paten w/peened upper surface, Dirk Van Erp, San Francisco, California, paten 5½" d., chalice 7" h., the set..............**690.00**

Chamberstick, *Martelé*, modeled in the form of a chrysanthemum flower, the stem forming the handle & rising from the leafy domed base, hung w/a bellflower form extinguisher, .950 standard, Gorham Mfg, Co., Providence, Rhode Island, 1899, 7⅛" h........................**7,475.00**

Child's feeding set: mug, bowl & underplate; each of circular form w/a frieze of emblems of nursery rhymes, each monogrammed "RT," Gorham Mfg. Co., Providence, Rhode Island, ca. 1908, underplate 7" d., 3 pcs. **2,300.00**

Cocktail shaker, cov., tapering cylindrical body raised on a low foot, sweeping angular handle, the spout w/cover on chain, decorated w/a foliate design around the upper portion & handle w/fluting above foot, Black, Starr & Frost, Ltd., New York, New York, 11" h........**1,150.00**

Cocktail shaker, vase form w/angled borders & incised line

decoration, harp-shaped handle, monogrammed "O'B," designed by Erik Magnussen, Gorham Mfg. Co., Providence, Rhode Island, ca. 1928, 12⅜" h...............................**6,095.00**

Silver Coffeepot with Applied Decoration

Coffeepot, cov., compressed globular base w/elongated neck, shaped tubular handle w/ivory insulators, shaped spout, the sides applied w/a copper tree branch, a lizard, three birds & a butterfly, w/hinged tapering cover w/shell thumbpiece, the lower body engraved w/a landscape, Gorham Mfg. Co., Providence, Rhode Island, 1881, 7⅛" h.................................**6,325.00** (Illustration)

Coffeepot, cov., ribbed baluster-

form w/engraved scrolling bor-
ders, monogrammed, Gorham
Mfg. Corp., Providence, Rhode
Island, late 19th c., 8½" h......**287.50**

Coffeepot, cov., baluster-form,
the foot border chased w/a
band of scrolling acanthus
below wavy acanthus, the body
chased w/foliate sprigs & flowerheads on a matted ground,
w/leaf-clad scroll spout & a
shaped tubular handle w/ivory
insulators, the hinged domed
cover w/ball finial, engraved
under base "LEDEL," Dominick
& Haff, New York, New York,
1882, 8¾" h..........................**690.00**

Coffeepot, cov., vasiform,
chased w/landscape scenes on
a stippled ground, mounted w/a
harp handle capped by a ram's
head, the hinged cover opening to the side, S. Kirk & Son
Co., Baltimore, Maryland, ca.
1900, 9¾" h........................**1,150.00**

Coffeepot, cov., vase-form on
spreading foot, tubular handle,
scroll spout, the hinged domed
cover surmounted by a bud
finial, engraved on side w/a
monogram, maker's mark of F.
Masi & Co., Washington. D.C.
ca. 1843, 10½" h................**1,380.00**

Coffeepot, cov., Athenic patt., of
shaped baluster form on mold-
ed base, the body *repoussé*,
chased & engraved w/strap-
work & flowers, w/curving ivory
handle & undulating rim, the
hinged domed cover w/ivory
baluster finial, Gorham Mfg.
Co., Providence, Rhode Island,
1902, 10¾" h.....................**6,900.00**

Coffeepot, cov., tapering cylindrical body w/tuck-in base, on
spreading circular foot, w/leaf-
clad scroll spout, wooden scroll
handle w/shell-form join, the
hinged domed cover surmounted by a bud finial, engraved on
side w/script initials "PCW" &
under the base "L" over "CI,"

Silver Coffeepot by Myer Myers

maker's mark of Myer Myers,
New York, New York, ca. 1750,
11" h................................**77,300.00**
(Illustration)

Coffeepot, cov., baluster-form,
raised on three paw feet headed by acanthus, *repoussé* &
chased overall w/flowers,
acorns & leaves, w/leaf-clad
scroll handle w/ivory insulators,
leaf-clad spout w/cap, the
hinged cover surmounted by a
heraldic lion & shield, maker's
mark of Loring Andrews & Co.,
Cincinnati, Ohio, ca. 1896-
1900, 11¼" h.....................**1,725.00**

Coffee set: cov. coffeepot,
creamer & sugar bowl; overall
chased garland design,
Dominick & Haff, Newark, New
Jersey, late 19th c., coffeepot
10" h., 3 pcs. **575.00**

Coffee set: cov. coffeepot,
sugar bowl, creamer & tray; flat
based tapering cylindrical bodies, the pot w/wooden handle,
the sides lightly engraved overall w/scrolls & flowers, the footed oval galleried tray w/match-
ing decoration, undersides
monogrammed "S.R.C." &
dated "1906," Barbour Silver
Co., Hartford, Connecticut, ca.
1906, tray 12" l., pot 6⅝" h.,
4 pcs **920.00**

Coffee urn, cov., w/stand & lamp, baluster-form raised on four plain bracket supports w/stiff leaf decoration & plain circular lamp, w/bead & dart die-rolled borders, the body part-fluted above flowerheads, w/a band of Greek key & beads, w/square ring handles w/ivory rail, the removable cover surmounted by an urn form finial, Gorham Mfg. Co., Providence, Rhode Island, 1886, 13" h. **1,495.00**

Comb, seven-tooth, the high back pierced & bright-cut w/various leaves, flowers & scrolls, Tiffany & Co., New York, New York, ca. 1870, 5⅞" l. **1,380.00**

Compote, applied rose design on spaced & reticulated rim & base, monogrammed, Woodside Sterling Co., New York, New York, early 20th c., 9¼" d. **517.50**

Compote, shaped & reticulated applied floral rim & base, Howard & Co., New York, New York, 12¼" d., 5⅜" h. **546.50**

Compote, shaped rim & base, overall chased & reticulated decoration, Graff, Washburn & Dunn, New York, New York, early 20th c. **402.50**

Compotes, applied scrolling rim, *repoussé* herbaceous border, monogram in center, raised on a conforming low foot, Tiffany & Co., New York, New York, 1875-91, 7³⁄₁₆" d., pr. **1,380.00**

Compotes, shaped circular body on a spreading foot, applied w/foliate scrolls, *repoussé* & chased overall w/architecture in a landscape, w/everted border, centrally engraved w/a monogram, Samuel Kirk & Sons, Baltimore, Maryland, 1903-07, 8¼" d., pr. **1,955.00**

Console set, 12½" l. oval dish & pair 8" d., 4½" h. pedestal dishes; Francis I patt., Reed & Barton, Taunton, Massachusetts, 3 pcs. **1,075.00**

Creamer, pear-form w/waved rim, raised on three hoof feet headed by cinquefoils, engraved w/contemporary initials "AES" on base, William Ball, Philadelphia, Pennsylvania, ca. 1760, 4⅛" h. **3,565.00**

Creamer, coin, pear-shaped body raised on a spreading base, scroll handle, 18th c., 5" h. **192.50**

Creamer, coin, urn-shaped, marked "Coin, Boston," 5¾" h. **495.00**

Creamer, baluster-form on spreading base w/ropetwist border, *repoussé* & chased w/basketweave decoration, the handle & rim applied w/ropetwist design, maker's marks of Grosjean & Woodward and Tiffany & Co., New York, New York, ca. 1860, 5¾" h. **1,955.00**

Creamer & sugar bowl, Aesthetic Movement, each engraved in the Oriental taste w/figures & birds, Tiffany & Co., New York, New York, 2½" h., pr. **345.00**

Creamer & sugar bowl, slightly rounded lower section, chased overall w/matted flowerheads & applied w/copper seagrass & birds & brass branches w/vine scroll handles, Dominick & Haff, New York, New York, 1880, across handles 5" l., pr. **1,035.00**

Creamer & sugar bowl, in the Japanese taste, each of vase-form on a spreading circular base, w/pierced ear handles applied w/foliage, the bases

w/geometric & swan decoration, the matte-finished bodies
engraved w/Japanese designs
including figures, tea equipage
& games, die-rolled borders,
each w/monogram "LHB" in a
circle, the interiors gilt, Tiffany
& Co., New York, New York,
1871-75, sugar bowl 5⅝" h.,
pr. **4,830.00**

Cup, cov., coin, two-handled,
domed foot & low stem supporting a slightly globular bowl,
the canted cover w/ornate
finial, chased overall w/castles
& flowers, name & date
inscribed inside footrim,
engraved crest, S. Kirk & Son,
1846-61, 9" h.........................**489.00**

Cup, cov., two-handled, vase-
form on spreading foot, the
lower body *repoussé* & chased
w/twisting flutes, w/leaf-clad
scroll handles & beaded rim,
the cover surmounted by a bud
finial, engraved on both sides
w/a coat-of-arms, engraved
under base "S.A.B.S. 1895,"
Howard & Co., New
York, New York, 1894 ....**1,265.00**

Cup, coin, inverted pear-shape
w/beaded handle & gadrooned
foot, Adolphe Himmel for Hyde
& Goodrich, New Orleans,
Louisiana, ca. 1853-61, 3" d.,
3" h. **825.00**

Cup, child's, hand-hammered,
cylindrical w/gently rounded
base, raised rabbit design,
applied C-scroll handle,
marked "Sterling, Hand
Wrought at the Kalo Shop,
48," 3" h................................**467.50**

Cup, coin, presentation-type,
engraved w/lappets & applied
w/a satyr mask on the handle,
engraved "Winfield Everett
Stanton - from - Father &
Mother October 27, 1867,"
Victorian, Gorham Mfg. Co.,
Providence, Rhode Island,
4" h. **275.00**

Three-handled Silver Cup

Cup, three-handled, flat base
sack-form w/chased blossom &
leaf bands, three hollow scroll
handles w/matching design,
No. 6137, ca. 1900, 6" h. ...**1,150.00**
(Illustration)

Cup, presentation-type, cylindrical w/rounded lower section,
raised band at mid-section,
raised on a low foot, ornate
scrolled handles, engraved
presentation inscription, Wm.
B. Durgin, Concord, New
Hampshire, 20th c., 7¾" h.....**402.50**

Cup, low domed foot supporting
a cylindrical stem beneath the
hemispherical bowl, flat-chased
w/strapwork, the stem partly
chased in tree-trunk form,
marked on the base & num-
bered 2044, Robert Jarvie,
Chicago, Illinois, ca. 1910,
7⅜" h. **1,955.00**

Cup, presentation-type, tapering
cylinder w/angular side handles, engraved presentation
inscription, gold-washed interi-
or, Reed & Barton, Taunton,
Massachusetts, 20th c.,
9" h. **172.50**

Cup, three-handled, silver-gilt,
waisted cylindrical body
embossed & chased w/a continuous circle of dancing mae-
nads surrounded by sprays of
leaves, the leaves repeated on

the double-scroll handles which extend to form the feet, Tiffany & Co., New York, New York, ca. 1890, 9" h. **3,450.00**

Cup, hand-wrought, three-handled, 14th Century patt., w/presentation inscription dated "May, 1908" & applied w/an enameled plaque insignia of the organization, Shreve & Co., San Francisco, California, ca. 1908, 13½" h. **1,725.00**

Cup, three-handled, the bulbous lower section partly chased w/scrolling foliage, raised on three paw feet, gilt interior, Tiffany & Co., New York, New York, 1902-07, 14⅝" h. **6,325.00**

Demitasse pot & tray, Plymouth patt., monogrammed "M," Nos. 2311 & A5486, Gorham Mfg. Co., Providence, Rhode Island, tray 14½" d., pot 10¾" h., 2 pcs **575.00**

Demitasse set: cov. coffeepot, cov. sugar bowl & creamer; Danish Modern style, each w/ebony handles, Gorham Mfg. Co., Providence, Rhode Island, coffeepot 6" h., 3 pcs. **747.00**

Demitasse set: cov. coffeepot, creamer, open sugar bowl &

tray; Colonial Revival style w/chased floral decoration, Gorham Mfg. Co., Providence, Rhode Island, ca. 1917, tray 12⅛" d., coffeepot 9¾" h., 4 pcs. **1,150.00**

Demitasse set: cov. coffeepot, sugar bowl, creamer & tray; applied floral & scroll design, Meriden Brittania Co., Ltd., Meriden, Connecticut, late 19th c., coffeepot 10" h., 4 pcs. **1,092.00**

Demitasse set: cov. Turkish-style coffeepot, cov. sugar bowl, creamer & tray; each decorated w/Persian-type designs, the tray w/pierced gallery & raised on paw feet, Tiffany & Co., New York, New York, coffeepot 11" h., 4 pcs. **4,830.00**
(Illustration: below)

Demitasse set: cov. coffeepot, gilt-lined open sugar bowl, gilt-lined creamer & tray; D'Orleans patt., monogrammed "R," the circular tray w/bracket handles, No. 55150, Towle Silversmiths, Newburyport, Massachusetts, tray across handles 15" l., pot 8¾" h., 5 pcs. **977.50**

Silver Demitasse Set by Tiffany

Desk set: paper knife, pen tray, perpetual calendar easel-back frame w/printed cards & stamp box; hand-wrought, mono-grammed "S," Shreve & Co., San Francisco, California, early 20th c., pen tray 9¾" l., 4 pcs. **690.00**

Dessert basket, boat-form w/lightly gilt frosted interior, the handle simulating a tooled & buckled leather strap joined to the body by applied sprays of morning glory, the tendrils extending around the rim & the body engraved w/spreading leaves to match, on a spread-ing foot, Gorham Mfg. Co., Providence, Rhode Island, 1872, 11½" l. **1,380.00**

Dessert knives, bright-cut deco-ration, engraved name & date, S. Kirk & Son, Baltimore, Maryland, mid-19th c., set of 12 ....**460.00**

Dessert stand, shaped circular form, the shallow bowl w/stepped & pierced floral-decorated borders enriched w/bright-cut decoration, the applied rim w/leaf & berry design, on a pedestal base w/matching rim mount, No. 1162L, Gorham Mfg. Co., Providence, Rhode Island, 12¾" d., 2⅝" h......................**690.00**

Dessert stands, Japanese style, rounded square form, the shallow bowl spot-hammered & applied w/sprays of wheat w/gold ears & silver stems overlapping the rim, raised on four polished silver Oriental-style bracket feet, Gorham Mfg. Co., Providence, Rhode Island, 1879, 6¼" w., pr. **2,875.00**

Dessert stands, circular w/applied cast openwork anthemion repeat border, raised on four recessed cast supports, verso w/engraved monogram "M.C.T.," No.

13937, possibly designed by Paulding Farnham, Tiffany & Co., New York, New York, ca. 1900, w/special mark for Exposition Universelle, Paris, France, 1900, 9½" d., pr. ...**2,185.00**

Dinner forks, coin, Fiddle Thread patt., John Polhemus for Tiffany & Co., New York, New York, mid-19th c., set of 6 ....**192.50**

Silver Service & Butter Plates

Dinner service: twelve each service plates & butter plates; shaped circular form w/gad-rooned body w/shells & acan-thus at intervals, Tiffany & Co., New York, New York, 1934-47, service plates 11" d., 24 pcs. ....**13,800.00** (Illustration)

Dinner service: cov. soup tureen, pair of sauce tureens w/covers & four salt dips; each of shaped oval form on a circu-lar foot upon four beaded pad supports, the rim chased w/a band of Vitruvian scrolls & ap-plied w/a string of beads, w/ram's-head ring handles, the domed covers w/beaded ring handles, the tureen w/plat-ed liner, engraved on one side w/initials & "June 23rd 1859," the sauce tureens engraved w/armorials & an inscription dated "June 23rd, 1859," Shreve, Brown & Co., Boston,

Massachusetts, 1857, soup tureen & cover 14" h., the set **8,625.00**

Dinner service: pair of ice bowls w/liners, pair of olive dishes, butter dish, cover w/pierced liner & tray, pair of tazze, gravy tureen, cover & stand, oil & vinegar stand, water pitcher, pair of water pitcher trays, pair of large meat platters, pair of square dish covers; silver-gilt, of rectangular & square form w/fluted angles & chased w/sprays of violets, w/shells at the angles & paw feet, each piece engraved "1865 Roebling-1890," Gorham Mfg. Co., Providence, Rhode Island, 1889 & later, 18 pcs. **12,650.00**

Dish, Francis I patt., footed, the lobed everted rim w/chased scroll & floral design, Reed & Barton, Taunton, Massachusetts, 20th c., 8" d............**345.00**

Dishes, Japanese style, shallow circular form w/spot-hammered surface, the *bombé* sides applied as follows: one w/a cricket in a copper basketweave semi-circle overlaid w/a spray of berried leaves, also w/a bug & an owl perched on a branch, both in copper; the other w/a cricket in a copper basketweave frame surrounded by brass floral sprays & a butterfly in flight, Gorham Mfg. Co., Providence, Rhode Island, 1880, 4¾" d., pr. **2,875.00**

Dishes, fruit, *Martelé,* shaped circular form w/undulating rim, the border *repoussé* & chased w/blossoms, fruit, berries & leaves, Gorham Mfg. Co., Providence, Rhode Island, ca. 1899, 6¼" d., set of 3 ....**2,073.00**

Dishes, sandwich, fan-shaped on four ball & leaf feet, the tab handle formed of acanthus scrolls & trelliswork, the bowl

repoussé & chased w/flowerheads & scrolls & pierced w/trelliswork, Tiffany & Co., New York, New York, 1902-07, 18¾" l., pr. **9,775.00**

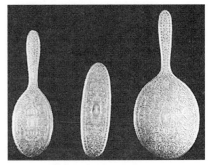

Lady's Silver Dresser Set by Tiffany

Dresser set: hand mirror, cov. powder jar, pin tray, hair brush, clothes brush & comb; decorated in the Persian taste, Tiffany & Co., New York, New York, early 20th c., 6 pcs. ....**1,210.00** (Illustration: three of six)

Dresser set: clothes brush, hair brush, nail buffer, hand mirror, button hook, nail file & comb; each piece molded in highrelief w/flowering Art Nouveau style rose branches, ca. 1900, 7 pcs. **402.00**

Egg cup, Arts & Crafts style, the hand-wrought tapering bowl & circular base w/hammered surface, Lebolt & Company, Chicago, Illinois, early 20th c., 2½" h....................................**110.00**

Entree dish w/reversible cover, Plymouth patt., monogrammed "M," No. A2782, Gorham Mfg. Co., Providence, Rhode Island, 1928, 10" l......**287.50**

Entree dish, cov., of oval form w/Greek key & beaded border, the fitted cover w/similar decoration w/later plated handle, engraved w/the initial "P," Tiffany & Co., New York, New York, 1856-70, 11" l. **1,380.00**

Entree dishes & covers, oval body on four square supports

Impressive Eight-branch Silver Epergne by Gorham

headed by acanthus, w/applied dentilated rim, the removable domed cover bright-cut engraved w/strapwork amid foliage, surmounted by acanthus scroll finial, Tiffany & Co., New York, New York, ca. 1870, 11" l., pr. **3,450.00**

Epergne, circular, the domed center pierced & cast w/flowers, shells & scrolls, fitted w/eight detachable reeded & floral branches supporting matching frames holding screw-in fluted gilt bowls, matching central bowl

engraved w/monogram, Gorham Mfg. Co., Providence, Rhode Island, ca. 1889, 24½" d., 12½" h.................**8,625.00**
(Illustration: above)

Epergne, on shaped square base, the scrollwork frame supporting a central two-handled vase surrounded by four foliate scroll branches holding slip-lock square deep dishes, partially chased w/flowers within scroll borders, Gorham Mfg. Co., Providence, Rhode Island, 1901, 19¾" h. **6,325.00**
(Illustration: below)

Vase-form Silver Four-dish Epergne

Late 19th c. Presentation Ewer

Ewer, presentation-type, ovoid body raised on a low foot, high scroll handle, vintage pattern decoration, engraved presentation inscription, Tiffany & Co., New York, New York, late 19th c., 14½" h. ....**11,500.00** (Illustration)

Ewers, presentation-type, baluster-form on spreading foot, chased w/stiff leaves & trailing grapevine, w/stepped rocaille rim, leaf-clad scroll handles, the front engraved w/a presentation inscription dated "1853," maker's mark of Robert & William Wilson, Philadelphia, Pennsylvania, ca. 1853, 15⅝" h., pr.........................**4,830.00**

Fernery, circular bowl w/straight shallow sides everted at the rim, decorated w/a chased & embossed repeat wave border at the base under a honeycomb peened finish, applied w/strapwork & loose ring handles, raised on four ball supports, monogrammed on the underside, Dominick & Haff, New York, New York, 1885, retailed by J.E. Caldwell & Co., 8" d., 3" h. ....**1,495.00** (Illustration: below)

Finger bowls, flared sides embossed & chased in high-relief w/birds perched among ferns, gilt interior, bases engraved w/contemporary chrysanthemum plant monograms "CCS," Tiffany & Co., New York, New York, ca. 1883, 5¼" d., set of 6 ....**5,750.00**

Flagon, cov., coin, cylindrical body decorated w/bands of chased & applied leaf & floral decoration, curved covered lip, C-scroll handle, domed hinged lid w/pineapple finial, Fletcher & Gardiner, Philadelphia, Pennsylvania, ca. 1820s, 11¾" h. ....**1,380.00** (Illustration: top next page)

Flagon, cov., in the Art Nouveau taste, the tall cylindrical body w/spreading base & scalloped border, w/*repoussé* foliage, rising to diagonal sweeping ribs, the handle issuing from a leaf,

Silver Fernery by Dominick & Haff

Early 19th c. Coin Silver Flagon

Silver Presentation Flask with Applied Decoration

w/cactus issuing from shrubbery, one side etched w/a mining site at the foot of a mountain, the other etched w/"L. H. Scott 1888," the circular hinged cap w/an etched inscription "Batopilas," Gorham Mfg. Co., Providence, Rhode Island, 1888, 7½" h........................**7,475.00** (Illustration)

Fruit bowl, circular w/shaped rim & lobed sides, Gorham Mfg. Corp., Providence, Rhode Island, 20th c., 9" d. **230.00**

Fruit bowl, applied scroll border, scrolling feet, Tiffany & Co., New York, New York, 1907-38, 9½" d..................**1,955.00**

Fruit bowl, quatrefoil-form w/machine-embossed panel decoration depicting fruit & flowers, No. A2223M, Gorham Mfg. Co., Providence, Rhode Island, 1901, 15¼" l., 2¼"h................................**1,725.00**

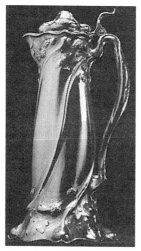

Flagon Designed for the 1900 Paris Exposition

w/chased foliate decoration, similar vines & leaves at the shoulder, undulating rim to fit the shaped domed cover & lipped spout, w/rolling thumbpiece, Gorham Mfg. Co., Providence, Rhode Island, 1900, designed by William C. Codman for the Paris Exposition of 1900, 15⅝" h.............................**96,000.00** (Illustration)

Flask, presentation-type, flattened shaped rectangular body w/serpentine outline, applied

Garniture set: footed compote & pair of candlesticks on marble bases; Greek key border around foot rims, engraved w/presentation inscription, Gorham Mfg. Corp., Providence, Rhode Island, 20th c., 3 pcs........................**920.00**

Goblet, coin, panelled bowl raised on a spreading foot, engraved "Fannie," mid-19th c., 6½" h. **247.50**

Goblets, water, typical plain form, Gorham Mfg. Co., Providence, Rhode Island, set of 12 ....**900.00**

Goblets, wine, wide band of foliage on a stippled ground, on a conforming domed foot, 20th c., set of 12 ....**1,610.00**

Gravy boat & underplate, Arts & Crafts style, hand-wrought paneled form w/hammered & undecorated surfaces, The Kalo Shop, Chicago, Illinois, early 20th c., 9" l., 4½" h. **440.00**

Gravy ladle, Arts & Crafts style, lobed bowl & trifid tip, The Kalo Shop, Chicago, Illinois, early 20th c., 7¼" l. **110.00**

Coin Silver Hot Water Urn

Hot water urn, coin, Renaissance Revival style, the globular body raised on four slender legs ending in claw feet, raised on a square base w/bracket feet, ornate ring handles, monogrammed "M," very slight dents, Gorham Mfg. Corp., Providence, Rhode Island, third quarter 19th c., 14¼" h. ....**4,312.50** (Illustration)

Hot water urn, two-handled vase-form, lightly flat-chased w/classical foliage on partly matted ground, the handles topped by female masks, the finial as a putto blowing a trumpet, the spigot terminating in a ram's head, the stand on three scroll feet & w/detachable lamp, Tiffany & Co., New York, New York, ca. 1875, 18¾" h. **5,462.00**

Ice bucket, oval, realistically formed as a wooden tub chased w/barrel staves & hoops, raised rim handles, applied on one side w/the initial "W," Tiffany & Co., New York, New York, 1858-70, 10½" l. **5,175.00**

Inkwell, square, sterling overlay decoration on bottle, sterling lid w/monogram, Black, Starr & Frost, New York, New York, late 19th c., 3" sq., 4" h. **431.00**

Julep cup, coin, slightly tapering cylinder w/molded foot, engraved "Leland," marked "Hildeburn & Bros., 12 Market Street, Phila.," 3⅜" h. (dents) **220.00**

Julep cup, cylindrical w/molded foot & rim, monogrammed, Mark J. Scearce, Shelbyville, Kentucky, 3¾" h. **242.00**

Julep cup, coin, tapering cylinder, engraved "Ohio State Board of Agriculture Premium" w/further decorative tooled detail, marked "Blynn & Baldwin," 3¾" h. **440.00**

Julep cups, cylindrical, each engraved w/a crest, S. Kirk & Son Inc., Baltimore, Maryland, mid-20th c., 3¾" h., set of 12 ....**1,955.00**

Ladle, coin, handle w/engraved monogram, marked "E. Kinsey, Cincinnati," 8" l. **225.00**

Ladle, coin, rounded handle

w/chased feathered edge, Newell Harding, Boston, Massachusetts, ca. 1822-32, 13½" l. **192.50**

Unusual Silver Trophy-type Ladle

Ladle, trophy-type, the bowl formed as the hull of a boat w/lines & a shell, w/applied zigzag border, the cylindrical mast rising from a loop handle & surmounted by a figure waving a hat & draped w/a sail, Tiffany & Co., New York, New York, 1870-75, 15" l. ....**3,680.00** (Illustration)

Three-handled Silver Loving Cup

Loving cup, three-handled, presentation-type, cylindrical w/gadrooned base & low foot, applied grapevine design, engraved presentation inscription, Tiffany & Co., New York,

New York, 20th c., 9" h. .....**2,645.00** (Illustration)

Loving cup, three-handled, presentation-type, Art Nouveau style, cylindrical w/reeded band near base & beneath rim, raised on a stepped foot & knopped stem, acid-etched & engraved presentation inscription, Gorham Mfg. Corp., Providence, Rhode Island, early 20th c., 12" h. **632.50**

Mirror, hand-type, square mirror back w/tapering cylindrical handle chased overall w/flowers & leaves, 19th c., 10¾" l. **172.50**

Models of peacocks, each realistically modeled, Heer Schofield Co., Baltimore, Maryland, 20" l., pr. **2,185.00**

Mug, child's, tapering cylindrical body w/engraved design, made by Moore, Tiffany & Co., New York, New York, 19th c., 3¼" h. **201.00**

Mug, coin, cylindrical w/dierolled rim & base, William Tenney, New York, New York, ca. 1840, 3½" h. **302.50**

Mug, of shaped baluster-form, *repoussé* & chased w/flowers, leaves & trailing vines, w/similar handle, Tiffany & Co., New York, New York, 1879-91, 3½" h. **1,495.00**

Mug, baluster-form, the body spot-hammered & w/three wide spirals, w/shaped & hammered handle, gilt interior, Tiffany & Co., New York, New York, 1880-85, 3½" h. **1,610.00**

Mug, cylindrical w/applied dierolled borders, the lower one w/Japanese landscapes & the upper w/geometric designs, the scroll handle w/stylized lotus terminals, Gorham Mfg. Co., Providence, Rhode Island, 1872, 3⅝" h. **460.00**

Mug, tapering cylindrical body

on spreading foot, simple scroll handle, the base engraved "Samuel Fisher," unmarked, mid-18th c., 4½" h. **518.00**

Mug, plain baluster-form w/double scroll handle, Reed & Barton, Taunton, Massachusetts, late 19th c., retailed by Shreve, Crump & Low, Boston, Massachusetts, 5¾" h. **259.00**

Napkin rings, decorated w/applied birds, insects & vegetation on a hammered ground, George W. Shiebler & Co., New York, New York, early 20th c., pr. **1,495.00**

Nut set: master bowl & four individual bowls; each in the form of a bushel basket w/ring handles, Gorham Mfg. Co., Providence, Rhode Island, ca. 1869, master bowl 3⁵⁄₁₆" d., individual bowls 2¹¹⁄₁₆" d., 5 pcs. **402.50**

Olive dish, modeled in the form of the fruit, leafy twig handle, Gorham Mfg. Co., Providence, Rhode Island, 1886, 5⅝" l. **1,150.00**

Ca. 1770 Silver Pepper Box

Pepper box, cov., cylindrical w/molded base & reeded scroll handle, the pierced cover w/molded bands & baluster finial, engraved on front "Miller," maker's mark of Elias Pelletreau, Southampton, New York, ca. 1770, 3⅜" h.........**8,625.00** (Illustration)

Pipe lighter, modeled in the form of a footed bowl w/everted waved rim & straight turned

wood handle, raised on three hoof feet headed by cinquefoils, Myer Myers, New York, New York, ca. 1760, 4⅝" d. **11,500.00**

Pitcher, globular hand-hammered body w/rolled rim & flaring lip, applied loop handle, raised initials "SH," marked "Sterling, August 8, 1916, Hand Wrought at the Kalo Shops, Chicago, New York, 9309," 6" h. **990.00**

Pitcher, of shaped baluster-form on circular undulating base, spot-hammered surface & handle, the body chased w/panels of strapwork & leaves, w/flaring undulating rim, Gorham Mfg. Co., Providence, Rhode Island, 1897, designed by William C. Codman, 6¼" h. **14,950.00**

Silver Pitcher Decorated in the Japanese Taste

Pitcher, of shaped baluster-form, decorated in the Japanese taste, the body spot-hammered, applied w/a copper & silver dragonfly, copper & green gold maple leaves, copper & silver moths, one w/*mokume* wings, a copper beetle on the handle, w/engraved trailing vines, Tiffany & Co., New York, 1878, designed by Edward C. Moore, probably for the Paris

Exposition of 1878,
6¾" h. **51,750.00**
(Illustration)

Pitcher, baluster-form body
w/spot-hammered surface,
applied w/a copper turtle &
crustacea, also applied w/silver
lily pads & buds & a salaman-
der, the handle chased w/two
bands of palmettes, Gorham
Mfg. Co., Providence, Rhode
Island, 1880, 6¾" h. **5,462.00**

Pitcher, water, of globular form,
entirely *repoussé* & chased
w/flowers & leaves, w/a band
of stylized leaves at the base of
the neck, the handle similarly
chased, the base engraved
w/monogram "EWP," Tiffany &
York, New York, 1872-91,
7" h. **6,900.00**

Pitcher, water, presentation-
type, vase-form on spreading
foot w/dentilated borders, the
shoulder w/a die-rolled band of
tooth & dart, w/leaf-clad scroll
handle, the front engraved w/a
presentation inscription, maker's mark of Thomas Fletcher,
Philadelphia, Pennsylvania,
ca. 1820, 7¾" h. **2,530.00**

Pitcher, water, baluster-form,
embossed & chased overall
w/water lilies w/overlapping
pads on a scalework ground,
Tiffany & Co., New York, New
York, ca. 1880, 7¾" h. **7,475.00**

Pitcher, water, urn-form shaped
oval body w/flat base, the sides
chased & embossed w/a variety of flowerheads & foliage,
hollow scroll handle, No. 6022,
Whiting Mfg. Co., Providence,
Rhode Island, late 19th c.,
7¾" h. **1,495.00**
(Illustration: top next column)

Pitcher, water, globular baluster-form on spreading foot, w/a
die-rolled band of acanthus
scroll & dart, shaped tubular
handle w/reeded bands, die-
rolled band at the shoulder

Floral-Chased Silver Pitcher

chased w/shield & dart,
Gorham Mfg. Co., Providence,
Rhode Island, ca. 1860,
7⅞" h. **1,380.00**

Pitcher, water, the bulbous body
w/frosted surface, inlaid in
vari-colored gold & copper w/a
pond scene showing a mallard
taking flight & a kingfisher w/a
minnow in its beak skimming
the surface, surrounded by a
butterfly, dragonfly, rushes, iris
plant & lily pads, the handle
chased to resemble raffia,
Theodore B. Starr, New York,
New York, ca. 1890,
8" h. **3,450.00**

Pitcher, water, ovoid body
w/wide chased scroll band, flat
base w/ring foot, flared collar
w/shaped rim edged in applied
scroll molding, hollow C-scroll
handle, George C. Shreve &
Co., San Francisco, California,
Bee Mark, ca. 1890, 8" h. **690.00**

Pitcher, presentation-type, of
shaped globular-form on a
molded base, part-fluted w/a
band of *repoussé* acanthus
vines & flowers, w/a similar
band of the neck, the handle
shaped as a branch, engraved
w/an intricate monogram
"CdeBM," the base engraved
"From many friends with Tiffany
& Co. Oct. 22 '89," Tiffany &

Co., New York, New York,
ca. 1889, 8¼" h. **4,025.00**

Pitcher, water, hand-wrought,
flat base, plain pyriform body
w/raised lip, C-scroll strap handle, Allan Adler, Los Angeles,
California, 8½" h...................**977.50**

Ornate Silver Water Pitcher

Pitcher, water, oval urn-form
w/spreading collet base,
scrolled rim w/flared spout &
hollow scroll handle, embossed
& chased w/blossoms,
engraved "G.C.H. 1886,"
Dominick & Haff, New York,
New York, 1886, retailed by
Bailey, Banks & Biddle
Company, Philadelphia,
Pennsylvania, 8⅝" h. **2,070.00**
(Illustration)

Pitcher, water, Old English patt.,
the body w/*repoussé* rocaille
decoration, raised on scrolled
feet, Poole Silver Co., Taunton,
Massachusetts, early 20th c.,
9" h......................................**489.00**

Pitcher, water, plain baluster-
form w/scrolled handle, R.
Wallace & Sons Mfg. Co.,
Wallingford, Connecticut,
early 20th c., 9¼" h. **259.00**

Pitcher, Rococo style, baluster-
form body decorated w/a
chased leaf & diamond quilted
design, the shaped rim
w/applied scrolling, raised on
ornate curved feet, mono-

Silver Pitcher & Serving Bowl

grammed, Frank W. Smith
Silver Co., Inc., Gardner,
Massachusetts, 19th c.,
9½" h. **1,150.00**
(Illustration)

Pitcher, cov., modeled in the
form of a churn, w/simulated
knotty wooden staves & polished hoops, embossed w/a
simulated riveted plaque
engraved w/a name & dated
"1865," the reeded scroll handle spreading into lily & other
water leaves, hinged domed
cover w/hinged flap & bud
finial, Edward C. Moore for
Tiffany & Co., 550 Broadway,
New York, New York, ca.
1865, 9½" h. **3,162.00**

**Silver Pitcher with a Nautical
Inscription**

Pitcher, presentation-type,

expanding cylindrical body
w/rounded shoulder, decorated
w/*repoussé* & chased design
including a band of seashells,
acid-etched inscription
"Larchmont Special Regatta,
For Forty Footers, Sept. 28th
1889, won by Liris, against
Mariquita, Gorillar and
Broncho," Whiting Mfg. Co.,
Providence, Rhode
Island, 9¾" h. **2,760.00**
(Illustration)

Pitcher, cov., baluster-form
w/reeded borders, the cover
w/bud finial, engraved w/con-
temporary monogram "SA," J.
& I. Cox, New York, New York,
ca. 1830, 9¾" h. **920.00**

Water Pitcher with Cattails Design

Pitcher, water, shaped baluster-
form, the body *repoussé* &
chased w/cattails & leaves, the
handle cast in the form of cattails, maker's marks of John C.
Moore and Tiffany & Co., New
York, New York, ca. 1853,
9¾" h. **7,475.00**
(Illustration)

Pitcher, water, Francis I patt.,
No. 570A, Reed & Barton,
Taunton, Massachusetts,
1951, 11" h. **2,185.00**

Pitcher, water, half-reeded
vase-form, chased w/floral
swags, monogram & date,

Lebkuecher & Co., Newark,
New Jersey, ca. 1900,
11¼" h. **805.00**

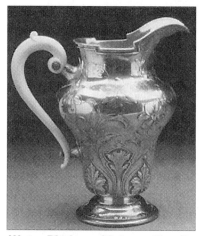

Water Pitcher with Ivory Handle

Pitcher, water, of inverted pear
shape, chased overall w/a floral & foliate design, scrolling
ivory handle, Gorham Mfg. Co.,
ca. 1900, retailed by Bigelow,
Kennard & Co., Boston,
Massachusetts, 11¼" h. **3,220.00**
(Illustration)

Pitcher, cov., coin, jug-type,
vasiform body w/scalloped
upper rim, fitted w/conforming
domed lid w/cast floral finial,
branch-form hollow handle, the
body chased & embossed
w/romantic architectural
scenes, Eoff & Shepard for
Ball, Black & Co., New York,
New York, 13" h. **1,610.00**

Pitcher, water, baluster-form,
chased w/a contemporary
monogram within a rococo cartouche, leafy scroll handle,
Wood & Hughes, New York,
New York, ca. 1845,
13½" h. **1,035.00**

Pitcher, water, of vase-form on
a stepped pedestal base decorated w/a band of die-rolled
speartips & interlaced circles,
the body engraved w/borders
of strapwork on a matted
ground, applied w/a mid-band

of similar speartip pattern, the neck w/engraved strapwork, the handle *repoussé* & chased w/stylized leaves, engraved on front w/a monogram below armorials, engraved under base w/inscription dated "1869," Tiffany & Co., New York, New York, ca. 1869, 13¾" h. **3,450.00**

Pitcher, water, vase-form, chased w/bands of formal foliage, leaf-capped reeded scroll handle, engraved w/contemporary & later inscriptions dated "1829" & "1916," Baldwin Gardiner, Philadelphia, Pennsylvania, 13¾" h. **1,725.00**

Ornate Footed Silver Water Pitcher

Pitcher, water, baluster-form on spreading circular foot, chased w/flowerheads & foliate scrolls, w/Greek key borders & leaf-clad scroll handle, engraved on front w/script monogram, maker's mark of J.E. Caldwell, Philadelphia, Pennsylvania, ca. 1885, 15¼" h. ....**1,380.00** (Illustration)

Pitcher, water, baluster-form w/engraved laurel bands & contemporary inscription, Whiting Mfg. Co., Providence, Rhode Island, ca. 1900, retailed by Galt & Brother, 15⅜" h. **1,035.00**

Pitcher, presentation-type, urn-form on spreading foot chased w/acanthus scrolls & leaves, w/a tied reed band below a fluted lower body, w/overlapping acanthus reeded bands at the shoulder, *repoussé* & chased w/acanthus below an applied grotesque mask under the lip, w/leaf-clad reeded handle terminating in leaves, engraved w/an inscription at the waist dated "December 24th 1884," Tiffany & Co., New York, New York, ca.1884, 18" h...........**7,475.00**

Pitchers, water, dome-footed baluster-form chased w/grapevine, monogrammed, twig handle & borders, by William Forbes for Ball, Black & Co., New York, New York, ca. 1850, 16½" & 17" h., pr......**4,025.00**

Plate, round w/Colonial Revival style *repoussé* rim, engraved central detail & monogram, Mt. Vernon Company Silversmiths, Inc., Mount Vernon, New York, ca. 1914, 8⅞" d. **115.00**

Plates, bread & butter, shaped hexagonal form w/hammered flat border, Shreve & Co., San Francisco, California, ca. 1909-22, 6" w., set of 12 ....**460.00**

Plates, circular w/serpentine border chased w/foliage & pierced w/paterae & latticework, Tiffany & Co., New York, New York, 1907-47, 9½" d., pr. **1,840.00**

Plates, dinner, scalloped shell & foliate scroll rim, the border chased w/spreading flowers at intervals, Howard & Co., New York, New York, 1886, 10⅜" d., set of 12 ....**5,175.00**

Plates, dinner, pierced rococo rim, monogrammed center, Redlich & Co., New York, New York, ca. 1909, retailed by Caldwell & Co., Philadelphia, Pennsylvania, 10½" d., set of 12 ....**5,750.00**

Plates, dinner, shaped circular form on reeded footrim, the rim applied w/foliate vines, the border chased w/architectural landscapes between fruit bouquets & foliage, the center engraved w/an elaborate script monogram "MEF," Samuel Kirk & Sons, Baltimore, Maryland, 1903-24, set of 12 ....**8,050.00**

Plates, service, shaped circular form w/applied hammered flat wire border, monogrammed "T," Shreve & Co., San Francisco, California, 1909-22, 10¾" d., set of 9 ....**1,610.00**

Plates, service, plain w/molded rim, crested center, border initialed "L," Tiffany & Co., New York, New York, ca. 1920, 10⅞" d., set of 12 ....**5,750.00**

Plates, service, Francis I patt., Reed & Barton, Taunton, Massachusetts, 20th c., 11" l., set of 4 ....**1,380.00**

Plates, service, St. Dunstan patt., Gorham Mfg. Co., Providence, Rhode Island, 20th c., 11" d., set of 12 .....**4,600.00**

Plates, bread, shaped rim, monogrammed, Richard Dimes Company, South Boston, Massachusetts, first half 20th c., set of 6 ....**172.50**

Plates, bread, Lord Saybrook patt., International Silver Co., Meriden, Connecticut, set of 12 ....**125.00**

Plates, service & dessert, the border embossed w/garlands of flowers & ferns on matted ground, the center w/foliate monogram, S. Kirk & Son Co., Baltimore, Maryland, early 20th c., eight 11" d. & eight 9⅛" d. plates, 16 pcs...........**6,900.00**

Platter, oval, the border *repoussé* & chased w/roses & other flowers, w/an applied rim

w/similar foliage, the border w/a reserve engraved "JHL," Gorham Mfg. Co., Providence, Rhode Island, 1896, 18" l....**4,830.00**

Platter, Georgian patt., shaped oval w/applied hollow molded scroll border, monogrammed "G," No. 7398, Shreve & Co., San Francisco, California, 1909-22, 19½" l.....................**460.00**

Platter, Georgian patt., No. 6173, Shreve & Co., San Francisco, California, 1909-22, 21" l. **747.50**

Platter, coin, the oval rim decorated w/acanthus, the body engraved w/a floral & scrollwork design, raised on four paw feet, monogram, Haddock, Lincoln & Foss, 19th c. (dent).....................**632.50**

Platters: meat, fish & circular; each w/foliate scroll rims, the borders chased w/sloping lobes w/flowers at intervals, monogrammed, Gorham Mfg. Co., Providence, Rhode Island, 1900-02, 22½", 17" l. & 15" d., set of 3 ....**2,875.00**

Platters, shaped oval body applied w/scrolling Art Nouveau flowers, two w/monogram, Mauser Mfg. Co., New York, New York, ca. 1900, graduated sizes from 15¾" to 22" l., set of 4 ....**3,450.00**

Porringer, circular w/reticulated handle, decorated w/an Arts & Crafts style design, Tiffany & Co., New York, New York, ca. 1917, 4½" d. **172.50**

Porringer, of typical rounded form, the keyhole handle engraved w/contemporary initials "IP to LC," Samuel Minott, Boston, Massachusetts, ca. 1780, 5" d. **1,840.00**

Porringer, coin, shallow bowl w/rounded sides, cast handle w/pierced design, unmarked

but attributed to Massa-
chusetts, 5¼" d. **605.00**

Porringer, of typical form w/wide
bowl, the keyhole handle
engraved w/contemporary initials "E S," marked on back of
handle ".REVERE," Paul
Revere, Jr., Boston,
Massachusetts, ca. 1760,
5⅞," d. **13,800.00**

Silver Porringer by Paul Revere II

Mid-18th c. Silver Porringer

Porringer, circular w/slightly
everted rim & pierced keyhole
handle engraved "R B to L B,"
maker's mark of Philip Syng,
Jr., Philadelphia, Pennsylvania,
1730-70, 7⅞" l. **3,680.00**
(Illustration)

Porringer, circular w/slightly
everted rim & pierced keyhole
handle engraved "H*A" over
"S*J 1765," maker's mark of
Thomas Townsend, Boston,
Massachusetts, 1725-60,
7⅞" l. **2,300.00**

Porringer, circular w/slightly flaring rim & pierced keyhole handle, engraved on handle
w/monogram "WMB," the front
engraved "James Breck
Perkins From his Grandfather,"
maker's mark of Paul Revere
II, Boston, Massachusetts,
1781, 8⅛" l. **18,400.00**
(Illustration: top next column)

Porringer, rounded body
w/slightly everted rim & pierced
keyhole handle, the handle

engraved w/initials "PB," maker's mark of John Germon,
Philadelphia, Pennsylvania,
ca. 1800, 8¼" l. **3,680.00**

Powder box, cov., engraved w/a
presentation inscription &
dated "May 5, 1907" on bottom,
Tiffany & Co., New York, New
York, 2¼" h. **176.00**

Punch bowl & undertray, the
bowl w/scalloped shell & flower
rim, the sides & shaped domed
foot *repoussé* w/a floral design,
the tray w/scroll rim w/rose
sprays at intervals, the center
w/a chased design, both pieces
engraved w/the arms, supporters & motto of the State of
Maryland, S. Kirk & Son,
Baltimore, Maryland, ca. 1900,
bowl 14¼" d., tray 20" d.,
2 pcs. **13,800.00**

Punch ladle, plain handle
w/engraved monogram,
Shreve, Crump & Low,
12" l. **192.50**

Salad serving set, parcel-gilt,
realistically formed as shells
lashed to a bamboo stem,
Gorham Mfg. Co., Providence,
Rhode Island, 1891 & 1892,
9½" l. **3,220.00**
(Illustration: top next page)

Salad serving set, Old English
patt., the handles chased

Unusual Silver Salad Serving Set

w/flowers & foliate, the gilt bowl
& tines w/bright-cut engraving,
Black, Starr & Frost, New York,
New York, ca. 1880, 12" l.,
pr. **920.00**

Salad serving set, spoon & fork
decorated w/a blossom pattern,
engraved monogram, Dominic
& Haff Co., Newark, New
Jersey, ca. 1905, pr. **259.00**

Salt & pepper shakers, modeled in the form of a dog,
monogrammed, Dominick &
Haff, Newark & New York,
1879, pr. **1,035.00**

Salt dips, round shallow bowl-
form raised on three paw supports headed by rams' heads,
w/applied Greek key border,
engraved w/initials "ISC,"
Tiffany & Co., New York, New
York, ca. 1870, 2¾" d.,
set of 4 ....**2,300.00**

Salt dips, shaped oval body
raised on bat's-wing supports,
the sides fluted w/applied
gadrooned rim, maker's mark
of James Howell, Philadelphia,
Pennsylvania, ca. 1810, 3⅞" l.,
set of 4 ....**5,060.00**

Salt dips, spoons & casters, the
oval trencher salt dip w/flaring
molded base, w/spoon, the
caster of baluster-form on
molded base, the slip-on
domed cover w/pierced foliate

decoration & surmounted by a
baluster finial, Arthur Stone
and Stone Associates,
Gardner, Massachusetts, two
pairs 1907-37, two pairs 1937-
57, the set **2,760.00**

Salt dips, coin, circular body
raised on a spreading foot, ca.
1850, cased set of 12...........**440.00**

Sandwich tray, circular
w/embossed floral edge, R.
Wallace & Sons Mfg. Co.,
Wallingford, Connecticut,
ca. 1925, 13⅝" d. **165.00**

Silver Sauceboat by Jacobi

Sauceboat, elongated oval body
on a circular foot, *repoussé* &
chased w/flowers & leaves on
a matted ground, w/molded rim
& leaf-clad dolphin-form handle, maker's mark of A. Jacobi,
Baltimore, Maryland, 1879-90,
8⅞" l. **978.00**
(Illustration)

Sauceboat on stand, of navette
form, on pedestal base
w/beaded & Greek key border,
w/applied bifurcated acanthus-
leaf handle, the rim w/similar
beading & Greek key borders,
the stand of oval form w/bead-
ing & Greek key border, both
engraved w/monogram "MBP,"
Tiffany & Co., New York, New
York, 1857-70, stand.........**1,150.00**

Sauceboats, modeled in the
form of a swan w/chased feather detailing, Gorham Mfg.
Corp., Providence, Rhode
Island, 8" l., pr. **1,092.00**

Sauceboats, oval, raised on a
stepped oval base, w/beaded

Ca. 1785 Silver Sauceboat

borders & upswept double
scroll leaf-clad handle, the side
engraved w/a foliate monogram, maker's mark of Daniel
Dupuy, Sr. or Jr., Philadelphia,
Pennsylvania, ca. 1785,
8¾" l., pr........................**19,500.00**
(Illustration: one of two)

Seafood salad servers, parcel-
gilt, the handles etched w/flow-
ers & leaves, the bowl &
prongs silver-gilt w/scalloped
edges etched w/seagrass &
lobster, each engraved on
reverse w/initials "ABR,"
Gorham Mifg. Co., Providence,
Rhode Island, ca. 1890,
11¼" l., pr.............................**978.00**

Serving bowl, Rococo style w/a
pierced & shaped scrolling rim,
the interior chased w/leaf &
diamond quilted design, monogrammed, Frank W. Smith
Silver Co., Inc., Gardner,
Massachusetts, 19th c.,

14½" h...............................**1,725.00**
(Illustration: top page 125)

Serving dish, cov., Art
Nouveau style, shaped oval
form, chased relief floral & foliate decoration, monogrammed,
convertible cover, Black, Starr
and Frost, New York, New
York, late 19th c., 12¾" l. **1,150.00**
(Illustration: below)

Serving dish, lobed body w/a
reticulated floral border, monogrammed, Dominick & Haff,
Newark & New York, 1897,
retailed by Bailey, Banks &
Biddle **489.00**

Sherbet cups, rounded bowl
raised on a spreading foot, the
rim applied w/trailing leaves,
repoussé & chased w/foliage
on a matted ground, engraved
w/monogram, w/glass liner,
Samuel Kirk & Sons, Baltimore,
Maryland, 1903-07, 3¾" h.,
set of 12 ....**2,990.00**

Soup ladle, Fiddle patt., monogrammed "F," Caleb Warner,
Salem, Massachusetts, 1810-
30, 12¼" l. **632.50**

Soup ladle, w/rounded end,
bright-cut & engraved w/con-
temporary monogram "MIS,"
the back of the bowl decorated
w/a spread-winged bird,
Joseph Lownes, Philadelphia,
Pennsylvania, ca. 1790,
13¼" l. **862.00**

Art Nouveau Silver Covered Serving Dish

Soup ladle, coffin end, engraved w/contemporary monogram "EDB," Richard Humphreys, Philadelphia, Pennsylvania, ca. 1795, 14½" l. **920.00**

Soup tureen, cov., Classical Revival style, boat-form, forked handles terminating in palmettes, border of interlaced ribbons enclosing flowerheads, engraved w/contemporary monogram "JW" surrounded by leaves, domed cover w/a border of shells & strapwork, oval rim finial, Tiffany & Co., 550 Broadway, New York, New York, ca. 1865, across handles 17" l. **6,325.00**

Soup tureens & covers, *bombé* oval form, raised on four paw feet headed by acanthus & resting on ball feet, the handles rising from female masks, the rim decorated w/shells & foliage, the finial formed as a lion *couchant guardant*, one engraved w/contemporary monogram "EBH," the other w/later monogram "EKR," Frederick Marquand, New York, New York, ca. 1825, across handles 16½" l., pr......................................**12,650.00**

Sugar bowl, cov., coin, urn-form on a low-footed square base, flaring open handles, stepped domed cover w/swan finial, William Seal, Philadelphia, Pennsylvania, ca. 1820, 5¾" h. **489.00**
(Illustration: top next column)

Sugar bowl, vase-form w/beaded borders, raised on a circular domed foot & slender stem, the flaring bell-form cover w/acorn finial rising from leaves, side engraved w/script monogram "AMS," Thomas Underhill & John Vernon, New York, New York, ca. 1785, 7⅜" h.........**1,035.00**

Sugar bowl, cov., urn-form

Ca. 1820 Coin Silver Sugar Bowl

raised on a circular foot upon a square pedestal, beaded borders, engraved w/a foliate wreath enclosing initials "AM," the domed cover w/an urn-form finial, maker's mark of Joseph Anthony, Jr., Philadelphia, Pennsylvania, ca. 1700, 9⅝" h. **2,300.00**

Sugar bowl, cov., urn-form on circular foot raised on a square pedestal, w/beaded borders, the domed cover surmounted by a pineapple finial issuing from leaves, the front engraved w/a monogram within foliate garlands, maker's mark of Joseph Lownes, Philadelphia, Pennsylvania, ca. 1795, 10" h. **1,725.00**

Tall Urn-form Silver Sugar Bowl

Sugar bowl, cov., urn-form on spreading foot raised on square pedestal, beaded borders, the domed cover surmounted by an urn finial, maker's mark of Samuel Richards, Jr., Philadelphia, Pennsylvania, ca. 1800, 10" h. ....**1,265.00** (Illustration: bottom previous page)

Sugar bowl, cov., vase-form w/beaded borders, raised on a square base supporting a trumpet-form standard, the sharply domed cover w/pineapple finial, engraved w/contemporary monogram "WEH," Van Voorhis & Schanck, New York, New York, ca. 1790, 10¼" h. **4,025.00**

Tablespoon, Old English patt., period monogram w/three script initials, Paul Revere, Jr., Boston, Massachusetts, ca. 1790, 8¾" l. **2,070.00**

Silver Tablespoon by Paul Revere II

Tablespoons, the terminal bright-cut w/chevron, the front engraved w/a monogram "DET" in script, maker's mark of Paul Revere II, Boston, Massachusetts, 1780-95, 8⅝" l., pr. ....**3,450.00** (Illustration: one of two)

Tablespoons, rounded ends, feather edge, engraved w/script monogram "CH," scroll-back bowl, four by Paul Revere, Boston, Massachusetts, ca. 1780 & two by Revere's apprentice, David Moseley, Boston, Massachusetts, ca. 1780, 8⅜" l., set of 6 ....**11,500.00**

Tankard, cov., tapering cylindrical body on a molded footrim, w/tubular scroll handle & scroll thumbpiece, the flat-topped hinged domed cover w/projecting lip, engraved on handle with the initials "W" over "DM," maker's mark of John Coney, Boston, Massachusetts, 1690-1700, 6¼" h. **23,000.00**

Late 18th Century Silver Tankard

Tankard, cov., tapered cylindrical body w/molded base & scroll handle, stepped domed cover w/scroll thumbpiece, handle monogrammed "M P," Freeman Woods, New York, New York, 1791-94, 7½" h. ....**21,850.00** (Illustration)

Tankard, cov., presentation-type, cylindrical on a spreading gadrooned foot, w/shaped handle & molded shoulder band, the hinged cover surmounted by a foliate shell-form finial, the front engraved w/a presentation inscription, maker's mark of Lincoln & Foss, Boston, Massachusetts, ca. 1841, 7⅝" h. **1,495.00**

Tazza, scrolling & floral reticulated rim w/conforming engraved design, Howard Sterling Co., Providence, Rhode Island, 7¾" d., 2¾" h. **230.00**

Tazze, pierced foliate scrolling border, Black, Starr & Frost, Ltd., New York, New York, 7" d., pr. **690.00**

Tea & coffee set: cov. coffeepot, cov. teapot, cov. sugar

Coin Silver Tea & Coffee Set

bowl & creamer; coin, octagonal paneled sides, ornate paw feet, C-scroll handles, bird finials, engraved decoration & monogram, R. & W. Wilson, Philadelphia, Pennsylvania, 1825-50, coffeepot 9⅜" h., 4 pcs ....**2,415.00** (Illustration: above)

Tea & coffee set: cov. coffeepot, cov. teapot, cov. sugar bowl & creamer; Engraved Ivy patt., urn-form bodies on spreading circular bases w/ivy leaf applications, the surfaces engraved w/panels of ivy leaf sprays, applied beaded borders, leaf-capped hollow han-

dles, domed lids w/bud finials, strapwork monogram "E.S.P.," Moore for Tiffany & Co., New York, New York, ca. 1870, coffeepot 9½" h., 4 pcs. .....**3,450.00** (Illustration: below)

Tea & coffee set: cov. teapot, cov. coffeepot, cov. sugar bowl & creamer; pedestal base & baluster-form bodies, domed lids w/cast floral spray finial, geometric handle w/ram's mask, chased & embossed w/architectural romantic landscapes & floral borders, monogrammed "J.P.," S. Kirk & Son, Baltimore, Maryland, 1880-90, coffeepot 14" h., 4 pcs. **5,462.00**

Engraved Ivy Pattern Tea & Coffee Set

Tea & coffee set: cov. teapot, cov. coffeepot, cov. two-handled sugar bowl, creamer & waste bowl; vasiform, chased w/foliate scrolls, engraved w/a monogram, Gorham Mfg. Co., Providence, Rhode Island, 20th c., 3¼" to 8" h., 5 pcs. **1,380.00**

Tea & coffee set: cov. coffeepot, cov. teapot, cov. sugar bowl, creamer & waste bowl, 14th Century patt., flat base urn-form bodies w/domed lids & C-scroll handles, monogrammed "H," No. 1984, Shreve & Co., San Francisco, California, coffeepot 8" h., 5 pcs. **1,725.00**

Tea & coffee set: cov. coffeepot, cov. teapot, cov. sugar bowl, creamer & waste bowl; plain hexagonal urn-form bodies w/peaked lids & harp-form handles, monogrammed "M," No. 65, Watson Co., Attleboro, Massachusetts, coffeepot 9½" h., 5 pcs. **690.00**

Tea & coffee set: cov. coffeepot, cov. teapot, cov. sugar bowl, creamer & waste bowl; Louis XIV patt., pedestal base urn-forms w/panel decoration, No. 76160, Towle Silversmiths, Newburyport, Massachusetts, coffeepot 10¾" h., 5 pcs. ...**1,265.00**

Tea & coffee set: cov. teapot, cov. coffeepot, cov. sugar bowl, creamer & waste bowl;

Prelude patt., plain pyriform bodies on collet bases, leaf-capped multi-scroll handles, International Silver Co., Meriden, Connecticut, coffeepot 10½" h., 5 pcs. **920.00**

Tea & coffee set: two cov. teapots, cov. coffeepot, cov. two-handled sugar bowl & creamer; globular w/faceted lower body, applied w/foliate bands, engraved w/a monogram & dated "1901," E. Stebins & Co., New York, 19th c., 8¼" to 13" h., 5 pcs. **3,450.00**

Tea & coffee set: cov. teapot, cov. coffeepot, cov. sugar bowl, creamer w/spout & waste bowl; decorated in the Persian taste, w/flowering fruit branches, the rim die-rolled w/geometric decoration, the elephant's-head handles w/ivory insulators, the spouts chased w/flutes & flowers, the hammered hinged domed covers w/reeded rectangular finials, each engraved on the base w/a presentation inscription dated "March 1st 1882," Gorham Mfg. Co., Providence, Rhode Island, 1881, coffeepot 7½" h., 5 pcs. **40,250.00**
(Illustration: below, two of five)

Tea & coffee set: cov. teapot, cov. coffeepot, cov. sugar bowl, creamer & waste bowl; engraved & applied ivy design, further decorated w/bands of

Gorham Silver Spouted Creamer & Sugar Bowl

Silver Tea & Coffee Set by Gorham

beading, covers w/cast putti finials, w/monogram & date, made by Moore, Tiffany & Company, New York, New York, 1860-64, 5 pcs. **6,325.00**

Tea & coffee set: cov. coffeepot, cov. teapot, cov. sugar bowl, creamer & waste bowl; compressed globular form, D-form handles, overall *repoussé* floral decoration, monogram & date on base, Gorham Mfg. Co., Providence, Rhode Island, 1890, 5 pcs. ....**5,175.00** (Illustration: above)

Tea & coffee set: cov. coffeepot, cov. teapot, cov. sugar bowl, cream pitcher, waste bowl & cov. kettle on lampstand; Regency style, plain *bombé* oblong urn-form bodies raised on bun feet, shell & gadroon borders, harp-form handles, wooden finials & kettle handle, monogrammed "A.A.G." in script, International Silver Co., Meriden, Connecticut, retailed by Shreve & Co., kettle 13" h., 6 pcs. **1,955.00**

Tea & coffee set: cov. teapot, cov. coffeepot, cov. sugar bowl, creamer, waste bowl & tray; paneled Colonial Revival style, monogrammed, Reed & Barton, Taunton, Massachusetts, 20th c., 6 pcs. **3,737.00**

Tea & coffee set: cov. teapot, cov. coffeepot, cov. sugar bowl, creamer, waste bowl & cov. kettle on lampstand; embossed w/architectural fantasies, rustic & lake views, S. Kirk & Son Co., Baltimore, Maryland, early 20th c., 6 pcs. **8,050.00**

Tea & coffee set: cov. teapot, cov. coffeepot, cov. two-handled sugar bowl, creamer, waste bowl & cov. teakettle on lampstand; slightly flaring paneled sides, Alvin Corp., Providence, Rhode Island, 20th c., 3½" to 13" h., 6 pcs. **1,495.00**

Tea & coffee set: cov. teapot, cov. coffeepot, cov. sugar bowl, creamer, waste bowl & tray; Plymouth (New Plymouth) patt., Gorham Mfg. Co., Providence, Rhode Island, 20th c., 6 pcs. **2,760.00**

Tea & coffee set: cov. teapot, cov. coffeepot, cov. hot milk jug, cov. sugar bowl, creamer, waste bowl & kettle on lampstand w/burner; each of navette-shaped baluster-form on spreading oval foot, bright-

Elegant Coffeepot by Tiffany

cut w/bands of foliate Vitruvian scrolls & ribbon swags, the lower body part-gadrooned, w/fluted lion's head spouts & upswept wooden bracket handles, the domed covers part-gadrooned & surmounted by wood finials, the sugar bowl w/ring handles issuing from lions' masks, the kettle stand on four lion's mask feet w/bracket supports, each engraved w/a monogram within a shield, engraved under bases "Mary Crowninshield Endicott November 1888," Tiffany & Co., New York, New York, ca.

1888, kettle on stand 13½" h., 7 pcs. ....**10,350.00** (Illustration: coffeepot)

Tea & coffee set: cov. coffeepot, cov. teapot, cov. sugar bowl, creamer, waste bowl, cov. kettle on lampstand & tray; George II style, ribbed spherical & ovoid bodies w/engraved panel decoration around shoulders, silver & ivory finials, the shaped rectangular tray w/pierced handles, the corners w/matching chased decoration, Theodore B. Starr, New York, New York, tray across handles 24" l., kettle 12½" h., 7 pcs. (kettle lacking finial) **4,312.00**

Tea & coffee set: cov. teapot, cov. coffeepot, cov. demitasse pot, cov. sugar bowl, large creamer, small creamer & cov. kettle on lampstand; vase form, etched w/collars of interlaced running foliage & chased at the base w/overlapping stiff leaves, monogrammed, Tiffany & Co., New York, New York, ca. 1915, kettle on stand 13" h., 7 pcs. **6,325.00**

Tea & coffee set: cov. teapot,

Silver Tea & Coffee Set with Tray

cov. coffeepot, cov. hot water jug, cov. sugar bowl, creamer, waste bowl & cov. kettle on lampstand; dome-footed baluster-form chased w/grapevine, monogrammed, twig handles & borders, by William Forbes for Ball, Black & Co., New York, New York, ca. 1850, kettle on stand 17¼" h., 7 pcs. **6,612.00**

Tea & coffee set: cov. teapot, cov. coffeepot, cov. sugar bowl, creamer, waste bowl, kettle on lampstand w/burner & tray; urn-form on oval feet, w/molded borders & leaf-clad scroll handles, the hinged domed covers surmounted by pineapple finials, the kettle w/an overhead swing handle, w/ivory insulators, the shaped oval tray w/molded rims & inset handles, Gorham Mfg. Co., Providence, Rhode Island, 1930, kettle on stand 13" h., tray 25⅛" l., 7 pcs. **7,475.00**
(Illustration: bottom previous page)

Tea & coffee set: cov. teapot, cov. coffeepot, sugar bowl, creamer, waste bowl, cov. teakettle on lampstand & two-handled tray; engraved w/a floral & scrollwork design, Meriden Britannia Co., Meriden,

Connecticut, late 19th c., tray across handles 31¼" l., 7 pcs. (very minor dents & scratches) **3,737.50**

Tea & coffee set: cov. teakettle w/lampstand, cov. teapot, cov. coffeepot, cov. hot milk pot, cov. sugar bowl, creamer & waste bowl; Chased Ivy patt., each of globular form on spreading circular base, ivory insulators, the covers w/similar decoration & pine cone finials, each engraved w/a monogram in a small oval reserve, Tiiffany & Co., New York, New York, 1870-75, teakettle on stand 12¼" h., 7 pcs. **19,550.00**
(Illustration: below)

Tea & coffee set: cov. teapot, cov. coffeepot, cov. sugar bowl, creamer, waste bowl, cov. kettle on lampstand & tray; globular bodies embossed overall w/flowers on matted ground, the two-handled rectangular tray engraved w/diaper surface & w/vacant husk wreath, Baltimore, Maryland, 20th c., tray across handles 27" l., 7 pcs. **11,500.00**
(Illustration: top next page, left)

Tea & coffee set: cov. teapot, cov. coffeepot, cov. hot water

Chased Ivy Pattern Silver Tea & Coffee Set

20th c. Silver Tea & Coffee Set

jug, creamer, cov. sugar bowl, waste bowl. cov. kettle on lampstand & rectangular two-handled tray; Chrysanthemum patt., engraved w/contemporary monogram "EE" in matching style, Tiffany & Co., New York, New York, tray across handles 30" l., coffeepot 9¼" h., 8 pcs. in fitted mahogany chest lined in red baize & w/Tiffany label **34,500.00**

Tea caddy, silver-gilt, inverted pyriform vessel on spreading circular base, fitted w/cap-form lid, chased w/flowers & scrolling foliage, engraved w/three-initial script monogram & dates for a fiftieth anniversary in 1904, No. 951, Howard & Co., New York, New York, 1903, 5½" h. **690.00**

Teakettle, cover & lampstand, of baluster form, w/circular base on four scroll supports, the body *repoussé* & chased w/Chinese figures in garden landscapes upon a matted ground, w/a band of draping leaves, w/branch-form handle w/ivory insulators, the spout applied w/foliage, the hinged cover w/radiating palm fronds & figural finial, the side engraved w/a monogram & the date "Jan. 24," maker's mark of Tiffany, Young & Ellis, New

Silver Teakettle on Lampstand

York, New York, ca. 1850, 12⅜" h. ....**6,325.00** (Illustration)

Teakettle, cover & lampstand, bulbous fluted urn-form w/fluted spout & hinged domed cover applied w/a border of ovolo & dart, surmounted by a foliate finial w/overhead swing handle w/ivory insulators, the stand on four scroll pad feet & openwork foliate scroll apron, pierced above w/geometric design centering a circular burner, w/pin & link chain, later engraved on shoulder w/monogram, maker's mark of Gerardus Boyce, New York, New York, ca. 1840, 14" h..........**1,725.00**

Teapot, cov., Arts & Crafts style, the moderne form w/hammered surface & mounted w/ivory insulators & finial, The T.C. Shop, Chicago, Illinois, ca. 1910-23, 5¾" h. **660.00**

Teapot, cov., straight-sided oval form, deeply fluted & engraved on both sides w/script initials "ET to EHT," straight tapered spout, flush-hinged cover w/domed center & fluted urn finial & marked "REVERE" rectangle, Paul Revere, Jr., Boston, Massachusetts, ca. 1798, 6" h. **34,500.00**

Teapot, cov., plain straight-sided oval body on collet base, domed lid w/urn finial, C-scroll hollow handle, decorated w/engraved & tooled bright-cut designs, Chas. W. Kennard & Co., Boston, Massachusetts, ca. 1870, 7" h. **862.50**

Teapot, cov., elongated Aladdin's lamp form w/spurred C-scroll handle, domed cover w/flower finial, overall *repoussé* floral decoration, The Stieff Company, Baltimore, Maryland, ca. 1900, 7" h. **632.50**

Teapot, cov., coin, plain baluster-form body, the cover w/fruit finial, Jones, Low & Ball, Boston, Massachusetts, ca. 1840, 9½" h. **345.00**

Teapot, cov., plain square body on a spreading foot, gadrooned rims, monogram, Frank M. Whiting & Co., North Attleboro, Massachusetts, late 19th - early 20th c., (small dent)......**230.00**

Tea set: cov. teapot, cov. sugar bowl & creamer; coin, each oblong body decorated w/large-scale gadrooning, the lids, shoulders & bases applied w/decorative bands of cornucopia & flowers, W. Jenkins, Philadelphia, Pennsylvania or New York, New York, ca. 1820-30, teapot 10" h., 3 pcs. .....**2,200.00** (Illustration: below)

Tea set: cov. teapot, cov. sugar bowl & creamer; the fluted sides w/repeating sytlized floral border, floral finials, N. J. Bogert, New York, New York, ca. 1830, 3 pcs...................**1,840.00**

Tea set: cov. teapot, cov. sugar bowl & creamer; boat-form w/molded collars, bright-cut w/bands of running foliage & w/crossed sprays of wheat, urn finials, marked on bases "GORDON" in serrated rectangle, Alexander S. Gordon, New York, New York, ca. 1800, teapot 7⅛" h., 3 pcs. **2,185.00**

Tea set: cov. teapot, cov. sugar bowl & creamer; coin, chased w/bunches of grapes & leaves, monogram, very slight dents, probably made by John Chandler Moore for Allcock, Allen & Co., New York, ca. 1850, 3 pcs...................**1,610.00** (Illustration: top next page)

Tea set: cov. teapot, cov. sugar bowl & creamer; quadrangular urn-form, partly lobed & applied w/die-rolled borders of running grapevine, engraved w/contemporary monogram "AS," John Crawford, New York, New

Coin Silver Tea Set by Jenkins

Coin Silver Tea Set with Vintage Design

York, ca. 1815, teapot 8¼" h.,
3 pcs. **1,610.00**

Three-piece Silver Tea Set by Eoff

Tea set: cov. teapot, cov. sugar
bowl & creamer; partly lobed
urn-form, straight gadroon borders, the finials formed as baskets of flowers rising from
spreading chased acanthus &
buds, Garrett Eoff, New York,
New York, ca. 1830, teapot
10¼" h., 3 pcs. **1,840.00**
(Illustration)

Tea set: cov. teapot & stand,
cov. sugar bowl & creamer; all
w/narrow beaded borders, urn
finials engraved w/contempo-
rary monogram "WCW," Daniel
Van Voorhis, New York, New
York, ca. 1790, teapot on
stand 7⅜" h., 4 pcs. **5,175.00**

Tea set: two graduated cov.
teapots, cov. sugar bowl & cov.
creamer; coin, pyriform bodies
w/scalloped upper rims, conforming lids w/variant figural
finials, branch-form hollow handles, the sides chased &
engraved w/leaf-tip & floral borders, Woodward & Grosjean,
Boston, Massachusetts, 1847-
52, retailed by Lincoln & Foss,
the larger pot 8½" h.,
4 pcs. **1,610.00**

Tea set: cov. teapot & stand,
cov. sugar bowl & creamer;
oval w/incurved angles, bright-
cut borders of ribbons &
engraved w/contemporary
monogram "EK," faceted urn
finials, J. Sayre, New York,
New York, ca. 1790-1800,
teapot on stand 8⅝" h.,
4 pcs. **5,462.00**

Tea set: cov. teapot, cov.
creamer, cov. sugar bowl &
waste bowl; coin, urn-form bodies w/peaked lids & finials,
w/bright-cut & engine-turned
decoration, beaded borders,

raised on waisted stems over circular bases, monogrammed "F.A.B," Gorham Mfg. Co., Providence, Rhode Island, ca. 1860, teapot 12½" h., 4 pcs. **1,840.00**

Tea set: large & smaller cov. teapots, cov. sugar bowl, creamer, waste lowl, cov. kettle on lampstand & tray; in the Federal-style, the straight-sided pieces each bright-cut w/festoons, w/beaded borders & pineapple finials, mono-grammed "AML," the matching oval tray w/cut-out handles, Gorham Mfg. Co., Providence, Rhode Island, ca. 1900, tray across handles 25½" l., 7 pcs. **5,462.00**

Tea tray, rounded rectangular body raised on six ball sup-ports, the border pierced w/shaped handles, maker's mark of Joel Sayre, New York, New York, 1802-18, 20½" l. **4,600.00**

Tea tray, shaped oval form w/two handles, the border *repoussé* w/foliate scrolling designs, International Silver Co., Meriden, Connecticut, 28" l. **3,335.00**

Tea tray, oval w/applied reeded handles chased w/acanthus, the field chased w/a band of foliate scrolls & grape bunches enclosing a coat-of-arms above the name "Keyser," the border chased & applied w/acanthus & shells, the reverse engraved w/a monogram, Tiffany & Co., New York, New York, 1902-07, 28¾" l. **7,475.00**

Tea tray, Roman patt., the applied handles chased w/tied laurel & beading, the border chased w/acanthus scrolls & flowerheads, the field engraved w/foliate scrolls & grape bunch-es, Tiffany & Co., New York, New York, 1880-91, across handles 29" l. **6,900.00**

Tray, the shaped circular gadrooned rim w/acanthus & shells at intervals, the field engraved w/two crests, raised on three scroll pad feet, mak-er's mark "J.L.," possibly for John Leacock, Philadelphia, Pennsylvania, ca. 1760, 6⅝" d. **3,220.00**

Tray, Japanese style, circular w/a spot-hammered surface, inlaid w/gold swallows w/cop-per beaks, eyes & legs, flying

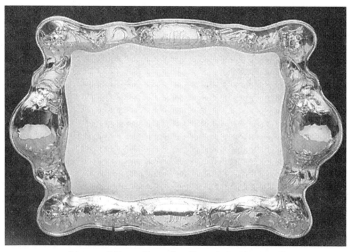

Large Silver Tray by Dominick & Haff

Late 19th c. Covered Silver Tureen

against a crescent moon, raised on four bead supports flanked by scrolls, stamped "PATENT APPLIED FOR," Tiffany & Co., New York, New York, ca. 1880, 9⅛" d. **12,650.00**

Tray, Chrysanthemum patt., round w/shaped rim, the border applied w/chrysanthemums & leaves raised on four cast & applied chrysanthemum supports, Tiffany & Co., New York, New York, 1880-91, 12" d. **3,450.00**

Tray, *Martelé*, the hammered body w/lobed ruffled rim, cast w/a band of spaced oak leaves within line borders, monogrammed, impressed *"MARTELÉ"* & w/maker's marks of Gorham Mfg. Co., Providence, Rhode Island, 20th c., 12⅛" d. **2,530.00**

Tray, Chrysanthemum patt., round w/shaped rim, the border applied w/chrysanthemums & leaves, Tiffany & Co., New York, New York, 1902-07, 13" d. **4,370.00**

Tray, circular, the center engraved w/foliate scrollwork, the reticulated border w/similar designs, Shreve, Crump & Low

Co., Inc., Boston, Massachusetts, 14" d. **1,035.00**

Tray, *Martelé*, shaped rectangular form, the border *repoussé* & chased w/berries, fruit & leaves, w/undulating rim, Gorham Mfg. Co., Providence, Rhode Island, 1899, 15¾" l. **7,475.00**

Tray, rectangular w/a shaped & chased poppy border, Whiting Mfg. Co., Providence, Rhode Island, 16" l. **690.00**

Tray, oblong w/raised serpentine rim, International Silver Co., Meriden, Connecticut, 12 x 17" **220.00**

Tray, Plymouth patt., monogrammed "M," No. A5480, Gorham Mfg. Co., Providence, Rhode Island, 20" l. **862.50**

Tray, the wide shaped border chased in high-relief w/full-blown irises, daffodils, poppies, tulips & carnations & lightly engraved twice w/the initial "M," the center surface plain, Dominick & Haff, New York, New York, 1901, retailed by Spaulding & Co., 32" l. ....**5,462.00** (Illustration: bottom previous page)

Tureen, cov., flat-sided body w/fluted ends, curving flattened

handles, the sides & cover
w/engraved floral & scrollwork
design, Meriden Britannia Co.,
Meriden, Connecticut, late
19th c., 12" l. **1,035.00**
(Illustration: top previous page)

**Silver & Copper Bud Vase
by Tiffany**

Vase, bud, tenpin-form, decorated in the Japanese taste, narrow applied band near base,
the spot-hammered surface
applied w/three copper & silver
relief panels w/Japanesque
scenes, applied w/silver
leaves, a gold butterfly & moth
w/*mokume* wings, further decorated w/engraved trailing tendrils, Tiffany & Co., New York,
New York, ca. 1878, designed
by Edward C.. Moore, probably
for the Paris Exposition of
1878, 6⅜" h. **9,200.00**
(Illustration)

Vase, Japanese style, cylindrical
body w/frosted surface,
engraved w/four quatrefoil
vignettes sketched w/the following scenes: a scholar climb-
ing to a pavillion, a fisherman
on a bridge, a bird on the
ground & a traveler by pine
trees; the scenes conjoined by
diagonal stripes simulating
cloth, also engraved w/a twig-
like monogram "CWC," the
base rim stamped w/cranes &

prunus flowers above a bamboo-form base, by Edward C.
Moore for Tiffany & Co., Union
Square, New York, New York,
1870-75, 7½" h..................**3,450.00**

Vase, chased & pierced
w/scrolling foliage, the circular
base applied w/scrolls, fitted
w/a green glass liner, Redlich
& Co., New York, New York,
early 20th c., 7⅝" h. **575.00**

Vase, cylindrical on spreading
foot, chased & applied w/bands
of scrolls w/ovolo at intervals,
enclosing chased & applied
roundels of scrolls & ovolo,
w/molded rim, Towle Silversmiths, Newburyport, Massachusetts, ca. 1910, retailed by
Bailey, Banks & Biddle, Philadelphia, Pennsylvania,
9⅝" h. **920.00**

Silver Yacht Trophy Vase

Vase, trophy-type, in the 17th c.
New York style, the tapering
cylindrical body on a spreading
base w/a chased band of flowers & leaves, the body chased
w/strapwork & foliage w/pen-
dant fruit & birds, w/a molded
rim, engraved on front w/an
inscription reading "NEW
YORK YACHT CLUB The
Cruise THIRD PRIZE won by
AVENGER 12 August 1913,"

Black, Starr & Frost, New York,
ca. 1913, 10⅜" h. **1,095.00**
(Illustration)

Silver Vase with Applied Decoration

Vase, baluster-form body raised
on three supports formed as a
lobster, a turtle & a frog upon a
leaf below a spreading footrim,
the spot-hammered body
applied w/seagrass & vines,
w/dragonflies & copper beetles
& gold butterflies, applied w/a
collar chased w/foliage & geometric design, Gorham Mfg.
Co., Providence, Rhode Island,
1880, 11⅛" h. **12,650.00**
(Illustration)

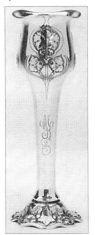

Impressive Silver Vase

Vase, Athenic-style, plain tapering stem expanding to a tulip-

form top w/applied clusters of
cast foliage enriched w/chased
details, on a skirt base w/wave
edge finished w/molded rim,
monogrammed "M.B.S.," No.
A3228, Gorham Mfg. Co.,
Providence, Rhode Island,
11⅞" h. **2,070.00**
(Illustration)

Vase, pierced & applied Rococo
floral & scroll design on rim &
base, 20th c., 12" h. **862.50**

Vase, trumpet-form, raised on a
spreading circular base, Tiffany
& Co., New York, New York,
12" h. **920.00**

Vase, tapered cylindrical body
etched w/the polished silhouette of an iris against a mottled
ground, Tiffany & Co., New
York, New York, ca. 1885,
12¾" h. **3,450.00**

Early 20th c. Presentation Vase

Vase, presentation-type, domed
foot supporting a conical body
w/narrow ring at base & wider
ring beneath the flaring petal-
form rim, *repoussé* & chased
floral decoration overall,
engraved inscription on rim
"Mr. & Mrs. Albert Davidson
from Baltimore Baseball Club
1914," The Stieff Company,
Baltimore, Maryland, early
20th c., 14¼" h. **1,495.00**
(Illustration)

Vase, paneled ovoid body, Black, Starr & Frost, Ltd., New York, New York, 14½" h. **690.00**

Large Amphora-form Silver Vase

Vase, tapering amphora-form applied w/scroll handles, decorated w/applied foliate bands at the shoulder & foot, Gorham Mfg. Co., Providence, Rhode Island, 16" h. ......**1,980.00** (Illustration)

Vase, three-handled, the rim embossed & chased w/pendant grapevine repeated on the strap handles, the body divided into panels by tendrils sprouting into clover leaves, engraved w/monogram, the dates "1884" & "1909" & donors' names, .950 standard, Gorham Mfg. Co., Providence, Rhode Island, ca. 1909, 19¼" h. **8,912.00**

Vegetable bowls, Georgian patt., No. 6218, Shreve & Co., San Francisco, California, 1909-22, 13" l., pr. **632.50**

Vegetable dish, cov., oval body on shaped collet base, bracket end handles, domed lid w/scrollwork open handle, No. A577, Gorham Mfg. Co., Providence, Rhode Island, 1904, across handles 12" l., 7½" h. **1,495.00**

Vegetable dishes, shaped oval form w/flat rim, monogrammed "M.H.," No. A9357, Gorham Mfg. Co., Providence, Rhode Island, 1914, 12½" l., pr. **374.00**

Vegetable dishes & covers, oval, the rim chased w/acanthus, *repoussé* & chased overall w/architecture scenes amid foliage & trailing vines, the domed cover surmounted by a foliate scroll & shell handle, Samuel Kirk & Sons, Baltimore, Maryland, 1925-32, 10½" l., pr. **6,325.00**

Vegetable dishes & covers, oval w/everted rim, domed lid w/foliate ring finial, overall embossed & chased foliate decoration on matted ground, the interior divided, Jacobi & Jenkins, Baltimore, Maryland, 11⅜" l., pr. ......**3,165.00** (Illustration: below)

Vegetable tureen, cov., two-handled, Chrysanthemum patt.,

Ornate Floral Chased Silver Vegetable Dishes

engraved w/arms, Tiffany & Co., New York, New York, 1902-07, across handles 11½" l. **6,325.00**

Vegetable tureens & covers, the oval body in the Adam taste w/ram's head handles & bud finials, the sides heavily engraved & w/vacant reserve, base stamped "DE LA LONDE," Bailey, Banks & Biddle, Philadelphia, Pennsylvania, 11¼" pr...............**5,750.00**

Whiskey flask, Art Deco style, flat rectangular form w/applied medallion, International Silver Co., Meriden, Connecticut, 7½" h. **110.00**

Wine cooler, cylindrical w/slightly rounded lower section raised on a spreading foot, w/two upswept handles, w/interior liner & collar, the side engraved w/armorials, the base w/a presentation inscription dated "1851," maker's mark of Jones, Ball & Poor, Boston, Massachusetts, 1847-51, 8" h. **8,050.00**

ENGLISH & OTHERS

The use of silver in England, both as a form of currency and also for decorative and utilitarian items, goes back to very early times. In the mid-1100s, in an effort to improve the realm's coinage, King Henry II brought in the Easterlings, who were coiners from eastern Germany & their silver coins were called "sterlings."

In 1300, King Edward I declared that wrought silver must be of the same standard as the coins of the realm. This marked the inception of the *sterling standard* in which 925 parts of silver per 1000 must be silver; the remaining 75 parts per 1000 would be an added metal, usually copper, which had been found to be the most satisfactory alloy, giving greater strength to the silver without changing the lustrous color.

Much fine work has been attributed to France, Germany and some of the Scandinavian countries, as well as other continental countries. It should be noted that much of this work was not marked either as to the maker, country or silver content. However, with study it is possible to learn to identify pieces by their style. On the other hand, you will find that English works are very clearly marked with a date-letter symbol indicating the year in which the item was made or assayed. They will also be marked with a town mark, indicating the location of the silversmith. Also included in this marking is the identifying symbol, initials or name of the smith.

Price Listings:

Argyle, cov., vase-form w/narrow beaded borders, engraved w/contemporary arms in bright-cut oval, reel-shaped cover, urn finial, raffia-covered handle, the interior w/an inner chamber w/detachable cap, George III period, Hester Bateman, London, England, 1780, 8¾" h. **$5,462.00**

Asparagus dishes, silver-gilt, in early Regence style, the border of raised strapwork & husks on a matted ground, engraved twice w/a monogram, G. Keller,

Late 19th c. Silver Baby Rattle & Whistle

Paris, France, ca.
1900, 17" l., pr...................**9,200.00**

Asparagus tongs, pierced floral design, Victorian, George Angell, London, England, 1863-64, 8" l........................**287.50**

Baby rattle, Humpty-Dumpty finial, w/inscription, hallmarked, Continental, late 19th c. **230.00**

Baby rattle & whistle, modeled in the Georgian taste w/chased decoration & attached bells at midsection, coral end, maker's Mark "GU," Birmingham, England, 1887, 3½" l............**330.00** (Illustration: bottom previous page)

Basin, oval w/embossed gadroon rim, the border flat chased w/a band of foliage interlaced w/strapwork, Johann Ludwig Schoap I, Augsburg, Germany, 1700-05, 17½" l. **7,475.00**

Basin, w/shaped oval molded rim decorated w/cartouches of flowers at intervals from which spread festoons of flowers chased in relief on matted ground, lobed & fluted well, unmarked, Portugal, third quarter 18th c., 20½" l........**2,070.00**

Basket, Louis XVI-style, circular, the base w/profile bust medallions of Louis XVI & Marie Antoinette, the sides w/scrolling foliage & flower-filled urns, handles at the sides, raised on four recessed scroll supports, maker's mark "GR," Germany, ca. 1890, across handles 13" l., 3" h.....**546.00**

Baskets, oval w/wirework sides, the base rim pierced w/vertical pales, one engraved w/contemporary arms, the other plain, George III period, John Scofield, London, England, 1793, 11⅞" l., pr.................**6,900.00**

Basting spoon, long-handled, George III period, maker's mark

"W.W.," England, 1798, 12½" l. **302.50**

Beaker, niello, decorated w/a nielloed view of the Moscow Kremlin, the surround nielloed w/scrolling foliage, w/molded lip, Ovchinnikov, Moscow, Russia, 1874, 3" h.............**1,610.00**

Beaker, cylindrical w/flared rim & molded foot, engraved w/foliage spreading from strapwork, also pricked w/contemporary initials, Commonwealth period, maker's mark "DR" pellet above & below, possibly Daniel Rutty, London, England, 1654, 3⅜" h......................**2,587.00**

Beaker, parcel-gilt, tapered cylinder, chased w/strapwork & husks on matted ground surround w/white silver coins, Johann Heinrich Graf(fe), Berlin, Germany, ca. 1725, 3½" h......................**2,587.00**

Beaker, parcel-gilt, tapered cylinder, embossed w/four rows of hearts on matted ground, the base engraved w/Cyrillic initials, maker's mark "GK" incuse, probably for Gottfried Kittel, Ohlau, Germany, ca. 1700, 3⅞" h................................**4,312.00**

Charles II Silver-gilt Beaker

Beaker, silver-gilt, of tapered cylindrical form, embossed w/full-blown flowering plants alternating w/pendent sprays of fruit, the rim initialed "MD" & dated "1611," Charles II period, maker's mark "TK" above a flowerhead, London, England, 1672, 4⅛" h. ....**2,300.00** (Illustration)

Beaker, partly silver-gilt, slightly tapering cylinder, engraved w/three scenes of figures, each within a baroque cartouche incorporating fruit & foliage, the rim inscribed w/the date "1754" & "Alexander, Son of Rogotnev," w/molded lip, Assay master Michael Borovshchikov, Moscow, Russia, 1754, 4⅝" h. **2,415.00**

Beaker, tapered cylinder, engraved w/flowers spreading downwards from strapwork at the lip, further engraved w/three birds picking at fruit, the foot stamped w/lozenges above a corded band, the base engraved w/two coats of arms suspended from a branch & w/initials "WD" & "AI," maker's mark "BR" in shield, Leeuwarden, Holland, 1634, 4⅞" h. **5,175.00**

Beaker, tall tapered body engraved w/crest & motto in plain reserve, reverse w/a like panel w/figural landscape, separated w/panels of bamboo & birds, finished w/multiple varied decorative bands, Chinese Export, marked w/indistinct three character mark, ca. 1880, 5¾" h. **632.50**

Beaker, trumpet-form, lightly tooled w/a band of flowers, raised on a lobed foot, maker's mark "CG," Vasa, Finland, 1826, 7" h. **1,150.00**

Beakers, silver-gilt, of cylindrical form w/flared rim, decorated w/a broad granulated band, engraved on the base w/a contemporary crest, George III period, maker's mark "I.C.,"

London, England, 1809, 3¾" h., pr. **2,875.00**

Russian Silver Beakers

Beakers, tapered cylindrical form, embossed w/eagles among rococo ornament, Moscow, Russia, 1760-86, 3" to 3⅜" h., set of 5 ....**4,600.00** (Illustration)

Beakers, tulip-shaped w/molded rim, engraved w/a vacant foliate cartouche, gilt interior, Victorian, F. Brown, London, England, 1876, 4" h., set of 5 ....**2,760.00**

Beer jug, of plain pear shape w/short spout, molded foot & double scroll handle, George II period, Richard Bayley, London, England, 1741, 7¾" h. **3,162.00**

Bell, table-type, w/molded borders, octagonal baluster handle ending in a stylized bud, George III period, Joseph Angell, London, England, 1814, 4¾" h. **2,415.00**

Bell, domed body w/widely flaring rim, baluster-form handle, George IV period, John, Henry & Charles Lias, London, England, 1825, 4¾" h. **1,495.00**

Bell, table-type, shaped square form w/molded borders & conforming baluster-form handle, Vincenzo Belli I, Rome, Italy, mid-18th c., 4¾" h. **2,875.00**

Bell, table-type, w/molded borders & turned ivory handle,

George III period, Phipps & Robinson, London, England, 1794, 5⅛" h. **2,070.00**

Bell, table-type, plain dome enclosed by three elongated shell & scroll supports conjoining beneath the flower-cluster finial, the body pricked w/later inscription dated "19 Nov 1800," unmarked except for later Prussian control mark, Germany, ca. 1760, 5¼" h. **2,070.00**

Bell, table-type, of typical form, w/molded borders, girdle & baluster-form handle, Cornelis Knuysting, Rotterdam, Holland, 1784, 5¾" h. **4,025.00**

Bear Bell Push by Fabergé

Bell push, modeled in the form of a seated bear w/realistically chased fur, the lower jaw hinged to function as a push, marked in Cyrillic "I.S.A." for the First Silver Artel & "Fabergé" w/Imperial warrant & 88 standard (91.66%), Fabergé, St. Petersburg, Russia, ca. 1910, 3¼" h. ....**16,100.00** (Illustration)

Berry spoons, Chased Vine patt., Victorian, Mitchell & Russell, Glasgow, Scotland, 1838, 10¼" l., pr. **575.00**

Biscuit box, cov., decorated to imitate basketweave & w/a simulated linen napkin, the slip-on cover engraved to simulate

wood grain, P. Loskutov, Moscow, Russia, ca. 1890, 6" h. **2,990.00**

Bonbonniere, cov., oval boat-form, chased w/flowers above scroll feet, multiple tendril handles, the finial formed as a spray of a flower & buds, Georg Jensen Silversmithy, Copenhagen, Denmark, number 262, post-1945, 7" l. **5,462.00**

Decorative Silver Book Binding

Book binding, parcel-gilt, the front chased w/an oval vignette of the visit of the Magi, the back w/the Holy Family & the infant St. John, the spine w/a tall spray of flowers issuing from a pot, the clasp cast w/flowerheads, containing a prayer book, *Scribanus, Amor Divinis,* Lyon, France, 1624, the unmarked Continental binding late 17th c., 4⅝" l. ....**1,380.00** (Illustration)

Book binding, the front & back covers both chased w/the lion of Judea in oval reserves surrounded by foliage & oak sprays on matted ground, the spine chased w/palmettes framed by scrolls, w/paper lining, Angelo Giannotti, Rome, Italy, ca. 1840, 6⅝" h. ....**3,450.00** (Illustration: top next page)

Bottle coasters, reticulated gallery, applied w/a reeded rim, on a turned wood base,

Ornate Italian Silver Book Binding

Georgian period, London,
England, late 18th - early
19th c., 5¼" d., set of 4 ......**2,587.00**

Bowl, cov., rounded sides
w/wide flaring rim, the rim
chased w/a running band of
blossoms, openwork berry &
tendril finial, Georg Jensen
Silversmithy, Copenhagen,
Denmark, 1925-32,
7½" d. **4,140.00**

Bowl, circular, decorated
w/chased elongated gadrooning, engraved w/a lion, coin in
base, gold-washed interior,
Victorian, Charles Stuart
Harris, London, England, 1884-
85, 4⅜" d. **172.50**

Bowl, footed, the lobed body
w/pierced handles, .830 fine,
Germany, 19th c., 4½" h. **489.00**

Bowl, modeled in the form of a
shell, the scrolled handle surmounted by an infant blowing a
horn astride a swan, w/shaped
neo-rococo foot, marked
"Fabergé" in Cyrillic w/Imperial
warrant & 84 standard (87.5%),
Fabergé, Moscow, Russia, ca.
1910, 4½" l. **3,162.00**

Bowl, round body on a short circular foot, decorated in the
Georg Jensen style w/applied
blossoms, Mexico, 20th c.,
4¾" h. **374.00**

Bowl, presentation-type, circular, decorated w/a chased bird
amid bamboo, gold-washed
interior, Chinese Export,
Chongwoo, Hong Kong,
20th c., 5⅛" d. **230.00**

Bowl, hemispherical form
w/flared rim & spreading foot,
engraved w/contemporary
crest, George III period,
Matthew West, Dublin,
Ireland, 1776, 5½" d. **1,610.00**

Bowl, circular w/relief & chased
tiger & wild boar hunting scene,
India, 12" d., 7¾" h. **1,150.00**

Bowl, shaped circular body, the
flat base of four petals rising to

Chinese Export Silver Basketweave Bowl

a lobed bowl suspending four green enameled leaves, the rim w/four applied tab handles w/green & blue enameled leaves, maker's mark of Adolf von Mayrhofer, Munich, Germany, across 8" l..........**1,725.00**

Bowl, reeded rim, chased & applied chrysanthemum design on an open basketweave ground, Chinese Export, possibly Sing Fat & Chao-Ch'ang, early 20th c., 8⅞" d. ....**920.00** (Illustration: bottom previous page)

Bowl, dessert, in the form of a shell supported by three dolphins & topped by a seated putto holding a swag, gilt interior, Germany, ca. 1900, 10¾" l. **2,587.00**

Bowl, flaring circular form w/rounded rim & two applied foliate & bead handles, on molded base, Georg Jensen Silversmithy, Copenhagen, Denmark, post-1945, across handles 13½" l. **2,300.00**

Box, cov., circular, the knop in the form of a stylized flower, Georg Jensen Silversmithy, Copenhagen, Denmark, 2¾" d....................................**460.00**

Box, cov., octagonal, the slip-on cover engraved w/a landscape surrounded by borders of scrolling strapwork on matted reserves, Martin Roth, Ulm, Germany, ca. 1730, 3½" l. **3,737.00**

Box w/hinged cover, oval, embossed & chased w/radiating panels of flowers, floral wreath-form handles, cover w/bird on flowering branch finial, Turkey, mid-19th c., 9¼" l. **2,760.00**

Box, cov., oval, the lid worked in *repoussé* w/cupids filling a basket w/flowers, the sides decorated w/alternating reserves of

Oval Silver Box with Cupids

fruit baskets & cornucopae, Continental, 12½" l. ....**2,645.00** (Illustration)

Bread & butter plates and butter pats, circular w/fluted borders, Prieto, Juarez, Mexico, .950 standard, plates 6" d., pats 3¾" d., set of 12 each ...**862.50**

Bread basket, boat-form, the sides of floral trellis within borders of laurel suspending four classical cameos & raised on four ribbon-bow feet, matching handles, Willem Pont, Amsterdam, Holland, 1783, across handles 13¼" l.......**10,925.00**

Butter dish on stand, cov., the bowl w/fixed stand & ball feet, the cover chased w/a mound of leaves enclosing cabochon oval ambers & w/matching bead finial, w/glass liner, Georg Jensen Silversmithy, Copenhagen, Denmark, post-1945, stand 6¾" d. **4,312.00**

Caddy set: comprising a pair of rectangular tea caddies & sugar box; the covers chased w/classical festoons & profile heads, the caddies w/slip-on caps chased w/swirled flowerheads, the sugar box w/finial in the form of putti at a tea party, in an ivory veneered case, pierced & carved w/flower sprays & diaper, w/chased silver claw-and-ball feet, plain escutcheon & shell-decorated bail handle, Hendrik Boshart, Middelburg, Holland, ca. 1780, case 9⅞" l., the set............**5,750.00**

Cake basket, oval w/fluted sides & swing handle, marked w/Cyrillic initials of workmaster Stephan Wakeva, "K. Fabergé" & Imperial warrant & .84 standard (87.5%), Fabergé, St. Petersburg, Russia, ca. 1900, 9¾" l. **2,530.00**

George III Silver Cake Basket

Cake basket, oval w/reticulated panels in alternating designs, separated by reverse punched beaded borders, later keyed swing scroll handle, cast scrollwork base w/four rocaille supports, engraved w/secondary armorial at center & crest on handle, George III period, S.

Herbert & Co., London, England, 1760, 10½" h.......**1,955.00** (Illustration)

Cake basket, tapered octagonal form, the flat border decorated w/grapevine, w/swing handle, gilt interior, Sazikov, Moscow, Russia, 1885, 11¾" l. **2,760.00**

Cake basket, oval, pierced w/alternating panels of scrollwork & repeating crosses divided by beading, pierced rim foot & swing handle, the center engraved w/contemporary crest, on rococo pedestal, George II period, S. Herbert & Co., London, England, 1758, 12¼" l. **2,300.00**

Cake basket, oval, pierced w/quatrefoils & foliage between rows of beading, matching swing handle, engraved w/contemporary cartouche enclosing later arms, repairs to handle, George III period, S. Herbert & Co., London, England, 1762, 12⅝" l. ....**2,070.00** (Illustration: lower right, below)

Cake basket, of oval form pierced w/alternating panels of diaper & scrollwork divided by

An Assortment of George III Period Cake Baskets

beading, openwork swing handle, engraved w/contemporary arms in rococo cartouche, on pierced rim foot, George III period, S. Herbert & Co., London, England, 1763, 13¾" l. ....**2,990.00** (Illustration: left, bottom previous page)

Cake basket, boat-form, applied w/four classical oval medallions in the manner of Wedgwood below a band of vertical pales interrupted by paterae, beaded rim & reeded swing handle, engraved w/later crest & baronet's badge, George III period, Hester Bateman, overstruck by John Robins, London, England, 1786, 14⅛" l. ....**2,300.00** (Illustration: upper left, bottom previous page)

Cake basket, of oval boat-form w/pierced & bright-cut border, reeded rim & swing handle, George III period, William Abdy, London, England, 1791, 14¾" l. ....**3,105.00** (Illustration: upper right, bottom previous page)

Candelabra, two-light, square base supporting vase-form stem, fitted w/a detachable two-light branch mounted in an urn-shaped socket, removable nozzles, one base loaded, Continental, maker's mark "GK," town mark a bird on a branch, ca. 1810, 8¼" h., pr. **2,300.00**

Candelabra, two-light, of slender vase-form, the shoulders decorated w/lion masks & swags the stem attached by three paw feet to the reel-shaped base, the branches w/formal foliate arms decorated w/paterae, galleried drip-pan & lyre-shaped finial topped by a garland, Dominico Massotti, Rome, Italy, ca. 1830, 17½" h. **8,050.00**

Candelabra, four-light, square base raised on claw feet, the standard modeled in the form of a classical maiden holding aloft a swag-draped rod mounted w/candle nozzles, Continental, 12" h., pr. ....**4,600.00** (Illustration: below)

Candelabra, five-light, shaped

Impressive Four-light Figural Silver Candelabra

octagonal base w/baluster stem & sconces, fixed nozzles, Tetard Freres, Paris, France, early 20th c., 10⅝" h., pr. ...**4,025.00**

Victorian Silver Six-light Candelabra

Candelabra, six-light, shaped domed base chased w/paneling, raised on leafy scroll feet & applied w/swags pendent from ram's heads, the swirled rococo stem spreading into asymmetric scrolled arms w/sconces at staggered heights, openwork leafy finial, the integral drip-pans in the form of triangular rococo cartouches, detachable nozzles, Victorian, R. & S. Garrard & Co., London, England, 1845, 27½" h., pr. ....**68,500.00** (Illustration)

Candelabra, seven-light, on shaped domed rococo base, the stem formed as a bower of coral branches, one enclosing a seated nude nymph attended by an infant triton & a putto holding rushes surrounded by fish & marine motifs, the other enclosing a seated triton blowing a conch surrounded by putti playing w/fish, foliate scroll branches rising to water-chased sconces, A. Bachruch,

Vienna, Austria, ca. 1880, pr. **20,700.00**

Candlesticks, circular molded base, banded urn-shaped stem & campana sconce, George II period, maker's mark "IS" below a flowerhead in shield, London, 1727, 5½" h., pr. **11,500.00**

Candlesticks, octagonal molded & faceted base engraved w/contemporary arms under helm & foliate mantle, octagonal baluster stem rising from circular knop to circular banded campana sconce, George I period, David Kilmaine, London, England, 1715, 6⅞" h., pr. **12,650.00**

Candlesticks, shaped square domed base engraved w/arms on drapery mantle below coronet, fluted octagonal stem & sconce, Antoni Grill II, Augsburg, Germany, 1732-33, 7" h., set of 4 ....**14,950.00**

Candlesticks, shaped domed base supporting a faceted hexagonal stem, banded campana sconce, Lorenzo Petroncelli, Rome, Italy, ca. 1760, 8¼" h., pr. **4,312.00**

Candlesticks, octagonal stepped base supporting an octagonal baluster-form stem w/two circular knops, the well engraved w/arms, engraved underneath "Dolly," Bernt Wolff, Nijmengen, Holland, 1733, 8¼" h., set of 4 ....**74,000.00**

Candlesticks, parcel-gilt, figural, in the form of a cupid seated on the back of an open-jawed crocodile & holding a grape-laden cornucopia, detachable nozzle, L.R. Ruchmann, Paris, France, ca. 1825, 8⅜" h., pr. ....**18,400.00** (Illustration: one of two, top next page)

Candlesticks, on shaped

Unique Figural Silver Candlestick

square base, octagonal stem rising to cushion-shaped shoulder, matching campana sconce, George II period, John Priest, London, England, 1752, 9⅜" h., pr...........................**4,600.00**

Candlesticks, circular saucer tripod base w/raised conical center under a thin beaded stem & tall cylindrical sconce, finished w/a plain circular bobeche, Spanish Colonial, early 19th c., one stamped "Vargas," 9½" h., pr...........**2,875.00**

Chinese Export Silver Candlestick

Candlesticks, square low-foot-

ed base, baluster-form standard w/upper & lower ring, scroll decoration, weighted, Chinese Export, unidentified mark on base, late 19th c., 10⅜" h., pr............................**747.50** (Illustration: one of two)

Candlesticks, lobed circular foot w/grapes attached at base supporting a spiral-twist stem topped by molded grapes, w/flaring drip-pan, Georg Jensen Silversmithy, Copenhagen, Denmark, post-1945, 11⅝" h., pr.............**13,800.00**

Candlesticks, in Louis XV taste, domed lobed foot supporting a lobed & fluted baluster-form stem, applied on the base & shoulders w/leaves & flat chased w/bands of rococo ornament, Victorian, R. & S. Garrard, London, England, 1839-40, 11⅞" h., set of 4 ....**9,488.00**

Canister, cov., parcel-gilt, the barrel chased w/two putti, one carrying a staff & leaf spray w/a pack on his back, the other carrying a staff & a single leaf, chased between w/flowering plants, screw-on cover w/lobate handle topped by a grotesque mask, Hans Scholler, Leipzig, Germany, 1661-63, 6⅜" h.................**17,250.00**

Casket, cov., rectangular, cast & chased w/Napoleonic scenes, raised on four spreadwinged eagles, the finial in the form of Napoleon on horseback, w/key, Hanau, Germany, late 19th c., 10¾" l. **5,175.00**

Casket, cov., rectangular, flat-chased w/rococo ornament, dragons & demi-lions, w/borders of acanthus, hinged cover w/wide matted band applied w/lion masks, leopard's heads & elephant's heads within beaded festoons, coiled serpent handles, the finial in the

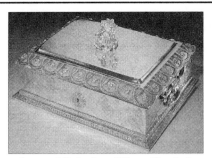

Large Victorian Silver Casket

form of a lion's head w/pendant ring, w/triple bolt lock, the lock casing secured by silver flowerhead screws, the inside of cover w/engraved plaque "C. Chubb & Son 57 St. Paul's Church Yard London Fecerunt," Victorian, Charles Reily & George Storer, London, 1844, fully marked & stamped w/Chubb's patent, 16½" l. ....**19,550.00** (Illustration)

Castor, the paneled sides engraved w/elaborate foliate scrollwork, maker's mark rubbed, London, England, 1837, 3½" h. **275.00**

Queen Anne Silver Caudle Cup

Caudle cup, two-handled, embossed w/a baroque cartouche centering a cable collar above a panel of sloping gadroons, stamped w/rows of leaves, the large scroll handles w/beading, Queen Anne period, Thomas Parr I, London, England, 1703, 4½" h.........**2,530.00** (Illustration)

Center bowl, Grapevine patt., oval w/shallow rounded sides & flaring rim, raised on a low foot w/pierced grape clusters & vine decoration, Georg Jensen Silversmithy, Copenhagen, Denmark, number 296A, 1932- 44, 14⅜" l. **9,200.00**

Centerpiece, shaped oval platform supporting standing winged putti holding a cast ribbon-tied garland of fruit & flowers enclosing a diamond & fancut oval glass bowl, B & Z, Germany, 1895-1915, .800 standard, 11½" w., 19" l., 10" h. **8,625.00**

Unique Temple-form Centerpiece

Centerpiece, in the form of an oval temple, w/fluted borders & six slender columns sheltering a figure of Apollo, all on four leaf-headed paw-and-ball feet, fitted w/a cut-glass bowl, George III period, William Hall, London, England, 1795, overall 16½" h. ....**3,105.00** (Illustration)

Centerpiece, boat-form chased w/pastoral scenes & swags of flowers, mounted on each end w/triple candle holders w/detachable nozzles, Hanau, Germany, ca. 1890, overall 26½" l. **4,025.00**

Chalice, silver-gilt, inverted bell-form cup w/applied foliate band & chased leaf-tips, on a vasiform stem over a similarly decorated stepped circular base, w/Latin presentation inscription dated "1909," later engraved w/an English armorial at the base, maker's mark "uAB," Rome, Italy, late 18th - early 19th c., 11" h. **1,265.00**

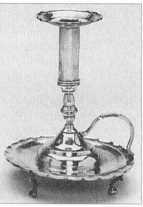

Spanish Colonial Silver Chamberstick

Chamberstick, scalloped edge saucer base w/domed center & bracket handle, on four scrolled supports, knopped stem & tall faceted sconce fitted w/scalloped edge nozzle, Spanish Colonial, 18th c., unmarked, 9¼" h. ....**2,587.00** (Illustration)

Early 18th c. Silver Chocolate Pot

Chocolate pot, cov., tapered cylindrical body w/molded borders, partly faceted swan's neck spout, engraved w/arms in baroque cartouche, high domed cover w/sliding large baluster finial, George I period, Pentecost Symonds, Exeter, England, 1718, 10¾" h.....**18,400.00** (Illustration)

Cigarette case, the cover applied w/monograms & charms including a United States silver half-dollar coin, Moscow, Russia, ca. 1910, 4½" l. **1,495.00**

Claret jug, cov., of spiral shell form w/conch finial, the handle formed as a merman blowing a shell, Puiforcat, Paris, France, late 19th c., 12½" h. **3,335.00**

Clock, desk model, barrel shape surmounted by two doves, the four supporting legs in the form of ram's heads & hooves, the square base w/a border of drapery, the hands in the form of a serpent, Andrei Bragin, St. Petersburg, Russia, ca. 1910, 5½" h.................................**8,050.00**

Art Nouveau Style Silver Clock

Clock, Art Nouveau style, architectural case, the large lower front panel embossed w/stylized female figure on a pendulum swing, upper section fitted w/a French movement, Victorian, Goldsmiths & Silversmiths Co., Ltd., London, England, 1900, 12¼" h.......**3,450.00** (Illustration)

Coffeepot, cov., pear-form w/short spout, the cover w/a baluster finial, engraved w/later arms, Louis XV period, maker's mark not clear, Paris, France, 1746, 5¾" h......................**2,588.00**

Coffeepot, cov., tapered cylindrical body engraved w/contemporary arms in baroque cartouche capped by a shell, slender swan's-neck spout & urn finial, George II period, Elizabeth Buteux, London, England, 1732, 7⅜" h.........**3,162.00**

Coffeepot, cov., of fluted barrel-form, chased w/a collar of sloping grapevine, raised on paw feet, detachable cover w/parrot finial, Johan Daniel Blomsterwall, Goteborg, Sweden, 1829, 8¼" h.........**1,610.00**

Lovely George II Period Coffeepot

Coffeepot, cov., baluster-form, eagle's head spout formed at the base as a gaping mask enclosing an inscription, all flanked by applied sprays of flowers, the upper handle terminal formed as a boar's head, the lower terminal as an applied spray of flowers, gadroon borders, domed cover chased w/leaves surrounding a later acorn finial, one side engraved w/a monogram, George II period, Henry Haynes, London, England, 1754, 9" l. ....**12,650.00** (Illustration)

Compote, plain flared circular bowl raised on a ring of scrolling foliage over a stepped base, designed by Johan Rohde, Georg Jensen Silversmithy, Copenhagen, Denmark, ca. 1925-30, 7¼" d., 5" h.........................**2,587.00**

Compote, flaring circular form, the hexagonal base w/six flattened-bead feet rising to an openwork stem w/six rectangular panels of blue & green enamel, designed by C.R. Ashbee, maker's mark of the Guild of Handicraft, London, England, 1906, 7⅛" h.........**4,830.00**

Cow creamer, realistically modeled, w/removable saddle blanket, Continental, 19th c., stamped w/French "Swan" mark, 8½" l. ....**2,875.00** (Illustration: top next page)

Creamer, squat globular body w/elongated lip, molded leaf handle, monogrammed, Emes & Barnard, London, England, 1813-14, 3⅜" h. (minor dents) **165.00**

Cruet set, miniature, the two-tiered stand raised on four slender legs ending in hoof feet, fitted w/three baluster casters & two silver-capped glass bottles, George I period, maker's mark "C.S." only, ca. 1725, 3⅝" l. **2,588.00**

Cruet set, the shaped platform on inverted acorn feet, pierced w/an apron of swan-flanked fountains, dolphin-flanked tridents & reed-flanked shells, central ring handle topped by

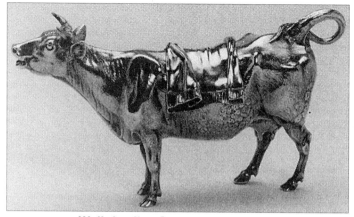

Well-detailed Silver Cow Creamer

swan's heads, repeated at the top of the pilaster supports, the center of the base applied w/a preening swan, fitted w/two cut-glass bottles w/stoppers, Directoire period, Francois Picard, Paris, France, 1798-1809, 10" l. **5,175.00**

Figural Elephant Cruet Stand

Cruet stand, modeled in the form of a caparisoned elephant w/architectural howdah topped by a seated Chinaman, fitted w/four bottle holders & two dishes, mounted on four artillery wheels, losses & repairs, now fitted w/four plated bowls replacing the bottles, Vienna, Austria, 1858,

10" l. **2,300.00**
(Illustration)

Cup, cov., silver-gilt, modeled as a bunch of grapes, tree trunk stem encircled by a tendril mounted w/a bird, vase of lilies finial, Wolf Straub, Nuremberg, Germany, ca. 1625, 10¾" h. **5,175.00**

Cup, cov., presentation-type, semi-ovoid body raised on a low foot, scroll handles, domed cover w/flame finial, engraved w/presentation inscription, George V period, Crichton Brothers, London, England, 1921, 11¼" h. **402.50**

Cup, two-handled, bell-shaped, engraved above the molded girdle on one side w/contemporary arms & on the other w/matching crest, harp-shaped handles, molded pedestal foot, George II period, Dublin, Ireland, 1740, 7¼" h. **4,025.00**

Dish, fluted circular body, the sides hand-hammered, designed by Josef Hoffmann, maker's mark of Wiener Werkstatte, Vienna, Austria, 5¼" d. **1,035.00**

Dish cross, beaded detail, George III period, probably William Pitts, London, England, 1783-84, 12½" l. **805.00**

Dishes, of scalloped shell form, engraved w/crest & mounted on whelk support, George II period, S. Herbert & Co., London, England, 1754, 5⅛" l., set of 4 ....**2,875.00**

Egg cup, novelty-type, modeled as a naked young boy holding an egg out of which emerges a squawking chick, white marble base, maker's mark (?)AD bird between, Paris, France, ca. 1880, 6⅜" h. **1,840.00**

Entree dish w/reversible cover, circular w/fluted sides, the base raised on four hemispherical supports, the cover w/bracket handles, Prieto, Juarez, Mexico, .950 standard, 12¼" d **546.00**

Entree dishes & covers, rectangular cushion-form, gadroon rim w/leaf-flanked shells alternating w/shells, the cover rim w/flowerheads in addition, the surfaces chased, probably at a later date, w/fluting & floral sprays on partly matted ground, oak branch handles, George IV period, Paul Storr, London, England, 1821, 11¾" l., pr.........................**11,500.00**

Epergne, the central oval body w/four slender pilasters ending in paw feet & topped by lion masks connected by an applied band of grapevine, w/central fountain-form finial, topped by an acorn, from which spread four branches, fitted w/a large oval cut-glass bowl & four smaller cut-glass bowls, George III period, Matthew Boulton & Co., Birmingham, England, 1806, 13" h.........**8,625.00**

Epergne, the stand on four scroll supports linked by cast aprons of flowering foliage, detachable central basket & four circular baskets on detachable branches, later gilt, George III period, Thomas Pitts, London, England, 1767, overall 19" w., 14¾" h. ....**9,200.00** (Illustration: below)

Ewer, cov., of vase-form w/headed collar, the cover w/leaf & berry finial, engraved w/arms under a coronet, Andreas Kolbany, Neusohl, Hungary, ca. 1785, 8¾" h.................................**1,725.00**

Ewer & basin, the low-footed ewer w/globular lower section

George III Period Silver-Gilt Epergne

French Silver Ewer & Basin

& waisted neck, the forked rustic handle capped by a spray of buds & leaves, the shallow basin w/narrow molded rim, both engraved w/foliate cartouches on an engine-turned ground, France, ca. 1860, basin 17¾" d., ewer 15½" h., the set ....**2,300.00** (Illustration)

Finger bowls, pierced & chased dragon design, w/glass liner, Chinese Export, Sing Fat & Chao-Ch'ang, early 20th c., 4⅝" d., pr.............................**460.00**

Flagon w/hinged cover, cylindrical w/molded base, chased in low- and high-relief on one side w/the racecourse & stands, the other side w/the ruins of the castle w/the Baden-Baden valley below, chased w/borders of flowers & ferns, made for the Baden-Baden races, Victorian, James B. Hennell, London, England, 1882, 11½" h. **5,750.00**

Flagon, cov., parcel-gilt, baluster-form, embossed & chased w/bands of fruit, a grotesque mask below the spout & four grotesque masks at the top of the foot, lobate scroll handle partly suggestive of a dolphin, mounted at the top of a leaf, hinged cover embossed w/fruit,

Augsburg, Germany, ca. 1670, 11¾" h. **3,162.00**

Impressive German Silver Flagon

Flagon, cov., silver-gilt, baluster-form body raised on a low rounded foot, shield terminal to the scroll handle, the flat stepped cover w/forked scroll thumbpiece, the side engraved w/contemporary arms, the base rim w/initials "CFGZS" & date "1714," Philipp Heinrich Schonling, Frankfurt-am-Main, Germany, ca. 1714, 13" h. ....**51,750.00** (Illustration)

Goblets, wine, rounded bowl raised on a fluted & openwork bead stem, designed by Harald Nielsen, Georg Jensen Silversmithy, Copenhagen, Denmark, post-1945, 5⅝" h., set of 4 ....**1,955.00**

Hanukkah lamp, on four lion rampant supports, box-form base w/hinged cover engraved w/lozengework, the backplate in the form of a crowned cartouche embossed w/a menorah flanked by lion rampant supporters, detachable servant light, maker's mark "III" in trefoil, Frankfurt, Germany, late18th c., 7" h. **10,350.00**

Late 19th c. Silver Hanukkah Lamp

Hanukkah lamp, the burners in the form of seated lions, flanked by lions on pedestals, the crowned backplate fitted w/pilot light & ewer, possibly Germany, late 19th c., .800 standard, 13" l., 11⅜" h......**2,587.00** (Illustration)

Ice pails, of tapered pail form, chased w/hoops & engraved w/pales, gadroon rim, partly openwork swing handle, engraved twice w/arms, one base stamped "STORR & MORTIMER 55," William IV period, Paul Storr, London, England, 1830, to rim 6¾" h.,pr..........................**74,000.00**

Incense burner, cov., globular, pierced w/stars below a bud finial surrounded by spreading leaves, on a tri-form base screwed to a circular plate w/embossed floral rim, three scroll rim, w/metal liner, Turkey, mid-19th c., 6¾" h................................**3,737.00**

Inkstand, shallow boat-form, beaded rim linking ram's head handles, on four foliate supports, fitted w/three silver-mounted cut-glass bottles of slightly later date, George III period, maker's mark "PD," possibly Phineas Daniell of Bristol, London, England, 1777, 9¼" l. **2,070.00**

Inkwell, naturalistically formed as a circular pond w/lily supports, the well rising from a lily pad, Victorian, Heath & Middleton, London, England, 1886, 6¾" d. **1,150.00**

Mid-19th c. Silver Lantern

Lantern, hexagonal form w/glazed sides, tooled w/stars & bosses, the domed cover pierced w/linked quatrefoils & w/a coat-of-arms & supporters, on three melon feet, matching finial, two glass panels missing, unmarked except for Dutch control mark, mid-19th c., 13½" h. ....**3,220.00** (Illustration)

Meat dishes, shaped oval w/gadroon rim, engraved w/arms & supporters, George II period, Edward Wakelin, London, England, 1759, 16⅜" l. **8,625.00**

Meat platter, oval, the rim decorated w/sloping lobes alternating w/buds w/leaf-flanked shells & anthemia at intervals, engraved twice w/arms, George IV period, Benjamin Smith II, London, England, 1826, 16⅜" l. **2,875.00**

Menorah, stepped domed circular base decorated w/cornu-

German Silver Menorah

copia, C-scrolls, diaper patterns & flowers, baluster-form shaft surmounted by a Star of David & supporting four pairs of cast scroll & floral arms w/urn-form sconces & a matching servant lamp, Germany, late 19th - early 20th c., .800 standard, 12¼" h..................**805.00** (Illustration)

Mirror, rococo scroll & cupid design enclosing a heart-shaped bevelled mirror plate, easel back, William Comyns, London, England, 1896-97, 17½" h.................................**747.50**

Model of a soldier, the figure representing a mounted soldier of the 9th (Queen's) Royal Lancers, finely & realistically modeled, the soldier fully equipped w/rifle, sword & lance, on a grassy base above an ebonized plinth w/regimental cypher & presentation inscription, Goldsmiths & Silversmiths Co., London, England, 1911, 15½" h.......**3,450.00**

Monteith, the deeply notched detachable rim above a flat-chased chinoiserie scene of posturing courtiers, birds & plants, Victorian, D. & J. Welby, London, England, 1893, rim 8¾" d.................**1,725.00**

Monteith, detachable scalloped rim topped w/putto heads, the sides chased w/two bands of vertical flutes bordered by stamped leaves, also chased w/two baroque cartouches enclosing contemporary arms & crest, hinged bail handles mounted on cast quasi-lion mask & scroll cartouches, gadrooned foot, Queen Anne period, Robert Timbrell, London, England, 1705, 11½" d.............................**42,550.00**

Mug, niello, of cylindrical form, the spreading base w/leaf decoration, the body w/niello *entrelocs* & vacant cartouches w/a band of Cyrillic inscription, Moscow, Russia, ca. 1890, retailer's mark of Tiffany & Co., New York, New York, 3¼" h................................**1,265.00**

Mug, tapered cylinder w/molded borders & scroll handle, Queen Anne period, Richard Green, London, England, 1707, 3⅞" h...............................**2,530.00**

Mug, baluster-form, the body engraved w/contemporary arms in rococo cartouche above an inscription, leaf-capped double-scroll handle, George II period, Thomas Whipham & Charles Wright, London, England, 1759, 6½" h...............................**9,775.00**

Mustard pot w/hinged cover, plain tankard-form on pedestal foot, the cover engraved w/contemporary initials, forked thumbpiece & scroll handle, maker's mark a crowned fleur-de-lis, probably for Johannes van der Lely, Leeuwarden, Holland, late 17th c., 4⅝" h...............................**2,530.00**

Pitcher, water, Cosmos patt., shaped baluster-form, the body part-fluted, w/fluted ebony handle, the base engraved w/a presentation inscription dated

"SEPT. 23, 1928," designed by Johan Rohde, Georg Jensen Silversmithy, Copenhagen, Denmark, 1925-32, 7¾" h. **4,025.00**

Pitcher, baluster-form w/trefoil lip & molded collar, the base engraved w/contemporary monogram "ST," George IV period, Richard Sibley, London, England, 1825, 8" h............**2,530.00**

Pitcher, water, vase-form, decorated in the Georg Jensen style w/applied blossoms, Mexico, 20th c., 11¼" h. **747.50**

Plates, dinner, shaped gadroon rim, border engraved w/two later crests, George III period, William & John Frisbee, London, England, 1811, 9½" d., set of 12 ....**9,775.00**

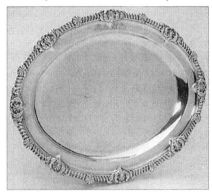

George IV Silver Platter

Platter, oval w/shell & gadroon border, engraved w/crest & motto, George IV period, Philip Rundell, London, England, 1823, 23" l. ....**2,300.00** (Illustration)

Porringer, double handled, engraved decoration & initials, George IV period, maker's mark "J.H.," Edinburgh, Scotland, 1825-26, 4⅝" d. **172.50**

Salt dips, circular w/rounded sides, raised on curving legs & paw feet, the sides chased &

engraved w/floral designs, Robert Hennel, London, England, 1872, 2¼" d., 1½" h., set of 4 ....**440.00**

Salt dips, the banded reeded rims w/shells at intervals, raised on three ram's mask & hoof feet linked by applied swags of flowers, George II period, maker's mark "IH" pellet below in shield, London, England, 1736, 3¼" d., set of 4 ....**4,888.00**

Sauceboat, the boat-shaped body w/shaped rim & a double scroll handle, raised on three hoof feet, George III period, Hester Bateman, London, England, 1790-91, 7" l. **316.00**

Sauceboats, *bombé* oval form, engraved w/a crest & raised on three lion mask & paw feet, waved rim & leaf-capped scroll handle parting from a stylized trefoil, George II period, John Moore, Dublin, Ireland, ca. 1750, 8¼" l., pr. **3,162.00**

Shell-form Silver Sauceboat

Sauceboats, fluted shell-form, raised on three paw feet headed by lion masks w/flowing manes, leaf-capped double-scroll handle parting from shell & scalework mount, the upper one capped by a flattened lion's head, engraved w/a crest, George II period, John Jacob, London, England, ca. 1738, 8⅝" l., pr. ....**17,250.00** (Illustration: one of two)

Saucepan, cov., cylindrical, detachable cover w/hinged

flap, wooden handle & finial,
George III period, John Emes,
London, England, 1800,
4⅝" h. **805.00**

Sconces, wall-type, one-light,
silver-gilt, formed as a baluster
urn on hoofed feet, draped
w/Husks, on plinth decorated
w/scrolled acanthus branches,
maker's mark "DD" w/torch
between, Paris, France, late
19th c., 10" h., pr...............**9,200.00**

Serving dish, circular w/shaped
gadroon rim, engraved w/arms,
George III period, William
Cripps, London, England,
1761, 15" d.........................**1,955.00**

Snuff box, cov., rectangular
w/applied rococo design,
monogrammed, George II period, maker obscured, London,
England, 1745, 2¾" l.............**230.00**

Snuff box, cov., silver-gilt, rectangular, the cover mounted
w/an oval bas-relief of a classical scene, the surface engine-
turned & w/raised border of
flowers & shells, Regency period, maker's mark overstruck by
another, London, England,
1817, 3¼" l. **1,265.00**
(Illustration: top next column)

Snuff box w/hinged cover, niello, rectangular w/in-curved

Silver-gilt English Snuff Box

sides, nielloed w/figures in garden settings, w/scrollwork border & thumbpiece, Assay-mas-
ter's initials "A.T.," Tobolsk,
Russia, 1771, 3¼" l. **805.00**

Soup ladle, Old English patt.
w/bright-cut decoration,
engraved w/crest within shield,
shell-form bowl, maker's mark
"FIS," Oporto, Portugal, ca.
1843-53, 13".........................**489.00**

Soup tureen, cov., two-handled,
partly lobed urn-form, straight
gadroon rim, the cover w/simi-
lar ring finial, George III period,
William Bennett, London,
England, 1805, across handles
11¾"..................................**4,312.00**

Soup tureen, cover & stand, of
bombé oval form w/shell handles, the cover w/artichoke
finial, flat-chased w/strapwork

20th c. Silver Covered Soup Tureen

on matted ground, Continental, early 20th c., stand 21¾" l., the set **4,312.00**
(Illustration: bottom previous page)

Spoon, Apostle-type, depicting St. John the Evangelist, inscribed w/initials on verso, gilt bowl, Enkbuizen, Holland, dated 1800, 7½" l. **374.00**

Stuffing spoon, plain w/engraved crest, George III period, possibly Thomas Nash II, London, England, 1796-97, 11¾" l. **144.00**

Sugar bowl, cov., the hemispherical low-footed bowl engraved w/contemporary arms, the crest repeated within a collared handle in the center of the domed cover, George I period, William Fleming, London, England, 1721, Britannia Standard, 3⅝" d................................**4,025.00**

Sugar bowl, cov., the hemispherical bowl engraved w/an ecclesiastical coat of arms between caryatid supports, domed cover chased w/leafage, the finial formed as a seated child blowing a conch, Gennaro Romanelli, Naples, Italy, ca. 1840, 7¼" h. **2,300.00**

Sugar box w/hinged cover, of *bombé* circular form raised on four trifid feet, the cover w/baluster finial, gilt interior, maker's mark "CII" in trefoil, town mark of horse above "12," probably Celle, Germany, ca. 1730, 5" l. **3,450.00**

Tablespoons, rat-tail bowl, terminal engraved w/contemporary arms, Early English patt., Queen Anne period, John Broake, London, England, 1711, 8" l., set of 12 ....**6,900.00**

Tablespoons, Fiddle Thread patt., engraved w/contemporary arms & coronet, Joannes Andreas Gerardus L'Herminott,

Maastricht, Holland, 1772-74, 8⅛" l., set of 12 ....**1,265.00**

Tankard, cov., miniature, parcel-gilt, the tapered beaker-shaped body engraved w/a band of arabesques within strapwork, spreading domed foot & cover chased w/lobes & strapwork, gilt baluster finial, twin-tailed double-sided mermaid thumbpiece, the scroll handle terminating in curled wires, North Germany or Baltic regions, ca. 1570-80, 5¼" h.............**5,750.00**

Tankard, cov., tapered cylindrical form w/three reeded bands, flat cover & openwork thumbpiece, English Colonial, Johnson & Cox, Madras, India, ca. 1810, 5⅝" h. **1,495.00**

Tankard, cov., tapering cylindrical body w/molded base, the barrel engraved w/contemporary arms between crossed plumes above an inscription, flat-domed cover w/lobate scroll thumbpiece, William & Mary period, maker's mark "IA" in monogram, London, England, 1689, 6½" h.......**18,400.00**

Tankard, cov., parcel-gilt, the barrel engraved w/three vignettes, one of Bacchus flanked by two of Cupid, sur-

Ornate German Silver Tankard

rounded by flowers & lobate ornaments, the hinged cover w/thumbpiece mounted w/later medal of the Empress Catherine I of Russia, dated 1726, engraved underneath w/a later inscription, Nathanael Presting II, Danzig, Poland, ca. 1680, 8¾" h. **8,050.00**

Tankard, cov., parcel-gilt, tapered cylindrical form, the body w/six ogee arched panels engraved w/portraits of fashionable European & near-Eastern figures, surrounded by embossed sprays of fruit, the finial formed as a figure holding a horseshoe on reel-shaped plinth, twin-tailed mermaid thumbpiece, the scroll handle applied w/a bearded bust above strapwork, the base inserted w/a 1554 coin depicting Ferdinand of Austria, maker's mark "P," Luneburg, Germany, ca. 1600-20, 9" h. ....**40,250.00** (Illustration: bottom previous page)

Tea & coffee set: cov. teapot, cov. coffee jug, sugar bowl & creamer; partly chased w/curving lobes w/gadroon borders, twin-serpent handles, jug engraved w/arms, the rest w/matching crests, George III period, William Burwash, London, England, 1813, jug 8½" h. **3,450.00**

Tea & coffee set: cov. teapot, cov. coffeepot, cov. sugar bowl & creamer; each w/a fluted shield-shaped body, Mexico, coffeepot 9" h., 4 pcs. **805.00**

Tea & coffee set: cov. teapot, cov. coffeepot, sugar bowl & creamer; of melon-form chased w/flowers & engraved w/contemporary crests & mottoes, oak branch handles, spouts & feet, the cast leaf-form covers w/acorn spray finials, stamped "STORR & MORTIMER, 311, 312," early Victorian, Paul

Storr, London, England, 1838, coffeepot 9" h., 4 pcs. **6,325.00**

Tea & coffee set: cov. coffeepot, cov. teapot, cov. sugar bowl & creamer; plain hexagonal urn-form bodies w/domed lids & harp-form handles, China, .900 standard, coffeepot 10¾" h., 4 pcs. **460.00**

Tea & Coffee Set by Elkington

Tea & coffee set: cov. teapot, cov. coffeepot, sugar bowl & creamer of baluster-form, engraved w/birds & bamboo, bamboo-form handles, seated Oriental figure finials, Frederick Elkington & Co., London, England, 1880, 4 pcs. ....**3,220.00** (Illustration)

Tea & coffee set: cov. coffeepot, cov. teapot, cov. sugar bowl, creamer & tray; in the 18th c. taste, panelled pyriform vessels chased w/strapwork & floral decoration, shaped oval tray w/matching chased border, Germany, 20th c., .800 standard, tray 17" l., coffeepot 8¾" h., 5 pcs. **2,070.00**

Tea & coffee set: cov. teapot, cov. coffeepot, cov. sugar bowl, creamer & tray; octagonal baluster form w/angular rosewood handles & block finials, the tray w/conforming handles, maker's mark "PB" lion between, Paris, France, retailed by Lopez y Fernandez, Madrid, Spain, ca. 1930, 5 pcs. **5,060.00**

Tea caddy, oval form, bright-cut w/festoons linking oval shields, one enclosing contemporary initial "U," beaded borders, stepped domed cover w/finial, George III period, Hester Bateman, London, England, 1783, 5¼" h........................**4,312.00**

George I Period Silver Tea Caddy

Tea caddy, of upright octagonal form w/molded borders, sliding cover & octagonally domed cap, engraved w/contemporary arms, George I period, John Farnell, London, England, 1715, 5½" h........................**8,050.00** (Illustration)

Teakettle, cover & lampstand, diamond-shaped, decorated w/applied & chased birds among blossoming prunus, bamboo-form feet, matching bamboo-form X-form stand, Chinese Export, Woshing 'An Ch'ang, late 19th c., 12" h................................**1,380.00**

Teakettle, cover & lampstand, lobed ovoid body w/wooden handle, the stand on four paw feet, w/burner, George III period, kettle marked Thomas Robins, London, ca. 1806-07, stand marked W.B., London, ca. 1807-08, overall 14" h................................**1,265.00**

Silver Teakettle on Lampstand

Teakettle, cover & lampstand, almost spherical-form, the shoulder flat-chased w/a band of diaper interrupted by baskets of flowers, engraved w/contemporary arms in rococo cartouche, raffia-covered swing handle rising from stylized shells, lampstand w/fixed lamp, three multiple-scroll supports linked by swags of flowers suspended from ribbon bows & shells, the arms repeated on the lamp cover, George II period, James Manners, London, England, 1736, 15½" h.....**10,925.00** (Illustration)

Teapot, cov., pear-shaped body on a low base, decorated in the Dutch 'Louis XIV' style w/fluting around mid-section & on shoulder, chained cover & duck-head spout, maker's mark not clear, Sneek, Holland, 1746 or 1763, 4¾" h....................**2,185.00**

Teapot, cov., straight-sided oval form, engraved on both sides w/crests in ribbon-suspended oval frames linked by bright-cut swags, also w/bright-cut borders, ivory scroll handle & button finial, George III period, Hester Bateman, London, England, 1780, 5" h...........**3,163.00**

Five-piece Queen Anne-style Silver Tea Set

Teapot, cov., pear-form w/lobed & ribbed angles, covered swan's-neck spout, faceted urn finial, leaf & scroll carved handle, Esaias Busch III, Augsburg, Germany, 5" h...........**6,900.00**

Teapot, cov., spherical, the flat cover w/flush hinge engraved w/flowerheads, the short spout issuing from shellwork, on three shell & scroll supports, gilt interior, Theodore Matthias Gennerup, Riga, Latvia, ca. 1770, 5¼" h.......................**2,587.00**

Teapot, cov., partly lobed circular body w/a collar of anthemia, twin-winged serpent handle, raised collar w/egg-and-dart rim, George IV period, Philip Rundell, London, England, 1820, 5½" h.......................**2,587.00**

Teapot, cov., octagonal pear-form, engraved on both sides w/arms in baroque cartouche topped by a crest, faceted swan's-neck spout, urn finial, George I period, London, England, 1718, 6⅜" h.......**17,250.00**

Tea set, bachelor's-type: cov. teapot, cov. sugar bowl & cov. cream pitcher; flat-based oval barrel bodies, half-fluted & w/engraved & chased bands, fluted domed lids w/knob finials, Victorian, Edward Hutton, London, England, 1892, teapot 5" h., 3 pcs. **575.00**

Tea set: cov. teapot, cov. sugar bowl & creamer; Cosmos patt., carved ebony handles, designed by Johan Rohde, Georg Jensen Silversmithy, Copenhagen, Denmark, number 45C, post-1945, 3 pcs. **2,875.00**

Tea set: large cov. teapot, small cov. teapot, cov. tea kettle on lampstand, cov. sugar bowl & creamer; Queen Anne-style, bulbous w/bands at the shoulders & on the covers, the kettle engraved w/arms, Britannia Standard, Crichton Bros., London, England, 1919-24, kettle on stand 13¾" h., 5 pcs. **3,163.00**
(Illustration: above)

Tea tray, oval, the shaped gadroon rim w/leaves & ovolos at intervals, reeded handles rising from acanthus, the panel feet cast w/stiff leaves flanked by quatrefoils, engraved w/contemporary arms, Regency period, Paul Storr, London, England, 1814, across handles 23⅞" l. **20,700.00**

Tea tray, two-handled, shaped oval w/shell & scroll rim, the surface engraved w/a band of baroque ornamentation, Victorian, Sheffield, England, 1901, across handles 28½" l. **3,163.00**

Tea tray, two-handled, shaped oval form, the wide rim cast & chased w/grapevine between oval cartouches, the surface engraved w/a band of foliate strapwork, Victorian, Stephen Smith & William Nicholson, London, England, 1853, across handles 30½" l. **5,175.00**

Silver Gilt Tea Urn in the Egyptian Manner

Tea urn, cov., silver-gilt, in the Egyptian manner, the hemispherical body supported on three winged sphinxes, standing on a triangular platform w/applied Egyptian ornament & ball feet, between the sphinxes a shallow urn-form lamp & cover on a slender column partly screened by shaped panels of anthemia & paterae, the eagle head spout w/relief foliate ornament, the top

w/cone finial & coiled serpent handle, the urn can be carried by two swing handles, the handles of which are concealed by classical masks & sunbursts & which form the beaded molding above a frieze of key pattern interrupted by beaded lozenges on a matted ground, the shoulder applied w/a band of trailing berried foliage on a matted ground, wavy rim above a gadroon border, detachable domed cover w/bud finial, George III period, Digby Scott & Benjamin Smith II, London, England, 1805. after a design by J.J. Boileau, 15" h. ......**85,000.00** (Illustration)

Tea urn, cov., plain oviform body w/vacant rococo cartouche & handles formed as floral pendants, beaded borders & flame finial, raised on a detachable square base w/openwork apron & claw-and-ball feet, George III period, maker's mark "DW" script, possibly for David Whyte, London, England, 1770, 21¼" h.......**3,738.00**

Toast rack, seven-bar, rectangular boat-form w/gadroon rim & shell grips, open scrollwork feet, minor repairs, George III period, Paul Storr, London, England, 1817, 11" l...........**3,450.00** (Illustration: top next page)

Tobacco box, cov., elongated octagonal form, finely engraved on the top w/two vignettes from the Old Testament, one of Joseph's brother showing the coat to his father, dated in a pediment "1756," & Joseph & Potiphar's wife, the base engraved w/two New Testament scenes: The Last Supper & the Ascension, Andreas van Oosterhout, Schoonhoven, Holland, ca. 1754, 5⅜" l. **4,025.00**

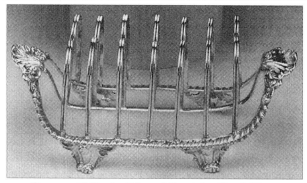

George III Period Toast Rack by Paul Storr

Tray, circular w/shaped edge, raised on three feet, Edwardian, unidentified maker, Sheffield, England, 1913-14, 8¼" d. **345.00**

Tray, square w/shaped angles decorated w/shells, molded rim & short central foot, Reynier Brandt, Amsterdam, Holland, 1745, 8⅞" w. **2,300.00**

George I Period Silver Tray

Tray, square w/a shaped molded rim, raised on four scroll supports, engraved w/a later crest, maker's mark "SM" crowned, probably for Samuel Margas, London, England, 1726, 9¼" w. ....**2,587.00** (Illustration)

Tray, silver-gilt, the heavy circular body engraved in the center w/the Imperial monogram of Czar Paul I, w/molded border, raised on three scroll supports,

Germann Gottlieb Unger, St. Petersburg, Russia, 1800, 11⅜" d. **5,175.00**

Tray, oval w/reeded rim & matching handles rising from leaves, the center engraved w/contemporary arms within an oval frame of husks, paterae & beads, George III period, John Crouch & Thomas Hannam, London, England, 1787, across handles 21⅞" **5,405.00**

Tray, rectangular w/shaped ribbon edge & two handles, the center engraved w/a crest, Edwardian, Fordham & Faulkner, Sheffield, England, 1907-08, in fitted oak box, 17½ x 24" ....**3,450.00** (Illustration: bottom next page)

Trays, shaped circular body w/applied cast scroll & foliate border, raised on four scrolled supports, George IV period, Robert Garrard II, Panton Street, London, England, 1828, 15½" d., pr...............**9,200.00**

Tureen, cov., circular on high flared foot, the rim applied w/three scalloped projected moldings, the domed cover w/white onyx knop scalloped to match, marked on base "STERLING, MADE IN MEXICO" & "JEAN PUIFORCAT," w/Puiforcat Mexican mark, ca. 1945, 10" d. ....**23,000.00** (Illustration: top next page)

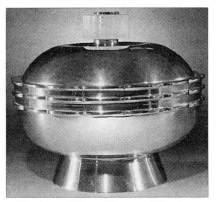

Mexican Silver Covered Tureen

Tureen, cov., silver-gilt, of oval *bombé* form, chased w/swags over lobes & flutes, the cover chased w/clusters of shells on similar ground, artichoke spray finial, unmarked, possibly Royal Workshops, Italy, third quarter 18th c., across handles 10½" l. **20,700.00**

Vase, silver-gilt, two-handled, derived from the Warwick Vase, the body applied w/large bacchic masks between thrysi, the neck w/repeating band of shells & anthemia, twisted branch handles, the rim chased w/Vitruvian scrolls within an egg-and-dart border, fluted pedestal foot, George IV period, maker's mark "R & E,"

London, England, 1828, 10¾" h. plus ebonized wood plinth **6,037.00**

Vase, ovoid on a spreading circular foot, w/upswept handles at the shoulder, hand-textured surface, gilt interior, Mario Buccellati, Milan, Italy, post-1935, 15¾" h......................**8,625.00**

Vegetable dish, cov., gadroon rim w/shells & foliage at intervals, the cover w/a matching chased band, engraved w/arms & w/heraldic eagle finial, George III period, James Scott, Dublin, Ireland, 1814, retailed by West, 12" d....................**2,588.00**

Vegetable dish w/reversible cover, oval w/fluted sides, the base raised on four hemispherical supports, the lid w/bracket handles, Prieto, Juarez, Mexico, .950 standard, 14" l. **805.00**

Vegetable dishes, covers & liners, Louis XV-style, circular bowl on a collet base w/interlacement band borders, mounted w/acanthus leaf handles, stepped domed lid mounted w/cast trophy of vegetables & grains as a handle, the bowl & cover chased w/strap-work

Large Edwardian Two-handled Silver Tray

Louis XV-style Vegetable Dish

panels on a pricked matte ground, Continental, probably French, without hallmarks, retailed by Tiffany & Co., New York, New York, across handles 11½" l., 6¾" h., pr. ....**5,175.00** (Illustration: one of two)

Wine coasters, shaped cylindrical sides w/reeded rim & turned wood base, centered w/a boss engraved w/crest framed in a garter band w/motto, George III period, Solomon Hougham, London, England, 1800, 5" d., 1¾" h., set of 4 ....**4,600.00**

Wine cooler, vase-form, partly lobed & with a cast collar of arches enclosing anthemia, ribbon-tied reeded handles rising from lion masks, engraved w/later monogram, lobed pedestal foot, detachable rim & liner, George III period, Paul Storr, London, England, 1806, 9⅜" h. **16,100.00**

Wine cooler, modeled in the form of a neo-classical urn, the sides chased & engraved w/stylized shells & leaves at the bottom, Italy, 19th c., 13" d., 11¾" h....................**1,540.00** (Illustration: top next column)

Wine cooler, square pedestal base supporting a campana-shaped body w/an applied collar of grapevine, engraved below w/a fox hunting scene, handles rising from bearded masks, egg-and-dart rims, detachable liner, Victorian,

Neo-Classical Wine Cooler

J. Dixon & Sons, Sheffield, England, 1873, 11¾" h.......**4,025.00**

Wine funnel, of typical form, maker & date obscured, Newcastle, England, early 19th c., 5½" h. **259.00**

Ca. 1760 Silver 'White Wine' Label

Wine label, cast & pierced in low-relief as a cherub holding two flasks among scrolls & vines, a central curved ribbon engraved "WHITE WINE," struck "WALSH" for Stephen Walsh, Cork, Ireland, ca. 1760, 2¼" w. ....**1,035.00** (Illustration)

Wine syphon, of typical arched form, w/a syringe-form plunger, inscribed, flattened bell-shaped tap, George III period, Phipps & Robinson, London, England, 1804, 15" l. **4,600.00**

STERLING SILVER FLATWARE

(Listed by item. Individual pieces unless otherwise noted.)

BABY FORKS

Marie Antoinette patt.,
Dominick & Haff **$30.00**

BERRY FORKS

Empire patt., Whiting Mfg.
Co. **30.00**

Violet patt., set of 6, R. Wallace
& Sons **165.00**

BERRY SPOONS

Chrysanthemum patt., Wm. B.
Durgin Co. **495.00**

Colfax patt., Wm. B . Durgin
Co. **85.00**

Dauphin patt., Wm. B. Durgin
Co. **345.00**

Egyptian patt., Whiting Mfg.
Co. **150.00**

Honeysuckle patt., Whiting
Mfg. Co. **225.00**

Ivory patt., Whiting Mfg. Co....**375.00**

Jefferson patt., Gorham Mfg.
Co. **85.00**

Louis XIV patt., Towle Mfg.
Co. **85.00**

Louis XV patt., Whiting Mfg.
Co. **150.00**

Orange Blossom patt., Alvin
Mfg. Co. **185.00**

Rustic patt., gold-washed,
Towle Mfg. Co. **65.00**

Versailles patt., Gorham Mfg.
Co. **175.00**

BONBON SPOONS

Grande Baroque patt., R.
Wallace & Sons **36.00**

BOUILLON SPOONS

Bridal Rose patt., Alvin Mfg.
Co. **45.00**

Buttercup patt., Gorham Mfg.
Co. **20.00**

Etruscan patt., Gorham Mfg.
Co. **24.00**

Georgian patt., Towle Mfg.
Co. **24.00**

Lily patt., Whiting Mfg. Co. **35.00**

Louis XIV patt., Towle Mfg.
Co. **25.00**

Madame Jumel patt., Gorham
Mfg. Co. **30.00**

Marguerite patt., Gorham Mfg.
Co. **18.00**

Mount Vernon patt., Lunt
Silversmiths............................**22.00**

Versailles patt., Gorham Mfg.
Co. **40.00**

Violet patt., R. Wallace &
Sons.......................................**28.00**

BUTTER PICKS

Bridal Rose patt., Alvin Mfg.
Co. **150.00**

Heraldic patt., Whiting Mfg.
Co. **65.00**

Irian patt., R. Wallace &
Sons.......................................**120.00**

Rose (Maryland) patt., The
Steiff Co. **45.00**

BUTTER SERVING KNIVES

Francis I patt., Reed &
Barton **65.00**

Jac Rose patt., Gorham Mfg.
Co. **20.00**

King Edward patt., Gorham
Mfg. Co. **28.00**

Lily of the Valley patt., Gorham
Mfg. Co. **27.00**

Mount Vernon patt., Lunt
Silversmiths...........................**24.00**

Nocturne patt., Gorham Mfg.
Co. **25.00**

Pantheon patt., International
Silver Co. **42.00**

Rose (Maryland) patt., The
Steiff Co. **50.00**

BUTTER SPREADERS,
Flat handle

Cambridge patt., Gorham Mfg.
Co. **16.00**

English Shell patt., Lunt
Silversmiths **10.00**

Georgian patt., Towle Mfg.
Co. **36.00**

King Albert patt., Whiting Mfg.
Co. **10.00**

King Edward patt., Whiting Mfg.
Co. **10.00**

Kings patt., R. Wallace &
Sons.....................................**20.00**

Lily of the Valley patt., Gorham
Mfg. Co. **18.00**

Louis XV patt., Whiting Mfg.
Co. **23.00**

Madame Morris patt., Whiting
Mfg. Co. **20.00**

Majestic patt., Alvin Mfg. Co. ...**21.00**

Manchester patt., Manchester
Mfg. Co. **18.00**

Mandarin patt., Whiting Mfg.
Co. **17.00**

Marie Antoinette patt.,
Dominick & Haff **25.00**

Marlborough patt., Reed &
Barton **20.00**

Maryland patt., Gorham Mfg.
Co. **22.00**

Melrose patt., Gorham Mfg.
Co. **21.00**

Mount Vernon patt., Lunt
Silversmiths...........................**16.00**

Nocturne patt., Gorham Mfg.
Co. **18.00**

Paul Revere patt., Towle Mfg.
Co. **22.00**

Plymouth patt., Whiting Mfg.
Co. **9.00**

Strasbourg patt., Gorham
Mfg. Co. **22.00**

Violet patt., Whiting Mfg.
Co. **25.00**

William & Mary patt., Lunt
Silversmiths...........................**12.00**

BUTTER SPREADERS,
Hollow handle

English Gadroon patt., Gorham
Mfg. Co. **18.00**

Melbourne patt., Oneida
Silversmiths...........................**16.00**

Versailles patt., Gorham Mfg.
Co. **18.00**

CAKE FORKS

Louis XIV patt., Towle Mfg.
Co. **80.00**

CAKE KNIVES

Louis XIV patt., Towle Mfg.
Co. **75.00**

CAKE SERVERS

Manchester patt., Manchester
Mfg. Co. **31.00**

Mandarin patt., silver plate
blade, Whiting Mfg. Co............**34.00**

CHEESE SCOOPS

Cambridge patt., Whiting Mfg.
Co. **45.00**

Kensington patt., Gorham Mfg. Co. **125.00**

Strasbourg patt., Gorham Mfg. Co. **120.00**

CHEESE SERVERS

Grande Baroque patt., R. Wallace & Sons.....................**38.00**

CHOCOLATE MUDDLERS

La Parisienne patt., Reed & Barton **135.00**

CITRUS SPOONS

Francis I patt., Reed & Barton **36.00**

Hampton Court patt., fluted, Reed & Barton **30.00**

Labours of Cupid patt., Dominick & Haff **75.00**

COCKTAIL FORKS

Audubon patt., Tiffany & Co. ...**50.00**

Chantilly patt., Gorham Mfg. Co. **12.00**

Grande Baroque patt., R. Wallace & Sons.......................**28.00**

Marlborough patt., Reed & Barton **20.00**

Melrose patt., Gorham Mfg. Co. **20.00**

Old Newbury patt., Towle Mfg. Co. **18.00**

Paul Revere patt., Towle Mfg. Co. **24.00**

Raleigh patt., Alvin Mfg. Co. **17.00**

Rose Point patt., R. Wallace & Sons.....................................**16.00**

Strasbourg patt., Gorham Mfg. Co. **22.00**

Versailles patt., Gorham Mfg. Co. **22.00**

COLD MEAT FORKS

Etruscan patt., Gorham Mfg. Co. **55.00**

Florentine patt., Alvin Mfg. Co. **140.00**

Francis I patt., Reed & Barton **81.00**

French Antique patt., pierced, Reed & Barton **64.00**

Grande Baroque patt., R. Wallace & Sons.......................**84.00**

Hampton Court patt., Reed & Barton **58.00**

Madame Jumel patt., Whiting Mfg. Co. **65.00**

Manchester patt., small, Manchester Mfg. Co.......................**31.00**

Marlborough patt., Reed & Barton **64.00**

Orange Blossom patt., Alvin Mfg. Co. **185.00**

CRACKER SCOOPS

Chrysanthemum patt., Wm. B. Durgin Co. **650.00**

CREAM LADLES

Dresden patt., Whiting Mfg. Co. **65.00**

Grande Baroque patt., R. Wallace & Sons.......................**41.00**

Hampton Court patt., Reed & Barton **37.00**

King Edward patt., Gorham Mfg. Co. **30.00**

Lily of the Valley patt., Gorham Mfg. Co. **34.00**

Louis XIV patt., Towle Mfg. Co. **45.00**

Louis XV patt., Whiting Mfg. Co. **45.00**

Radiant patt., Whiting Mfg.
Co. **45.00**

CREAM SOUP SPOONS

Camellia patt., Whiting Mfg.
Co. **15.00**

Damask Rose patt., Gorham
Mfg. Co. **32.00**

Francis I patt., Reed &
Barton **32.00**

Grande Baroque patt., R.
Wallace & Sons.....................**36.00**

Lily of the Valley patt., Gorham
Mfg. Co. **22.00**

Marlborough patt., Reed &
Barton **28.00**

Nocturne patt., Gorham Mfg.
Co. **35.00**

Old French patt., Gorham Mfg.
Co. **32.00**

CUCUMBER SERVERS

Fairfax patt., Wm. B. Durgin
Co. **55.00**

Lily patt., Whiting Mfg. Co. **250.00**

Morning Glory patt., Alvin Mfg.
Co. **85.00**

Paris patt., Gorham Mfg.
Co. **165.00**

DEMITASSE SPOONS

Arabesque patt., Whiting Mfg.
Co. **24.00**

Audubon patt., Tiffany & Co. ...**55.00**

Blossom patt., Georg Jensen,
1904-08, 3⅜" l., set of 12 ...**1,495.00**

Francis I patt., Reed &
Barton **24.00**

Grande Baroque patt., R.
Wallace & Sons.....................**24.00**

Hampton Court patt., Reed &
Barton **18.00**

Lily patt., Whiting Mfg. Co. **25.00**

Louis XIV patt., Towle Mfg.
Co. **15.00**

Louis XV patt., Whiting Mfg.
Co. **15.00**

Madame Jumel patt., Whiting
Mfg. Co. **10.00**

Marlborough patt., Reed &
Barton **21.00**

DESSERT FORKS

Audubon patt., Tiffany & Co. ...**80.00**

Chantilly patt., Gorham Mfg.
Co., in original case, set of
12 ....**605.00**

DESSERT SERVING SPOONS

Japanese patt., Gorham Mfg.
Co., 1870-80, 10" l. **690.00**

DESSERT SPOONS

Francis I patt., Reed &
Barton **60.00**

Frontenac patt., International
Silver Co. **45.00**

King Edward patt., Whiting Mfg.
Co. **18.00**

Louis XIV patt., Towle Mfg.
Co. **52.00**

Mignonette patt., Lunt
Silversmiths...........................**20.00**

Old French patt., Gorham Mfg.
Co. **36.00**

Strawberry patt., Wm. B.
Durgin Co. **40.00**

Versailles patt., Gorham Mfg.
Co. **55.00**

DINNER FORKS

Angelo patt., Wood &
Hughes....................................**60.00**

Bridal Rose patt., Alvin Mfg. Co. **38.00**

Camellia patt., Whiting Mfg. Co. **20.00**

Corinthian patt., Gorham Mfg. Co. **65.00**

Damask Rose patt., Gorham Mfg. Co. **25.00**

Etruscan patt., Gorham Mfg. Co. **38.00**

Francis I patt., Reed & Barton **54.00**

King Edward patt., Gorham Mfg. Co. **35.00**

Kings patt., R. Wallace & Sons **48.00**

Lily of the Valley patt., Whiting Mfg. Co. **60.00**

Louis XIV patt., Towle Mfg. Co. **35.00**

Louis XV patt., Whiting Mfg. Co. **25.00**

Louis XV patt., Wood & Hughes......................................**50.00**

Madame Jumel patt., Gorham Mfg. Co. **32.00**

Manchester patt., Manchester Mfg. Co. **24.00**

Mandarin patt., silver plate blade, Whiting Mfg. Co...........**27.00**

Marie Antoinette patt., Dominick & Haff **42.00**

Marie Antoinette patt., Gorham Mfg. Co. **50.00**

Melrose patt., Gorham Mfg. Co. **44.00**

Old Colonial patt., Towle Mfg. Co. **35.00**

Orange Blossom patt., Alvin Mfg. Co. **80.00**

Paul Revere patt., Towle Mfg. Co. **45.00**

Rose Point patt., R. Wallace & Sons......................................**35.00**

William & Mary patt., Lunt Silversmiths..........................**20.00**

DINNER KNIVES

Buttercup patt., Gorham Mfg. Co. **49.00**

Cambridge patt., Gorham Mfg. Co. **49.00**

Damask Rose patt., Gorham Mfg. Co. **25.00**

Etruscan patt., Gorham Mfg. Co. **36.00**

Grand Duchess, Towle Mfg. Co. **34.00**

Kings patt., R. Wallace & Sons......................................**48.00**

Louis XVI patt., Towle Mfg. Co. **38.00**

Madame Jumel patt., Gorham Mfg. Co. **32.00**

Majestic patt., silver plate blade, Alvin Mfg. Co. **41.00**

Marie Antoinette patt., Dominick & Haff **35.00**

Old Colonial patt., Towle Mfg. Co. **32.00**

Orange Blossom patt., Alvin Mfg. Co. **85.00**

Rose Point patt., R. Wallace & Sons......................................**35.00**

EGG SPOONS

Audubon patt., gold-washed bowl, Tiffany & Co. **75.00**

Mayfair patt., Dominick & Haff **14.00**

FISH FORKS

Old French patt., Gorham Mfg. Co. **55.00**

FISH SERVING FORKS

Ivory patt., Whiting Mfg. Co....**475.00**

FISH SERVING SETS — 2 PC.

Luxembourg patt., Gorham
Mfg. Co. **250.00**

Undine patt., Wood &
Hughes................................**495.00**

FRUIT KNIVES

Grande Baroque patt., hollow
handle, R. Wallace & Sons **41.00**

Melrose patt., Gorham Mfg.
Co. **28.00**

GRAPEFRUIT SPOONS

Audubon patt., Tiffany & Co. ...**95.00**

GRAVY LADLES

Angelo patt., Wood &
Hughes................................**115.00**

Cambridge patt., Gorham Mfg.
Co. **65.00**

Chantilly patt., Gorham Mfg.
Co. **45.00**

Chrysanthemum patt., Tiffany
& Co. **395.00**

Egyptian patt., Whiting Mfg.
Co. **125.00**

Francis I patt., Reed &
Barton **80.00**

Hampton Court patt., Reed &
Barton **58.00**

Italian patt., Tiffany & Co........**250.00**

King Edward patt., Gorham
Mfg. Co. **58.00**

King Edward patt., Whiting
Mfg. Co. **130.00**

Louis XIV patt., Towle Mfg.
Co. **48.00**

Manchester patt., Manchester
Mfg. Co. **31.00**

Mount Vernon patt., Lunt
Silversmiths...........................**50.00**

Nocturne patt., Gorham Mfg.
Co. **55.00**

Versailles patt., Gorham Mfg.
Co. **145.00**

Violet patt., R. Wallace &
Sons..**95.00**

GUMBO SPOONS

Cambridge patt., Gorham Mfg.
Co. **25.00**

Manchester patt., Manchester
Mfg. Co. **28.00**

Mandarin patt., Whiting Mfg.
Co. **24.00**

Orange Blossom patt., Alvin
Mfg. Co. **50.00**

ICE CREAM FORKS

Louis XIV patt., Towle Mfg.
Co. **40.00**

Nocturne patt., Gorham Mfg.
Co. **35.00**

Violet patt., R. Wallace &
Sons..**90.00**

ICE CREAM KNIVES

Luxembourg patt., Gorham
Mfg. Co. **225.00**

Versailles patt., Gorham Mfg.
Co. **250.00**

ICE CREAM SPOONS

Lorraine patt., Alvin Mfg. Co. ...**35.00**

Paul Revere patt., Towle Mfg.
Co. **32.00**

Peony patt., R. Wallace &
Sons..**38.00**

Rose (Maryland) patt., The
Steiff Co. **28.00**

ICED TEA SPOONS

Buttercup patt., Gorham Mfg.
Co. **33.00**

Chantilly patt., Gorham Mfg.
Co. **22.00**

Hampton Court patt., Reed &
Barton **26.00**

Louis XIV patt., Towle Mfg.
Co. **24.00**

Marie Antoinette patt.,
Dominick & Haff **28.00**

Nocturne patt., Gorham Mfg.
Co. **25.00**

Rose patt., R. Wallace &
Sons.......................................**30.00**

Virginian patt., Gorham Mfg.
Co., set of 5............................**137.50**

ICE TONGS

Florentine patt., Tiffany &
Co. **695.00**

JELLY SERVERS

Francis I patt., Reed &
Barton **36.00**

Grande Baroque patt., R.
Wallace & Sons.......................**38.00**

Lily of the Valley patt., Gorham
Mfg. Co. **28.00**

LEMON FORKS

Grande Baroque patt., R.
Wallace & Sons.......................**30.00**

Hampton Court patt., Reed &
Barton **25.00**

King Edward patt., Gorham
Mfg. Co. **18.00**

LETTUCE FORKS

Cottage patt., Gorham Mfg.
Co. **55.00**

Lily patt., Whiting Mfg. Co. **285.00**

Renaissance patt., Dominick &
Haff **175.00**

LUNCHEON FORKS

Buttercup patt., Gorham Mfg.
Co. **15.00**

Camellia patt., Whiting Mfg.
Co. **18.00**

Chantilly patt., Gorham Mfg.
Co. **18.00**

Chrysanthemum patt., Wm. B.
Durgin Co...............................**95.00**

Etruscan patt., Whiting Mfg.
Co. **18.00**

Francis I patt., Reed &
Barton **36.00**

Hampton Court patt., Reed &
Barton **30.00**

King Edward patt., Whiting Mfg.
Co. **24.00**

Lily of the Valley patt., Gorham
Mfg. Co. **26.00**

Majestic patt., Alvin Mfg. Co. ...**28.00**

Mandarin patt., Whiting Mfg.
Co. **24.00**

Melrose patt., Gorham Mfg.
Co. **28.00**

Mignonette patt., Lunt
Silversmiths............................**18.00**

Nuremburg patt., Alvin Mfg.
Co. **45.00**

Old Colonial patt., Towle Mfg.
Co. **22.00**

Orange Blossom patt., Alvin
Mfg. Co. **55.00**

Plymouth patt., Whiting Mfg.
Co. **15.00**

Rambler Rose patt., Reed &
  Barton **18.00**

Rose Point patt., R. Wallace &
  Sons.......................................**32.00**

Strawberry patt., Wm. B.
  Durgin Co..............................**45.00**

Versailles patt., Gorham Mfg.
  Co. **30.00**

Violet patt., R. Wallace &
  Sons.......................................**28.00**

William & Mary patt., Lunt
  Silversmiths...........................**18.00**

LUNCHEON KNIVES

Chantilly patt., Gorham Mfg.
  Co. **18.00**

Etruscan patt., Whiting Mfg.
  Co. **16.00**

Francis I patt., silver plate
  blade, Reed & Barton.............**27.00**

Frontenac patt., International
  Silver Co. **40.00**

Grande Baroque patt., silver
  plate blade, R. Wallace &
  Sons.......................................**31.00**

Kings patt., R. Wallace &
  Sons.......................................**22.00**

Lily of the Valley patt., Gorham
  Mfg. Co. **22.00**

Majestic patt., silver plate
  blade, Alvin Mfg. Co...............**34.00**

Mandarin patt., silver plate
  blade, Whiting Mfg. Co...........**23.00**

Old Colonial patt., Towle Mfg.
  Co. **22.00**

Parallel patt., Georg Jensen
  Silversmiths...........................**65.00**

Plymouth patt., Whiting Mfg.
  Co. **12.00**

Rambler Rose patt., Reed &
  Barton **15.00**

William & Mary patt., Lunt
  Silversmiths...........................**15.00**

MEAT FORKS

Jac Rose patt., Gorham Mfg.
  Co. **55.00**

Nocturne patt., Gorham Mfg.
  Co. **65.00**

MUSTARD LADLES

Dauphin patt., Wm. B. Durgin
  Co. **60.00**

Versailles patt., Gorham Mfg.
  Co. **125.00**

NUT PICKS

Audubon patt., Tiffany &
  Co. **150.00**

Broomcorn patt., Tiffany &
  Co. **65.00**

Grecian patt., Gorham Mfg.
  Co. **45.00**

Grecian patt., Whiting Mfg.
  Co. **28.00**

NUT SPOONS

Lily patt., round, Whiting Mfg.
  Co. **110.00**

OLIVE FORKS

Marguerite patt., Wood &
  Hughes...................................**23.00**

OLIVE SPOONS

Fairfax patt., Wm. B. Durgin
  Co. **25.00**

OYSTER LADLES

Audubon patt., gold-washed
  bowl, Tiffany & Co................**450.00**

Fairfax patt., Wm. B. Durgin
  Co. **175.00**

Japanese patt., Tiffany & Co.,1871-80, 10¾" l. **1,150.00**

PASTRY SERVERS

Francis I patt., hollow handle, Reed & Barton **38.00**

Hampton Court patt., hollow handle, Reed & Barton............**38.00**

Louis XVI patt., Towle Mfg. Co. **85.00**

PICKLE FORKS

Cambridge patt., Gorham Mfg. Co. **30.00**

Francis I patt., Reed & Barton **34.00**

Grande Baroque patt., R. Wallace & Sons **27.00**

Hampton Court patt., Reed & Barton **25.00**

Lily patt., long handle, Whiting Mfg. Co. **125.00**

Lily of the Valley patt., Gorham Mfg. Co. **24.00**

Louis XVI patt., Towle Mfg. Co. **30.00**

Manchester patt., Manchester Mfg. Co. **17.00**

PUNCH LADLES

Beacon patt., Manchester Silver Co. **150.00**

Norfolk patt., Gorham Mfg. Co. **225.00**

SALAD FORKS

Broomcorn patt., Tiffany & Co. **115.00**

Buttercup patt., Gorham Mfg. Co. **37.00**

Camellia patt., Whiting Mfg. Co. **17.00**

Chantilly patt., Gorham Mfg. Co. **25.00**

Chrysanthemum patt., Tiffany & Co. **190.00**

Damask Rose patt., Gorham Mfg. Co. **30.00**

Essex patt., Wm. B. Durgin Co. **18.00**

Etruscan patt., Gorham Mfg. Co. **24.00**

Fontana patt., Towle Mfg. Co. **25.00**

Francis I patt., Reed & Barton **36.00**

Grand Duchess patt., Towle Mfg. Co. **30.00**

Louis XIV patt.,Towle Mfg. Co. **36.00**

Louis XV patt., Whiting Mfg. Co. **40.00**

Marie Antoinette patt., Dominick & Haff **32.00**

Melbourne patt., Oneida Silversmiths **24.00**

Pantheon patt., International Silver Co. **36.00**

Richmond patt., Alvin Mfg. Co. **30.00**

Rose (Maryland) patt., The Stieff Co. **25.00**

Rose Point patt., R. Wallace & Sons.....................................**34.00**

Strawberry patt., Wm. B.Durgin Co. **75.00**

Violet patt., R. Wallace & Sons.....................................**50.00**

Windham patt., Tiffany & Co....**65.00**

SALAD SERVING FORKS

Bridal Rose patt., Alvin Mfg. Co. **250.00**

Francis I patt., Reed &
Barton **100.00**

Melrose patt., Gorham Mfg.
Co. **97.00**

SALAD SERVING SPOONS

Bridal Rose patt., Alvin Mfg.
Co. **250.00**

SALAD SERVING SETS - 2 PC.

Audubon patt., gold-washed
bowls, 10" l., Tiffany &
Co. **2,250.00**

Cambridge patt., Gorham Mfg.
Co. **325.00**

Canterbury patt., Towle Mfg.
Co. **225.00**

Francis I patt., Reed &
Barton **395.00**

Hampton Court patt., fluted,
Reed & Barton **197.00**

Lily of the Valley patt., Gorham
Mfg. Co. **375.00**

Melrose patt., Gorham Mfg.
Co. **217.00**

SAUCE LADLES

Athenian patt., Whiting Mfg.
Co. **35.00**

Rose (Maryland) patt., The
Stieff Co. **55.00**

Washington patt., R. Wallace &
Sons **30.00**

Winthrop patt., Tiffany &
Co. **175.00**

SOUP LADLES

Empire patt., large, Whiting
Mfg. Co. **395.00**

Honeysuckle patt., Whiting
Mfg. Co. **265.00**

Rosette patt., Gorham Mfg. Co.,
ca. 1868,13" l. **137.50**

SOUP SPOONS, OVAL

Buttercup patt., Gorham Mfg.
Co. **25.00**

Georgian patt., Towle Mfg.
Co. **28.00**

Ivy patt., Whiting Mfg.
Co. **35.00**

Louis V patt., Whiting Mfg.
Co. **25.00**

Louis XV patt., Wood &
Hughes...................................**45.00**

Manchester patt., Manchester
Mfg. Co. **21.00**

Marie Antoinette patt., Gorham
Mfg. Co. **44.00**

Old Colonial patt., Towle Mfg.
Co. **28.00**

Old French patt., Gorham Mfg.
Co. **32.00**

Rose patt., R. Wallace &
Sons.......................................**24.00**

Strasbourg patt., Gorham Mfg.
Co. **30.00**

Violet patt., R. Wallace &
Sons.......................................**30.00**

STEAK CARVING FORKS

Mandarin patt., Whiting Mfg.
Co. **30.00**

STEAK CARVING SETS - 2 PC.

Grande Baroque patt., R.
Wallace & Sons **67.00**

SUGAR SHELLS

Francis I patt., Reed &
Barton **38.00**

Hampton Court patt., Reed &
Barton **26.00**

Orange Blossom patt., Alvin
Mfg. Co. **60.00**

SUGAR SPOONS

Canterbury patt., Towle Mfg.
Co. **38.00**

Dauphin patt., Wm. B. Durgin
Co. **85.00**

Egyptian patt., Whiting Mfg.
Co. **45.00**

Fontainebleau patt., Gorham
Mfg. Co. **40.00**

Francis I patt., Reed &
Barton **38.00**

Georgian patt., Towle Mfg.
Co. **38.00**

Grande Baroque patt.,
R. Wallace & Sons **40.00**

Honeysuckle patt., Whiting
Mfg. Co. **55.00**

King Edward patt., Gorham
Mfg. Co. **28.00**

Les Cinq Fleurs, Reed &
Barton **26.00**

Lion (Coeur de Lion) patt.,
gold-washed, Frank W. Smith
Co. **127.00**

Marlborough patt., Reed &
Barton **30.00**

Nocturne patt., Gorham Mfg.
Co. **25.00**

Pantheon patt., International
Silver Co. **35.00**

Rose (Maryland) patt., The
Stieff Co. **35.00**

Rose Point patt., R. Wallace &
Sons.......................................**20.00**

SUGAR TONGS

Francis I patt., Reed &
Barton **105.00**

Lily patt., claw tips, Whiting Mfg.
Co. **95.00**

Louis XIV patt., Towle Mfg.
Co. **45.00**

Louis XV patt., Whiting Mfg.
Co. **38.00**

Madame Jumel patt., Whiting
Mfg. Co. **35.00**

Medici patt., Gorham Mfg.
Co. **150.00**

Olympian patt., Tiffany &
Co. **195.00**

TABLESPOONS

Angelo patt., Wood &
Hughes...................................**95.00**

Arabesque patt., Whiting Mfg.
Co. **95.00**

Buttercup patt., Gorham Mfg.
Co. **85.00**

Chantilly patt., Gorham Mfg
Co. **45.00**

Corinthian patt., Gorham Mfg.
Co. **50.00**

Grande Baroque patt., pierced,
R. Wallace & Sons **84.00**

Hampton Court patt., Reed &
Barton **60.00**

Hawthorne patt., Gorham Mfg.
Co. **55.00**

Francis I patt., Reed &
Barton **81.00**

Imperial Queen patt., Whiting
Mfg. Co. **95.00**

King Edward patt., Gorham
Mfg. Co. **58.00**

Kings patt., R. Wallace &
Sons.......................................**38.00**

Louis XV patt., Whiting Mfg.
Co. **55.00**

Louis XV patt., Wood &
Hughes **50.00**

Madame Jumel patt., Whiting
Mfg. Co. **65.00**

Madame Royale patt., Wm. B.
Durgin **56.00**

Manchester patt., Manchester
Mfg. Co. **31.00**

Marie Antoinette patt.,
Dominick & Haff **45.00**

Marlborough patt., Reed &
Barton **54.00**

Maryland patt., Alvin Mfg. Co...**27.00**

Nocturne patt., Gorham Mfg.
Co. **55.00**

Old Colonial patt., Towle Mfg.
Co. **45.00**

Pantheon patt., International
Silver Co. **38.00**

Raleigh patt., Alvin Mfg. Co. **24.00**

Strasbourg patt., Gorham Mfg.
Co. **26.00**

Versailles patt., Gorham Mfg.
Co. **75.00**

TEASPOONS

Buttercup patt., Gorham Mfg.
Co. **15.00**

Cambridge patt., Gorham Mfg.
Co. **12.00**

Camellia patt., Whiting Mfg.
Co. **10.00**

Chrysanthemum patt., Tiffany
& Co. **115.00**

Corinthian patt., Alvin Mfg.
Co. **22.00**

Damask Rose patt., Gorham
Mfg. Co. **18.00**

Eloquence patt., Lunt
Silversmiths **14.00**

English Gadroon patt., Gorham
Mfg. Co. **15.00**

English Gadroon patt., Whiting
Mfg. Co. **12.00**

English Shell patt., Lunt
Silversmiths...........................**12.00**

Etruscan patt., Gorham Mfg.
Co. **14.00**

Etruscan patt., Whiting Mfg.
Co. **12.00**

Francis I patt., Reed &
Barton **23.00**

Grande Baroque patt., R.
Wallace & Sons **20.00**

King Edward patt., Whiting
Mfg. Co. **20.00**

Kings patt., Dominick & Haff **23.00**

Lily patt., Watson, Newell &
Co. **21.00**

Lily patt., Whiting Mfg. Co. **25.00**

Lily of the Valley patt., Gorham
Mfg. Co. **30.00**

Louis XIV patt., Towle Mfg.
Co. **14.00**

Louis XV patt., Wood &
Hughes.....................................**20.00**

Lucerne patt., R. Wallace &
Sons..**17.00**

Madame Jumel patt., Whiting
Mfg. Co. **14.00**

Majestic patt., Alvin Mfg. Co. ...**20.00**

Manchester patt., Manchester
Mfg. Co. **11.00**

Mandarin patt., Whiting Mfg.
Co. **16.00**

Marguerite patt., Alvin Mfg.
Co. **25.00**

Marie Antoinette patt.,
Dominick & Haff **14.00**

Marlborough patt., Reed &
Barton **17.00**

Marquise patt., Tiffany & Co. ...**30.00**

Maryland patt., Alvin Mfg. Co...**14.00**

Mazarin patt., Dominick &
Haff **14.00**

Melbourne patt., Oneida
Silversmiths **16.00**

Melrose patt., Whiting Mfg.
Co. **14.00**

Michelangelo patt., Oneida
Silversmiths **18.00**

Mignonette patt., Lunt
Silversmiths **14.00**

Mount Vernon patt., Lunt
Silversmiths **12.00**

Old French patt., Whiting Mfg.
Co. **12.00**

Old Colonial patt., Towle Mfg.
Co. **15.00**

Pantheon patt., International
Silver Co. **18.00**

Plymouth patt., Whiting Mfg.
Co. **9.00**

Poppy patt., Alvin Mfg. Co. **28.00**

Raleigh patt., Alvin Mfg. Co. **12.00**

Rambler Rose patt., Reed &
Barton **12.00**

**Renaissance (Bearded Man)
patt.,** Dominick & Haff.............**32.00**

Rose Point patt., R. Wallace &
Sons.......................................**12.00**

Tara patt., Reed & Barton.........**12.00**

Versailles patt., Gorham Mfg.
Co. **25.00**

Violet patt., R. Wallace &
Sons.......................................**20.00**

Violet patt., Whiting Mfg. Co. ...**12.00**

Wedgwood patt., Alvin Mfg.
Co. **20.00**

TEA STRAINERS

Repoussé patt., Samuel Kirk
& Sons **225.00**

TOMATO SERVERS

Chrysanthemum patt., Wm. B.
Durgin Co. **275.00**

Francis I patt., Reed &
Barton **91.00**

Hampton Court patt., Reed &
Barton **91.00**

Louis XIV patt., Towle Mfg.
Co. **95.00**

Nocturne patt., Gorham Mfg.
Co. **85.00**

Sir Christopher patt., R.
Wallace & Sons **195.00**

Victorian patt., Wm. B. Durgin
Co. **85.00**

MISCELLANEOUS

Olympian Pattern Asparagus Server

Asparagus server, Olympian
patt., the handle chased w/a
scene of Venus on her chariot
w/putti riding dolphins, w/trail-
ing water leaves, the prongs
w/chased fluting, engraved on
reverse w/initials, Tiffany &
Co., New York, New York,
1878-91, 9½" l. **920.00**
(Illustration)

Pie knife, Windham patt., serrated, Tiffany & Co. **395.00**

Serving fork, Versailles patt.,
Gorham Mfg. Co. **135.00**

Serving spoon, Bernadotte patt., Georg Jensen Silversmiths...........................**235.00**

Tomato Vine Pattern Soup Ladle

Soup ladle, Tomato Vine patt., the handle chased w/tomatoes, vines & leaves in relief lapping over to the back, the oval bowl w/a wide scalloped rim, the back engraved w/a monogram "LGS," Tiffany & Co., New York, New York, 1872-91, 12¼" l. ....**1,265.00** (Illustration)

Soup spoon, Old Colonial patt., Towle Mfg. Co. **25.00**

Strawberry fork, Louis XV patt., Whiting Mfg. Co. **25.00**

Stuffing spoon, King George patt., Gorham Mfg. Co. **395.00**

Sugar sifter, Virginia patt., Gorham Mfg. Co. **295.00**

Lap-Over-Edge Pattern Table Crumber

Table crumber, Lap-over-Edge patt., the handle bright-cut engraved w/bamboo branches & spider web, the shaped blade w/chased designs, Tiffany & Co., New York, New York, 1880-91, 12¾" l. ....**1,380.00** (Illustration: below left column)

Vegetable spoon, Grape patt., Dominick & Haff **150.00**

SILVER FLATWARE SETS

Acanthus patt., dinner service: twelve each tablespoons, luncheon spoons, teaspoons, coffee spoons, demitasse spoons, dinner forks, luncheon forks, fish forks, pastry forks, fish knives, dinner knives & luncheon knives, four cold cut forks, two each vegetable serving spoons, jelly spoons & salt spoons, one each large serving spoon, gravy ladle, serrated serving spoon, sugar spoon, meat fork, large salad serving spoon, large salad serving fork, small salad serving spoon, small salad serving fork, cake knife, tomato server, pastry server, small serrated knife & pierced server; knives & serving pieces w/stainless steel blades, tines or bowls, designed by Johan Rohde in 1917, Georg Jensen Silversmiths, Copenhagen, Denmark, various dates, 168 pcs. **12,650.00**

Acorn patt., dinner service: six luncheon forks, six pastry forks, eight teaspoons & eight luncheon knives w/stainless steel blades; Georg Jensen Silversmithy, Copenhagen, Denmark, post-1945, 26 pcs. **2,875.00**

Acorn patt., dinner service: twelve each dinner knives, dinner forks, luncheon knives, luncheon forks, fish knives, fish forks, pastry forks, cocktail

forks, soup spoons, tablespoons, dessert spoons, iced
tea spoons, teaspoons, coffee
spoons, demitasse spoons,
grapefruit spoons, fruit knives,
fruit forks, steak knives, butter
spreaders & lobster picks,
three each serving forks &
serving spoons, one each
sauce ladle, sardine server,
bottle opener, letter opener,
pickle fork, pie slice, fish slice
& jam spoon; Georg Jensen
Silversmithy, Copenhagen,
Denmark, 1921 & after,
272 pcs. **21,275.00**

Albert Pattern

Albert patt., dinner service:
twenty-four each dinner knives,
dinner forks, luncheon knives,
luncheon forks, fish knives, fish
forks, soup spoons, dessert
spoons, teaspoons, coffee
spoons, grapefruit spoons, lobster picks, fruit forks & mango
forks, two pairs of fish servers,
two serving spoons & one
sugar sifter & slice; Goldsmiths
& Silversmiths Co., Ltd., and
Garrard & Co., London,
England, 1933-79,
344 pcs. **19,550.00**
(Illustration: three of 344)

Arcadia Pattern

Arcadia patt., dinner service:
twelve each dinner knives, dinner forks, dessert spoons, luncheon forks & salad forks,
eleven teaspoons & eight luncheon knives; Georg Jensen
Silversmithy, Copenhagen,
Denmark, post-1945,
79 pcs. **5,520.00**
(Illustration: three of 79)

Back Tipt patt., dinner service:
eight each dinner knives,
dessert knives, dinner forks,
luncheon forks, salad forks,
butter knives & soup spoons,
ten teaspoons, two berry
spoons & one each gravy ladle,
lemon fork, cake server, cold
meat fork, olive fork & seafood
fork; Watson Company,
Attleboro, Massachu-
setts, 74 pcs. **1,092.00**

Bernadotte patt., dinner service: twelve each tablespoons,
luncheon spoons, ice cream
spoons, coffee spoons, demitasse spoons, dinner forks, luncheon forks, salad forks, fish
forks, fish knives, dinner
knives, luncheon knives & butter knives, two each large
servers, cold meat forks & fish
servers, one each cake server,

vegetable server, gravy ladle, meat fork, salad spoon, salad fork, cheese slice & cheese knife; some pieces w/stainless steel blades, tines or bowl, designed by Sigvard Bernadotte in 1930, Georg Jensen Silversmithy, Copenhagen, Denmark, post-1945, 170 pcs. **16,100.00**

Bittersweet Pattern

Bittersweet patt., dinner service: eight each dinner forks, salad forks, cake forks, tablespoons, soup spoons, teaspoons, dinner knives & butter spreaders; Georg Jensen Silversmithy, Copenhagen, Denmark, 64 pcs. ....**5,750.00** (Illustration: three of 64)

Brocade patt., dinner service: eight each salad forks, luncheon knives, luncheon forks, butter knives, teaspoons & iced tea spoons, four dessert spoons & one each sugar shell & master butter server; International Silver Co., Meriden, Connecticut, 54 pcs. **632.50**

Castilian patt., dinner service: twenty-four dinner knives, eighteen teaspoons, twelve each luncheon knives, cheese knives, soup spoons, butter knives, bouillon spoons, dinner knives, luncheon forks, salad forks, cocktail forks, grapefruit spoons, iced tea spoons & dessert forks, three serving forks; engraved w/monogram

"NAY," Tiffany & Co., New York, New York, 20th c., 195 pcs. **9,775.00**

Chateau Rose patt., dinner service: 12 each luncheon forks, soup spoons, salad forks, seafood forks, luncheon knives, teaspoons, 10 butter spreaders & a cake server; Alvin Corp., Providence, Rhode Island, ca. 1940, 83 pcs. **805.00**

Clinton patt., dinner service: thirty-six teaspoons, twenty-four cocktail forks, eighteen each dinner forks, luncheon forks, salad forks, bouillon spoons, soup spoons, demitasse spoons, dinner knives, luncheon knives & butter spreaders plus a two-piece carving set & eight serving pieces; Tiffany & Co., New York, New York, 232 pcs. ..**9,775.00**

Cluny patt., dinner service: thirty-six teaspoons, eighteen each dinner knives, luncheon knives, iced tea spoons cocktail forks, salad forks, grapefruit spoons, dinner forks, butter spreaders, luncheon forks, soup spoons & dessert knives, twelve steak knives, seven tablespoons, six each sauce ladles, pairs of salad servers, dessert serving spoons, serving forks & fish knives, four each pie slices & paté slices, two cake combs & pair of ice tongs, basting spoon, crumb scoop & asparagus server; silver-gilt, some pieces monogrammed, Gorham Mfg. Co., Providence, Rhode Island, ca. 1890 & later, 297 pcs. **16,100.00**

Commonwealth patt., dinner service: eight each table forks, salad forks, cocktail forks, dessert forks, demitasse spoons, dessert spoons, grapefruit spoons, soup spoons, butter spreaders, 9½"

knives & 8¾" knives, twelve five o'clock spoons, ten tea-spoons, two-piece salad serving set, two-piece fish serving set & one each cold meat fork, large serving spoon, cake saw, cake server, gravy ladle, sugar spoon, sugar tongs, butter serving knife, lemon fork, jelly knife, cheese knife, jelly spoon, ice tongs & roast carving fork & knife; hand-wrought, Porter Blanchard, Calabasas, California, 129 pcs. **8,050.00**

Devon patt., dinner service: twelve each dinner forks, salad forks, cake forks, seafood forks, soup spoons, teaspoons, grapefruit spoons, demitasse spoons, dinner knives & luncheon knives, sixteen butter spreaders & six fruit knives; Reed & Barton, Taunton, Massachusetts, 142 pcs. ...**2,185.00**

Eloquence patt., dinner service: sixteen each salad forks, cocktail forks, iced beverage spoons, dessert spoons, cream soup spoons, luncheon knives, butter spreaders & steak knives, fifteen luncheon forks & teaspoons, thirteen demitasse spoons, twelve place spoons, three tablespoons, pierced tablespoons, butter serving knives & cake knives, two two-piece salad serving sets, buffet spoons, buffet forks, gravy ladles, sauce ladles, bonbon spoons, sugar spoons, jelly servers, olive forks & sugar tongs, one cheese serving knife; Lunt Silversmiths, Greenfield, Massachusetts, 218 pcs. **4,312.00**

English Gadroon patt., dinner service: ten each luncheon forks, salad forks, luncheon knives & butter spreaders, eight cocktail forks, twenty-three teaspoons, six demitasse spoons, two tablespoons, one each cream soup spoon, gravy

ladle & cake server; Gorham Mfg. Co., Providence, Rhode Island, 92 pcs. **1,265.00**

Federal Cotillion patt., dinner service: twelve each luncheon forks, salad forks, ice cream forks, luncheon knives & butter spreaders, sixteen teaspoons, eight demitasse spoons, two-piece steak carving set, one berry spoon, salad serving fork, tablespoon, gravy ladle, pierced flat server, cold meat fork, bonbon spoon, sugar tongs, cream ladle, sugar spoon, jelly server, butter serving knife, lemon fork, olive fork, cake server & cheese server; Frank Smith Silver Co., Gardner, Massachusetts, 110 pcs. ...**2,300.00**

Francis I patt., dinner service: eight each dinner knives, dinner forks, soup spoons, teaspoons, butter knives, luncheon forks & seafood forks, plus one each sugar spoon, salad serving set, gravy ladle & two serving spoons; Reed & Barton, Taunton, Massachusetts, 1907, 62 pcs. **1,725.00**

Francis I Pattern

Francis I patt., dinner service: forty-two teaspoons, twenty-four each luncheon forks, salad forks, luncheon knives & butter

spreaders (twelve w/silver blades), twenty bouillon spoons, twelve each dinner knives, soup spoons, demitasse spoons, coffee spoons, dinner forks, cocktail forks & ice cream forks, eight grapefruit spoons plus fourteen serving pieces, w/two wood cases, Reed & Barton, Taunton, Massachusetts, 20th c., 276 pcs. **9,200.00**
(Illustration: three of 276)

Heiress patt., dinner service: twelve cocktail forks, butter spreaders, iced beverage spoons, soup spoons & luncheon knives, eighteen salad forks, nineteen luncheon forks, twenty-four teaspoons, two serving spoons & cold meat forks & one gravy ladle, butter serving knife & sugar spoon; Oneida Silversmiths, Sherril, New York, in fitted wooden case, 128 pcs. **920.00**

Imperial Chrysanthemum Pattern

Imperial Chrysanthemum patt., dinner service: twenty-four each table forks & dessert forks, twenty-one tablespoons, twelve each dessert spoons,

teaspoons, fruit spoons, demitasse spoons, fish forks, cocktail forks, fish knives & butter knives, four condiment spoons & one each fish server, fish slice, serving fork, punch ladle & lobster server plus twenty-four table knives & twelve dessert knives & fruit knives w/stainless steel blades; the terminals chased w/flowerheads & leaves, also engraved w/a monogram, in fitted wooden case, 222 pcs. **5,750.00**
(Illustration: five of 222)

King Albert patt., dinner service: twelve each dinner knives, dinner forks, salad forks, ice cream forks, teaspoons, dessert spoons, cocktail forks & butter knives plus carving knife, meat fork, serving spoon, cheese knife, berry spoon & sugar castor spoon; Whiting Mfg. Co., Providence, Rhode Island, 102 pcs. **1,425.00**

Kings patt., dinner service: twelve each dinner forks, dinner knives, butter spreaders & dessert spoons, 24 each teaspoons & salad forks plus 7 serving pieces; engraved monogram, Towle Silversmiths, Newburyport, Massachusetts, ca. 1904, 103 pcs...............**1,265.00**

King William patt., dinner service: eight each luncheon forks, salad forks, butter spreaders, dessert spoons, cream soup spoons & luncheon knives; monogrammed, Tiffany & Co., New York, New York, 1907-47, in a fitted wooden case, 48 pcs. **977.50**

Lap-Over-Edge Etched patt., etched w/plants, animals & fish, some identified on the back: twenty-four each teaspoons & luncheon forks, twelve each dinner knives, luncheon knives, butter spreaders, dinner forks, dessert spoons &

Lap-Over-Edge Etched Pattern

dessert knives, ten table-spoons, one sauce ladle & butter knife; engraved w/name Scoville in script on back, Tiffany & Co., New York, New York, ca.1885,132 pcs. .....**20,700.00** (Illustration: four of 132)

Louis XIII Richelieu Pattern

Louis XIII Richelieu patt., dinner service: twelve each dinner knives, dinner forks, lunch knives, lunch forks, table-spoons, dessert spoons, lobster forks, teaspoons, fish knives, fish forks, demitasse spoons, three butter knives, two serving forks & one each

soup ladle, sauce ladle, slice, cake knife & cheese knife; monogrammed, w/rattail bowls, trifid ends & cannon-handled knives w/ stainless steel blades, Puifor-cat, Paris, France, 20th c., in three fitted trays stamped w/maker's name, 144 pcs. ....**28,750.00** (Illustration: three of 144)

Mansion House patt., dinner service:12 each dinner knives, butter knives, dinner forks, luncheon forks, soup spoons & teaspoons plus13 serving pieces; Heirloom, Oneida Silversmiths, Sherrill, New York, 85 pcs. **690.00**

Old English Pattern

Old English patt., dinner service: thirty-six each dinner knives & dinner forks, twenty-four each luncheon knives, luncheon forks & dessert spoons, twelve each fish knives, fish forks, dessert knives, dessert forks, tablespoons & tea-spoons, four sauce ladles, pair of salad servers, pair of fish servers, one gravy spoon & four-piece carving set; Francis Higgins, London, England, 1936, 229 pcs. in fitted oak cabinet w/five drawers & double doors ....**20,700.00** (Illustration: three of 229)

Old English Feather Edge
patt., dinner service: twelve
each dinner knives, dinner
forks, salad forks, soup
spoons, dessert spoons & teaspoons, together w/twelve
chese knives w/bone handles;
Garrard & Co., Ltd., London,
England,1962-63, 84 pcs...**4,025.00**

Old French patt., dinner service:12
each bread & butter plates, luncheon
knives, dinner knives, fruit forks, luncheon forks, demitasse spoons,
dessert forks, salad forks, iced tea
spoons, egg spoons, citrus spoons,
soup spoons, cream soup spoons,
teaspoons & tablespoons,11 each
dinner forks & cocktail forks,10 butter
knives & 2 master butter knives;
Gorham Mfg. Co., Providence,
Rhode Island, ca.1915, 220 pcs. in
mahogany case..................**4,675.00**

Old Newbury patt., dinner service: eight each luncheon
forks, dessert spoons & dinner
knives, seven luncheon forks &
cocktail forks, six butter spreaders & teaspoons & one each
vegetable spoon, pastry server,
cold meat fork & serving spoon;
hand-wrought, Old Newbury
Crafters, Newbury-port,
Massachusetts, 54 pcs. **1,265.00**

Pine Tree patt., dinner service:
twelve each dinner forks, salad
forks, cocktail forks, butter
spreaders, teaspoons, bouillon
spoons & dinner knives, two
tablespoons, two-piece salad
serving set, one gravy ladle &
cake server; International
Silver Co., Meriden, Connect-
icut, in fitted case, 90 pcs.......**747.50**

Plymouth patt., dinner service:
twelve each dinner forks, luncheon forks, salad forks w/gilt
tines, cocktail forks, teaspoons,
soup spoons, demitasse
spoons w/gilt bowls, butter
spreaders, dinner knives & luncheon knives, three tablespoons & one each cream
ladle w/gilt bowl, olive spoon

w/gilt bowl, pickle fork, butter
serving knife, salad serving
fork w/gilt tines & cake server;
monogrammed "H.W.B.,"
Gorham Mfg. Co., Providence,
Rhode Island, 129 pcs. **920.00**

Repoussé patt., dinner service:
eight each luncheon forks,
salad forks, butter spreaders,
teaspoons, coffee spoons &
luncheon knives plus two serving spoons & ladles & one
each serving fork, berry spoon,
pickle fork, slice, sugar shell,
butter knife, jelly slice & meat
fork & knife; monogrammed, S.
Kirk & Co., Baltimore,
Maryland, 61 pcs...............**2,875.00**

Romance of the Sea patt., dinner service: eight each dinner
knives, butter knives, soup
spoons, salad forks, dinner
forks & teaspoons; R. Wallace
& Sons Mfg. Co., Wallingford,
Conn., 48 pcs. in a fitted
wooden case.....................**1,035.00**

Rose patt., dinner service; eight
each luncheon forks, salad
forks, butter spreaders, bouillon spoons, demitasse spoons
& luncheon knives, eleven
small teaspoons, seven teaspoons, three tablespoons,
two-piece steak carving set &
one jelly server, sugar spoon,
butter pick, lemon fork & gravy
ladle; monogrammed "C," Stieff
Co., Baltimore, Maryland, in
fitted case, 76 pcs. **1,035.00**

Royal Danish patt., dinner service: twelve each luncheon forks, demitasse spoons, soup
spoons & butter spreaders, ten
tablespoons & dinner knives,
nine dinner forks & teaspoons,
eight cocktail forks & luncheon
knives, seven salad forks, five
dessert spoons, two large serving spoons & one salad serving
fork, gravy ladle, large cold
meat fork & pickle fork; International Silver Co., Meriden,
Connecticut, 120 pcs. **2,185.00**

Strasbourg patt., dinner service: eight each dinner knives, dinner forks, salad forks & butter knives, sixteen teaspoons, three serving spoons & one each ladle, berry spoon, slotted spoon & meat fork; gold-washed, Gorham Mfg. Co., Providence, Rhode Island, in wooden cutlery box, 55 pcs. plus box.............................**1,330.00**

Suffolk patt., dinner service: twelve each dinner forks, salad forks, cocktail forks, teaspoons, soup spoons, grapefruit spoons w/gilt bowls, demitasse spoons, butter spreaders & dinner knives w/silver plate blades plus one each large serving spoon, pastry server, lettuce fork & sugar spoon; monogrammed "B," Alvin Corporation, Providence, Rhode Island,112 pcs.......................**977.50**

Tapestry patt., dinner service: 12 each luncheon forks, dessert spoons, salad forks, luncheon knives dessert knives, 24 teaspoons plus 9 serving pieces; Reed & Barton, Taunton, Massachusetts, ca.1964, 93 pcs.................**1,380.00**

Versailles Pattern

Versailles patt., dinner service: twelve each salad forks, dinner

forks, teaspoons, soup spoons, dinner knives & butter spreaders, ten small teaspoons & eight seafood forks; monogrammed, Gorham Mfg. Co., Providence, Rhode Island,1888, 90 pcs............**2,300.00** (Illustration: three of 90)

Versailles patt., dinner service: twelve each dinner knives, luncheon knives, bouillon spoons, teaspoons, dinner forks, luncheon forks & ice cream spoons, eleven each demitasse spoons & salad forks, eight butter knives plus twelve serving pieces; Gorham Mfg. Co., Providence, Rhode Island, early 20th c., 126 pcs. **4,255.00**

Winchester patt., dinner service: twelve each dinner forks, salad forks, teaspoons, cream soup spoons, dinner knives & butter spreaders, two tablespoons & one cold meat fork; Shreve & Co., San Francisco, California, in fitted wooden case, 75 pcs.....................**1,092.00**

Windsor patt., dinner service: eight each luncheon forks, teaspoons, demitasse spoons, luncheon knives, salad forks, soup spoons & butter spreaders plus a meat fork & knife; monogrammed, Old Newbury Crafters, Inc., Newburyport, Massachusetts, retailed by Cartier, 58 pcs. (one handle separate from knife) **1,265.00**

Woodlily patt., dinner service: eight each luncheon forks, salad forks, butter spreaders, cream soup spoons & luncheon knives, sixteen teaspoons, two tablespoons & one gravy ladle & butter serving knife; Frank Smith Silver Co., Gardner, Massachusetts, in fitted wooden case, 60 pcs. **1,150.00**

SILVER PLATE

It appears that as early as 1801, experiments took place in England which proved that a current of electricity passing through a conducting liquid decomposed the ingredients of that liquid and caused their elements to be set free at the two immersed electric poles. This principle led to the inception of the electroplating industry. At first there seemed to be no direct use for the electroplating process, but between 1836 and 1838, the G.R. & H. Elkington firm of Birmingham, England took out various patents for the process, and anyone interested in the method was required to go to Birmingham to study and pay a royalty and guarantee he would not deposit less than 1,000 ounces of silver per year.

John Mead is thought to be the first person to utilize silver plating in the United States. Another early manufacturer of silver plated ware in this country was Rogers Bros. in Hartford, Connecticut. It was this firm that really entrenched the silver plating industry in the United States. Another early silver plating company was the Meriden Britannia Company, located in Meriden, Connecticut. The International Silver Company of Meriden, Connecticut was incorporated in 1898 and included a number of independent New England silversmiths.

Originally, the manufacture of silver plated goods was located in New England and the northeastern states, mainly New York, Connecticut and Massachusetts. The use of the process spread out to Maine, Maryland, New Jersey, Pennsylvania and Rhode Island, and by the late 19th century to Illinois, Ohio, Indiana and Wisconsin, and finally to California.

Silver plated wares today can be found in different grades. The prime quality items are found in jewelry stores and jewelry departments in large department stores. There is, of course, an abundance of lower quality and lower priced wares which are available in discount stores, bargain basements and souvenir-type gift shops. It should be noted, however, that any piece with a reputable mark will be of the same quality whether retailed in a jewelry store or as an advertising premium.

Antique silver plated wares are to be found in the same items as the solid sterling pieces. Lovely tea sets, flatware, serving pieces, vases and other decorative wares are all available. Their style and beauty are the equal of sterling silver pieces, but the price is considerably lower.

Hollowware:

Asparagus stand, the pierced tray joined by the supports cast in the form of asparagus spears, Blackstone Silver Co., Bridgeport, Connecticut, 7¾" w., 5½" h. **$176.00**

Bun warmer, oval w/swing cover, engraved reserve & monogram on cover, J.H. Potter, 19th c., 14¼" l., 9" h........**230.00**

Butter dish, cov., compressed oval body w/retracting lid, raised on a low foot, overall floral engraving, 19th c., 8¾" l. **110.00**

Button, Indian in relief & "Massachusetts," back marked "Warrented (sic) Treble Plated," together w/old tattered note "Button from coat of Gen. James Warren," 1" d. **165.00**

Cachepots, baluster-form, fluted & chased w/laurel swags, France, ca. 1900, 12" h., pr. .**6,612.00** (Illustration: top next page)

Candelabra, three-light, Modernist style, pierced curved ramp form, centering a sphere, supporting three semi-ovoid candlecups, 9¾" l., 5" h., pr. **115.00**

Silver Plate Cachepots & Centerpiece

Candelabra, four-light, triform base surmounted w/griffin half-figures, tall fluted columnar shaft to three bracket-form arms & vasiform upper shaft all fitted w/urn-form sconces w/nozzles, England, 1861, 20¾" h., pr.............................**920.00** (Illustration: below)

Silver Plate Neoclassical Candelabra

Candelabra, nine-light, square stepped base supporting the stem formed as a putto standing on the shoulders & hands of a seated putto, Roman lamp-form branches w/ivy-clad

sconces, w/detachable nozzles, w/seventeen alternative liners, Christofle, Paris, France, third quarter 19th c., 26" h., pr......................................**5,750.00**

Candlesticks, baluster-form, Queen Anne-style, late 19th c., 8¾" h., pr...............................**345.00**

Candlesticks, oval lobed base, matching vasiform stem & campana-form sconce w/detachable nozzle, Gorham Mfg, Co., Providence, Rhode Island, 20th c., 11" h., set of 4 ....**805.00**

Candlesticks, neoclassical design, weighted, England, 19th c., 12" h., pr..................**920.00**

Candlesticks, oval spreading base supporting a lyre-shaped standard flanked by lion's heads, 12" h., pr...................**632.00**

Candlesticks, columnar-form, Corinthian-style candlecup over fluted stem, the square base chased w/ram's heads at the corners, suspending foliate swags, w/acanthus rims,

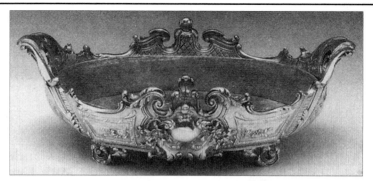

Louis XV-style Centerpiece

weighted, England, 20th c.,
12¼" h., set of 4 ....**1,610.00**

Centerpiece, Louis XV-style,
shallow boat-form w/heavy
scrollwork at ends & sides,
raised on four ornate feet,
France, third quarter 19th c.,
19¾" l. **2,875.00**
(Illustration: top)

Centerpiece, figural, rococo-
style, central architectural base
flanked w/two winged children
representing the arts, each sit-
ting above shell-form side
bowls, all in a scrolling frame-
wark w/mask supports, a vasiform stem holding the center-
drilled diamond-cut clear glass
circular bowl, secured w/a
boss-headed screw, Continental, 19th c., bowl 16¼" d., frame
24" l., overall 20½" h. **4,600.00**

Centerpiece, the oval body
raised on four scroll supports,
the ends mounted w/winged
putti holding branches, detachable liner, Christofle, Paris,
France, ca. 1875, across hand-
les 26¼" l. **8,625.00**
(Illustration: previous page front, with
cachepots)

Chamber pot, cov., dragon handle, possibly South America,
8¾" d...................................**460.00**

Chandeliers, six-light, Regence-
style, w/chased borders of
swirled foliage & strapwork,
electrified, 17½" h., pr. **5,750.00**

Late 19th c. Coach Lamps

Coach lamps, the squared body
beneath a circular tiered upper
portion decorated w/ribbon
bows, coronet finial, repairs,
now fitted for electricity, late
19th c., 29½" h., pr.............**3,162.00**
(Illustration)

Silver Plate Coach Lamps

Coach lamps, hexagonal form
w/a two-tiered cresting, raised
on a tall hexagonal standard,
chased w/foliage, electrified,
35" h., set of 3 ....**2,875.00**
(Illustration: two of three)

French Silver Plate Cocktail Set

Cocktail set: six goblets & tray; the goblet w/conical bowl raised on a conical & triangular stem, the rectangular mirrored tray w/angled handles, each impressed "DESNY - PARIS - MADE IN FRANCE - DEPOSE," ca. 1925, tray across handles 20½" l., goblets 4¾" h., the set ....**6,037.00** (Illustration)

Coffee set: two pots, sugar bowl, creamer & tray; Baroque patt., R. Wallace & Sons, Wallingford, Connecticut, tray 28¾" l., 5 pcs. **247.50**

Entree dish, cov., oval w/ gadroon decorated borders, retailed by Tiffany & Co., New York, New York, 1854-70, 12" l. **192.50**

Georgian-style Covered Entree Dish

Entree dishes, cov., Georgian style, rectangular, the top w/foliate handle & gadroon decoration, 9 x 11", pr. ....**440.00** (Illustration: one of two)

Epergne, in the William IV style, the lobed foliate stem on four foliate-capped claw feet, issu-

ing four reeded arms, each supporting a cut-glass bowl, centering a cage-form support, w/sides molded w/foliage & shells, supporting a conforming large cut-glass bowl, England, 19" l. **2,070.00**

Egyptian Revival-style Epergne

Epergne, Egyptian Revival style, the standard mounted w/eagle heads, fitted w/original frosted & cut-glass tray & conical vase, the whole resting on a three-part base mounted w/cast sphinxes, England, 1867, 21" h. ....**760.00** (Illustration)

Fish serving set, leaf decoration, late 19th c., in case, knife 12½" l., 2 pcs. **201.00**

Julep cup, cylindrical body flaring slightly at rim, marked "Homan & Co., Cincinnati," 3⅛" h. **88.00**

Knife rests, each cast as a different stylized animal or bird, impressed "GALLIA," in original box, the original tissue showing arrangement of knife rests in the case, each 3¾" l., set of 12 ....**2,990.00**

Mirror plateau, inset mirrored top surrounded by a frame depicting grapevines, 18½" d. **1,150.00**

Nut bowl, cast as a stylized squirrel w/its tail raised, designed by Louis Sue, by Gallia for Christofle, impressed "GALLIA 5989," ca. 1920, 7" l., 7½" h. **2,185.00**

Pitcher, the faceted cylindrical body w/a squared foot, peaked spout & angular handle, decorated at the base w/overlapping triangles, designed by Louis Sue for Gallia, impressed "GALLIA 5978" & w/the firm's mark, 7" h. **690.00**

Punch bowl, footed, the sides chased w/foliate scrollwork, the rim applied w/cast C-scrolls & stylized shells, Birmingham Silver Co., Yalesville, Connecticut, early 20th c., 16" d., 12" h. **577.50**

Early 20th c. Roast Cart

Roast cart, oblong, the two-handled pan w/hot water compartment & gravy recesses, pivoting domed cover, the mahog-

any table mounted w/a utensil tray, folding dish rack & removable lamp, on four fluted supports above nickel casters, cover engraved twice "Excelsior, Casablanca," France, early 20th c., stand 33¼" l. ....**5,750.00** (Illustration)

Shell-form Spoon Warmer

Spoon warmers, realistically modeled to depict a variety of seashells, each on a rockwork ground, assorted set of 5 ...**2,070.00** (Illustration: one of five)

Tazze, conical base beneath slender cylindrical stem supporting shaped flat body, faux ivory curled handles at rim, 6¼" d., 5¼" h. plus handles, pr. **66.00**

Tea & coffee set: cov. coffeepot, two cov. teapots, cov. sugar bowl, cream pitcher & waste bowl; neoclassical urn-form, monogrammed "S," Gorham Mfg. Co., Providence, Rhode Island, 1870-71, coffeepot 9¼" h., 6 pcs. **517.50**

Teapot, cov., rounded oval form raised on four paw feet headed by acanthus, curved spout, angular handle, cover w/griffin finial, Victorian, Reed & Barton, Taunton, Massachusetts, 6⅞" h. (some wear) **49.50**

Tray, shaped circular form w/engraved decoration & crest, late 19th c., 19¼" d. **172.50**

Silver Plate Covered Urn

Urn, cov., modeled in the classical style w/low slightly domed foot, applied w/ram's head handles & swags of fruit above the swirled lower section, the swirled cover w/bud finial, late 19th c., 29¼" h. ....**3,737.00** (Illustration)

Vegetable dish, cov., wide rectangular rim w/rounded corners, applied w/stylized tulips, Apollo Silver Co., New York, New York, 13½" l. **66.00**

Vases, openwork trumpet-form body raised on a spreading leaf & scroll spreading base, w/blue glass liner, Victorian, Harrison Fisher, Sheffield, England, late 19th c., 15¾" h., pr. **632.00**

Flatware:
(Listed by pattern)

ALDINE (1895 Rogers Bros.)

Berry spoon, gold-washed bowl..**30.00**

Cheese scoop, gold-washed bowl..**40.00**

Pie forks, set of 6 ....**45.00**

ARBUTUS (Wm. Rogers & Son)

Bouillon spoon **15.00**

Butter knife, twisted handle **20.00**

Butter pick..............................**22.00**

Cocktail fork.............................**10.00**

Cold meat fork **25.00**

Cream soup spoon.................**20.00**

Dinner fork **15.00**

Gravy ladle **25.00**

Luncheon fork **15.00**

Salad fork.................................**24.00**

Sauce ladle..............................**20.00**

Sugar spoon **18.00**

Tablespoon **15.00**

Youth fork **20.00**

BERKSHIRE (1847 Rogers Bros.)

Bonbon spoon, gold-washed bowl..**75.00**

Demitasse spoon......................**8.00**

Jelly trowel..............................**48.00**

Sugar tongs **25.00**

CARNATION (W. R. Keystone)

Citrus spoon **20.00**

Cream ladle **25.00**

Pie server **45.00**

Salad fork...............................**25.00**

Strawberry fork......................**25.00**

CHARTER OAK (1847 Rogers Bros.)

Charter Oak Pattern

Baby food pusher....................**95.00**

Berry spoon **65.00**

Butter knife, flat......................**25.00**

Citrus spoon 25.00

Cream ladle 45.00

Fruit knife 35.00

Dinner fork, hollow-handled 40.00
(Illustration: bottom previous page)

Dinner knife, hollow-handled
(resilvered blades) 15.00

Luncheon fork 38.00
(Illustration: center previous page)

Luncheon knife, hollow-
handled 27.50

Salad fork 36.00
(Illustration: top previous page)

Salad serving fork 75.00

Salad serving set..................175.00

Soup ladle 125.00

Soup spoon, round bowl 40.00

COLUMBIA (Wm. A. Rogers)

Berry spoon 30.00

Butter knife, twist handle 19.00

Citrus spoon 22.00

Cream ladle 40.00

Fruit spoon...............................13.00

Ice spoon...............................147.50

Salad fork 45.00

Salad serving fork 150.00

Strawberry fork........................65.00

Sugar tongs 75.00

FLORAL (1835 R. Wallace)

Cocktail fork............................10.00

Cold meat fork 30.00

Ice cream spoon 45.00

Pie server 75.00

Salad fork 36.50

Seafood fork 22.00

Soup spoon, oval bowl............15.00

Soup ladle, large 95.00

Strawberry fork........................50.00

Stuffing spoon 70.00

GROSVENOR (Oneida Community)

Butter knife, flat..........................7.00

Carving set, large, 3 pcs. 110.00

Cream soup spoon..................10.00

Dinner fork, hollow-handled 14.00

Dinner knife.............................10.00

Fruit knife 16.00

Fruit spoon.................................9.00

Ice cream spoon 20.00

Ice tea spoon 16.00

Luncheon fork 15.00

Salad fork 10.00

Sherbet spoon 16.00

Sugar tongs 35.00

HOLLY (E.H.H. Smith)

Bouillon spoon 45.00

Carving set, 3 pcs. 350.00

Cold meat fork 90.00

Demitasse spoon.....................35.00

Ice cream fork 90.00

Luncheon fork 30.00

Luncheon knife.........................20.00

Soup ladle 300.00

Tablespoon 35.00

Tomato server.........................225.00

KING CEDRIC (Oneida Community)

Iced tea spoons, set of 12 ....40.00

Jelly server....................................5.00

Place setting, 4 pcs.................56.00

Tablespoon 32.00

Teaspoon 12.00

LA VIGNE (1881 Rogers)

Butter spreader........................20.00

Citrus spoon, gold-washed
  bowl..25.00

Soup ladle 165.00

Sugar tongs 100.00

Dinner fork 9.00

Dinner knife..............................12.00

Luncheon fork 10.00

Soup spoon..............................12.00

Strawberry fork........................60.00

Sugar tongs 90.00

Tablespoon 10.00

Teaspoon 7.00

Tea strainer............................175.00

MARTINIQUE (Lady Beautiful)

Butter spreader, individual.........6.00

Dinner fork 8.00

Iced tea spoon 7.00

Salad fork....................................8.00

Soup spoon, oval bowl...............7.00

Teaspoon 5.00

Vegetable serving spoon........12.00

OLD COLONY (1847 Rogers Bros.)

Cold meat fork 20.00

Dinner fork, hollow-handled 12.50

Dinner knife, hollow-handled ...20.00

Ice cream fork 30.00

Ice cream spoon 35.00

Iced beverage spoons,
  set of 6 ....25.00

Salad serving fork 65.00

Strawberry fork........................30.00

STEEL

Although small amounts of steel have been made since the Iron Age, the modern steel industry was not developed until the mid-19th century when Englishman Henry Bessemer created the *Bessemer process* for refining iron. American ironmaker William Kelly independently developed a similar process about the same time. The new method of steel production was based on the discovery of the British metallurgist, Robert Mushet. In 1857, Mushet found that when you added an alloy of iron, carbon and manganese, called *spiegeleisen,* during the refining of iron, it helped remove oxygen and control the carbon content of the steel.

The Bessemer method was the main form of steel production in Britain and the United States until the early 20th century, and made them leaders in the industrialized world. Eventually a more efficient method of refining steel, the open-hearth method, replaced the Bessemer method. Today, even more modern and efficient methods are used in Japanese and European steel mills, causing serious setbacks for outdated American plants.

Since the late 19th century, steel has been a major material in the building of modern American society - everything from railroads to household appliances and automobiles to tablewares. Below, we list a small selection of early decorative objects made from this durable and versatile alloy.

Price Listings:

Calipers, sheet, lady's leg-shaped, decorated w/simple engraved designs, 4¼" l........**$99.00**

Console table, the rectangular top inset w/a rectangular frosted glass pane, above a rectangular apron w/checkerboard design, the recessed squares painted black, supported by six flattened oval-shaped legs, mounted on a stepped rectangular base, attributed to George Fry for the G. Fox Department Store, ca. 1937, 24 x 60", 30¼" h................**7,130.00**

Console table, Art Moderne style, the thick amber glass top raised on a U-form base composed of five wide struts etched w/a pattern of concentric circles, mounted on a stepped plinth, the surface mottled w/orange varnish, America, ca. 1930, 19" w., 79" l., 33½" h...................**26,450.00**

Ember tongs, hand-wrought, polished, 17¾" l....................**176.00**

Fireplace set: fender, shovel, tongs & poker; the fender cut w/foliate scrolls & w/a beaded border, w/urn finials, the tools w/conforming finials, polished, George III period, England late 18th c., fender 5' 8½" l., the set **2,300.00**

Food chopper, cast, rectangular blade marked "Cast Steel," w/turned walnut handle, 6" w. **22.00**

Food chopper, hand-wrought, w/heart cut-out & turned wood handle, 5 x 6¾" **357.50**

Fork, hand-wrought, two-tine, simple flat handle, marked "F.B.S. Canton, O. Pat. Jan. 26, '86" (1886), 16¾" l.............**82.50**

Harpoon, whaling-type, hand-forged, ferrule end for wooden handle w/old rope wrapping, head stamped "J.D.D." & scratched incised "W.D.B.," 32" l. **275.00**

Harpoon, whaling-type, hand-forged, blade stamped "Cast Steel," w/old wooden handle, 119" l. **330.00**

Spatula, hand-wrought, tulip cut-out in blade, 17½" l. (small break in blade design)..........**236.50**

Sugar nippers, hand-wrought, small size, w/keeper, 6⅞" l....**110.00**

Sugar nippers, hand-wrought, good detail w/some decorative tooling, polished, 9¾" l. **104.50**

Weathervane, sheet, cut figure of running fox, old worn & weathered green, brown & grey paint, w/directionals, 30" l., 23" h..................................**550.00**

TIN & TOLE

Tin is a soft silvery-white metal with a low melting point. It is imported into the United States from the major tin producing countries, including Malaysia, Indonesia, Bolivia, Thai-land, the former U.S.S.R., China and Brazil.

The first American tinsmiths took up residence in Berlin, Connecticut, in 1738. Prior to this time, tin was scarce and expensive. Tinplate (sheet iron rolled very thin and coated with layers of molten tin) was not produced in the U.S. until tin was discovered near Goshen, Connecticut in 1829. Early peddlers traveled the rural areas, first on foot and later using brightly painted green and yellow carts that opened up to display their wares. It is reported that they covered areas from Canada to New Orleans and to the Lake Erie and Detroit region.

The early wares carried by the

peddlers were plain, undecorated utilitarian wares such as basins, candle molds and sconces, pitchers, pails, coffeepots, cream whippers, cookie cutters, graters and other such items.

Tole wares appeared in England at Pontypool, near the Welsh border, around 1720. In the 1760s the colorfully decorated ware made its way to France, where it was an immediate success. Some tole had a "japanned" background. Japanning refers to painting the surface with asphaltum, which is a transparent black substance with a tar base. A good deal of the American tole ware had the dark brown or black background, but some work from Maine had a bright blue background, while other areas might use a cream or mustard yellow ground. Some pieces from Pennsylvania have a red or orange background. The designs of American tole were primarily stylized floral or fruit decoration in brilliant shades of red, green, blue, yellow and white. These decorated wares include document boxes, coffeepots, canisters and tea caddies, bread trays, apple and serving trays, candle sconces, jardineires and many other decorative or utilitarian items.

Today, collectors prize the country appeal of early plain and punched tin wares and brightly colored tolewares. Since there has been a great collector interest in these wares for over sixty years there are numerous quality reproductions on the market, so careful study is necessary to select the best early examples.

Price Listings:

Apple tray, tole, quatrefoil-form, worn original dark brown japanning over a crystallized ground, white rim band w/floral decoration in red, green & black, 11¼ x 11½" (old dark over-varnish) **$192.50**

Apple tray, tole, quatrefoil-form, original dark brown japanning over crystallized surface w/white rim band w/yellow

'comma' designs & floral decoration in red, green & black, 11½ x 12" (some wear & re-varnishing) **632.50**

Architectural ornament, tin, molded in high-relief in the form of a ferocious lion w/ornate scrolling mane, depicted w/his mouth open,overall green patina, probably New York, early 20th c., 75½" w., 34" h. **2,875.00**

Bank, tin, "Golden Shell," cylindrical, decorated w/drawings of hippo & spotted leopard, Emloid Co., Arlington, N.J., 2" d., 34" h. (very minor denting, rust & scratches) **412.50**

Book ends, tole, cut-out silhouette depicting a fruit basket, worn original paint, 9¼" w., 5¾" h., pr.............................**715.00**

Box, cov., tole, book-shaped, worn original yellow w/floral decoration in red, white & green, initial "W" on back, 3¼" l. **192.50**

Bread tray, tole, rectangular w/flaring sides & rounded ends, original dark brown japanning w/gold crystallized center, border of stylized floral design in red, yellow & green on a white band, 12⅜" l................**302.50**

Bread tray, tole, dished rectangular body w/rounded ends, original stylized floral decoration in red, green, yellow, white & black on a worn dark brown ground, 12⅝" l...................**2,365.00**

Bread tray, tole, rectangular dished form w/rounded ends, original dark brown japanning over crystallized ground, white rim band w/floral decoration in red, green & black, 13½" l. (areas of wear & scratches) ..**165.00**

Bread tray, tole, rectangular dished form w/rounded ends, original black paint w/yellow rim

& stylized floral center in red, yellow, green & white, 13½" l. (some wear) **357.50**

Bulb kit, tin, "Cadillac," rectangular box painted in orange, blue & beige, "for all Cadillac-La Salle Motor Cars, Part No. 42677," 2½ x 3½", 1½" h. (minor paint chips & scratches) **82.50**

Covered Tole Butter Tub

Butter tub, cover & underplate, tole, the reticulated oval rim w/a conforming lid above a shaped body, matching underplate on ball feet, decorated in brown & yellow, Continental, 5" h........**517.00** (Illustration)

Can, cov., tin, "Ace CX2 Motor Oil," red, white & black letter ing, qt., 4" d., 5½" h.................**30.00**

Can, cov., tin, "Ace Motor Oil," red, white & black lettering, qt., 4" d., 5½" h...........................**135.00**

Can, cov., tin, "Ace Wil-Flo 10W-30 Motor Oil," red & white lettering, red, blue, green & brown scene w/car, qt., 4" d., 5½" h.....................................**121.00**

Can, cov., tin, "Harley Davidson Pre-Luxe Motorcycle Oil," pictures motorcycle, w/contents, qt., 4" d., 5½" h. (minor denting) **25.00**

Can, tin, "Opaline Motor Oil," green, cream & black, classic car pictured, pour spout attached, minor denting & scratches, gal., 6" w., 11" h.....................................**650.00** (Illustration)

'Opaline Motor Oil' Gallon Can

Can, cov., tin, "Polarine Motor Oil," yellow, blue, pink, green, red, cream & brown, automobile on a country road pictured, gal., 8" w., 11" h. (minor scratches & denting) **475.00**

'Pure As Gold Motor Oil' Can

Can, tin, "Pure As Gold Motor Oil," red, yellow, white, black & blue, "Pep Boys" pictured, w/contents, qt., 4" d., 5½" h...................................**250.00** (Illustration)

Can, cov., tin, "Raleigh's Good Health Talcum," rectangular w/various scenes from nursery rhymes on all sides, 3" w., 7½" h. (very minor scratches) **121.00**

Can, tin, "Sinclair Motor Oil," green & cream pinstripe w/black lettering, very minor

'Sinclair Motor Oil' Can

soiling & scratches, w/contents, qt., 4¼" d., 4¾" h....................**285.00** (Illustration)

Can, cov., tin, "Woodfield's Fresh Oysters," scene of sailing ship & lighthouse, red & green on a yellow ground, gal., 6¾" d., 7¼" h. (very minor scratches & denting) **55.00**

'Zingo Sweets' Can

Can, cov., tin, "Zingo Sweets," old racing car pictured, brown, orange & blue, minor scratches & rust, "The Meeker Can Co., Cin, O. 2178," 12½" d., 10" h.....................................**192.50** (Illustration)

Candle mold, tin, ten-tube, w/side handle, 10" h..............**137.50**

Candle mold, tin, twelve-tube w/side handle, 10" h................**60.50**

Candle mold, tin, twelve-tube, w/large handle on side,10" h...**93.50**

Candle mold, tin, twelve-tube, w/large single handle at end, 11¼" h. (some old resoldering) **93.50**

Candle mold, tin, twenty-four tube, w/double ear handles, 10" h. (battered, replaced steel wick rods) **159.50**

Candle sconce, tin, rectangular reflector w/rounded top, decorated w/tooling, crimped edges, 9½" h. **137.50**

Candle sconce, tin, round reflector & drip pan w/crimped detail, 12" h. **330.00**

Candle sconces, tin, rectangular w/crimped circular crest & tooled designs, 13½" h., pr. ..**440.00**

Candle stand, tin, weighted conical base supporting a tall slender standard fitted w/an adjustable pan w/two candle sockets, old olive green repaint over earlier red, 37" h...........**440.00**

Candlestick, tole, hogscraper-type, low domed base w/cylindrical stem w/push-up & lip hanger, painted w/a red & yellow floral design w/striping on a black ground, 6½" h. **302.50**

Candlesticks, tole, Directoire-style, square base supporting a stem painted w/a rustic cottage in gilt against a scarlet ground, w/inset drip-pan, France, early 19th c., 7½" h., pr. (restored) **920.00**

Candlesticks, tin, weighted capstan base, cylindrical standard, push-up w/brass knob, 9¼" h., pr. (old soldered repairs) **605.00**

Canister w/hinged lid, tole, rectangular, original green paint w/gold stenciling, decoupage of oval portrait of a woman & paper label "Allspice," 9¾" h. ..**38.50**

Canisters, tole, cylindrical w/rounded shoulder & low-

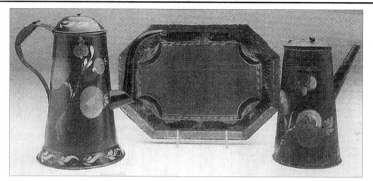

Pennsylvania Tole Coffeepots & Tray

domed cover, labeled "Crown Stores Pure Teas," England, 19th c., 17½" h., set of 4 ....**1,955.00** (Illustration: two of four)

"Crown Stores Pure Teas" Canisters

Regency-style Chestnut Urn

Chestnut urns, cov., tole, Regency-style, low slightly

domed foot supporting the con- ical body w/ring handles, black & gold decorated, paint loss, England,19th c., 21¼" h., pr. ....**1,265.00** (Illustration: one of two)

Chocolate mold, tin, modeled to represent Charlie Chaplin as "The Little Tramp," 7½" h. **104.50**

Chocolate mold, tin, figure of a lady rabbit in wedding dress, two-part, 6¾" h. **110.00**

Chocolate mold, tin, rooster, two-part, 5½" h. **71.50**

Coffeepot, cov., tole, miniature, original gold stenciling on red painted ground, 2¾" h. (some wear) **104.50**

Coffeepot, cov., tole, tapering cylindrical body w/straight spout, slightly rounded top, black ground w/stylized poly- chrome floral decoration, some wear, Pennsylvania, early 19th c., 8½" h. ....**575.00** (Illustration: top right)

Coffeepot, cov., tole, tapering sides w/molded base, goose- neck spout, strap handle, slightly domed cover, the sides decorated in polchrome w/stylized flowers, a band of leaves around the base, all against a dark brown ground, minor dents, Pennsylvania, early 19th c., 10" h. ....**1,495.00** (Illustration: top left)

Early 19th c. Tole Coffeepot & Syrup Jug

Coffeepot w/hinged lid, tole, tapering cylindrical body w/molded base, low domed lid, gooseneck spout & applied strap handle, decorated w/large red & yellow stylized fruit designs on a black japanned ground, probably Pennsylvania, early 19th c., 10½" h. ....**2,875.00** (Illustration: right)

Coffeepot, cov., tole, tapering cylinder w/molded base, gooseneck spout & high loop handle, decorated w/hand-painted fruit, flowers & foliage in yellow, white, green, black & red on original dark brown japanned ground, domed cover w/tooled finial, 10¾" h. (tip of spout & handle battered) **605.00**

Coffeepot, cov., tin, 'wrigglework,' conical w/hinged lid & scrolled strip finial, gooseneck spout, strap handle incised w/serpents maker's mark, the sides decorated w/a spreadwinged American eagle grasping an American flag in its talons & flanked by tulip buds & blossoms, the reverse w/flowers & leafage above a border of swags & tassels, the base w/incised wrigglework flowerheads, probably Pennsylvania, early 19th c., 11" h. ....**8,050.00** (Illustration: top next column)

Interesting 'Wrigglework' Tin Coffeepot

19th c. Tole Sugar Bowl & Coffeepot

Coffeepot, cov., tole, tapering cylindrical body w/domed hinged lid, applied strap handle, gooseneck spout, decorated w/bands of blue, red, yellow & green flowers & foliage on a dark brown ground, some paint loss & scrapes, probably Pennsylvania, mid-19th c., 11½" h. ....**805.00** (Illustration: above right)

Colander, tin, bowl-shaped w/punched stars, open handles, 10½" d. **44.00**

Cookie cutter, tin, heart beside a hand, flat backplate pierced w/single hole, 3½" h. **660.00**

Cookie cutter, tin, short-legged stylized horse, flat backplate pierced w/two holes, 7¼" l. ...**247.50**

Cookie cutter, tin, rooster, flat backplate pierced w/a single hole, 7" l. **77.00**

Cookie cutter, tin, stag, large, flat backplate pierced w/two holes, 7½" h. **330.00**

Cookie cutter, tin, large woman w/full skirt, flat backplate pierced w/two holes, 11" h. (light rust) **115.50**

Decoy, tin, stick-up field-type, Canada goose w/old weathered paint, 21" l. (light rust) ...**159.50**

Colorful 'GulfOil' Tin Display

Display, tin, "GulfOil," rectangular box supporting two cans of household lubricant flanking circular plaque w/logo, orange, blue & cream, minor scratches & soiling, 9½" w., 11½" h. .....**330.00** (Illustration)

Document box, cov., tole, miniature, rectangular w/low-domed cover w/brass bail handle, worn original yellow w/floral decoration in red, orange, black & green, 3" l. **165.00**

Document box, cov., tole, miniature, original gold stencil-

ing on red ground, 3" l. (some wear) **71.50**

Document box, cov., tole, miniature, rectangular w/low-domed cover centered by a ring handle, original dark brown japanning w/white band & decoration in red & blue, 4¼" l. (loose seam in lid, minor wear) **137.50**

Document box, cov., tole, miniature, rectangular w/low-domed cover centered by a loop handle, original brown japanning w/floral decoration in red, yellow, green & white, 4¼" l. (loose seam in lid, minor wear) **110.00**

Document box, cov., tole, flat top w/ring handle, worn original brown japanning w/white band & floral design in red, yellow & green, 6½" l. **165.00**

Document box, cov., tole, rectangular w/low-domed cover centered by a brass bail handle, worn old brown japanning w/ghost image of striping & 'comma' designs beneath, white band & floral design in green, red & black, 6¾" l. (some wear).....**115.50**

Document box, cov., tole, the rectangular domed lid w/wire ring handle decorated w/yellow foliate corner spandrels above a conforming case w/yellow foliate swag decoration beneath a yellow band w/red berries & green leaves on a black ground, the underside w/illegible inscription & dated "1836," New York, first half 19th c., 4" deep, 8" w., 6¼" h. **230.00**

Document box, cov., tole, rectangular w/low-domed cover, original dark brown japanning w/yellow striping & yellow 'comma' designs on lid, front & ends w/wide white band w/floral design in red, yellow, green & black, 8¼" l.......................**220.00** (Illustration: top next page)

Tole Document Box

Document box, cov., tole, rectangular w/low-domed cover centered by a loop ring handle, original dark brown japanning w/scalloped semi-circular white reserves on front & sides w/floral decoration in yellow, red, green & black, yellow striping & 'comma' designs on lid, 9" l. (lid a bit battered & hasp incomplete) **335.50**

Tole Document Box with Florals

Document box, cov., tole, rectangular w/low-domed cover, original brown japanning decorated w/an exuberant floral design on front & ends in red, white, green & yellow w/yellow 'comma' designs on lid, hasp incomplete, 10" l. ....**478.00** (Illustration)

Tole Decorated Dome-top Document Box

Document box, cov., tole, rectangular w/low-domed cover, original brown japanning w/floral decoration in red, white, green & yellow, yellow striping & 'comma' design on lid, 10" l. ....**605.00** (Illustration: bottom previous column)

Document box, cov., tole, rectangular w/low-domed cover w/original brass bail handle, worn original dark brown japanning w/white band w/stylized floral decoration in red & green w/yellow 'comma' designs.......**71.50**

Hat box, tole, oval w/conical top, black w/a *faux bois* design, cast w/the Royal seal & "Cieve's," England, 19th c., 10" h.....................................**99.00**

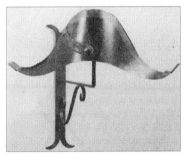

Tole Hat Maker's Sign

Hat maker's sign, tole, the Napoleonic formed hat fitted w/gold braiding & decoration, mounted on a scrolled wrought-iron support, painted in tones of iron-red & highlighted w/gilding, 26¼" l. ....**3,737.00** (Illustration)

Hot water urn, cov., tole, baluster-form body raised on tripod supports, w/spigot, high domed cover w/ball finial, scarlet ground painted w/gilt chinoiseries, Continental, possibly Holland, early 19th c.,18" h. ..**1,150.00**

Jardiniere, tole, the rectangular flared body decorated w/a chinoiserie design painted in polychrome & highlighted w/gilding, raised on acanthus-cast paw feet on a rectangular plinth, 13½" w., 11¼" h. **1,840.00**

Kerosene jug, cov., cylindrical base w/conical upper section w/spout, loop handle, screw-on cap & bail handle w/wooden handgrip, w/embossed brass label "W.S. Miley & Son...shoe findings and kerosene goods. Haverhill, Mass.," black repaint on tin, 11" h. (repairs)..............**60.50**

Lamps, tole, in the form of a red-painted attenuated urn w/scrolled brass handles, on a red stepped base cast w/leaves, further brass trim at base of lamp & connector, Charles X period, France, second quarter 19th c., 18" h., pr. (adapted, electrified) **6,900.00**

Lantern, tin, stepped cylindrical body w/stellate top & bull's-eye lens, original dark brown japanning w/gold trim, embossed brass label "Peter Gray & Sons, Boston, Mass.," removable font w/kerosene burner, 8½" h...................................**115.00**

Lantern, tin, Paul Revere-type, cylindrical w/conical top, punched decoration of a cross in a Gothic arch design w/cutout stars, old blue paint, 12" h. plus replaced ring handle (hasp an old, poorly soldered replacement) **467.50**

Lantern, tin, punched decoration, cylindrical body w/conical top & ring handle, 13½" h. plus handle (light rust) **159.50**

Lantern, tin, kerosene-type w/clear globe, "Dietz Fire Dept Tubular," 14" h. (burner replaced) **137.50**

Lantern, hanging-type, tin, square w/glazed sides, the sloping top & base decorated w/pierced star & flower designs, worn old red paint, font w/kerosene burner &

chimney, 16" h. plus replaced wire hanger.............................**247.50**

Lighting shelf, tin, for Betty lamps & candlesticks, back w/punched design w/large star, 13½" w., 15" h. (wear & some rust) **275.00**

Lunch pail, cov., tole, round, original gold stenciled floral design on red painted ground, 5" d., 4" h. (wear) **159.50**

Tin Oval Lunch Pail

Lunch pail, cov., tin, oval w/painted stripes at mid-section, the domed cover w/cast pewter finial, swivel bail handle, 9½" l. ....**33.00** (Illustration)

Magic lantern, tin, chromolithographed label w/children watching slides, w/original gunmetal japanning w/gilt trim, labeled "Perfek & J.S." & "Made in Germany," together w/eleven worn glass slides, in original wooden box **82.50**

Match holder, tole, hanging-type w/crimped crest above the rectangular pocket, worn original dark brown japanning w/floral decoration in red, blue, green & white, 7¾" h. (ground very worn in places) **82.50**

Model of a hat, tin, anniversary-type, paint decorated, 4¾" h. **144.00**

Monteith, tole, oval w/crenelated rim, red stenciled in gold w/a band of grape clusters & leaves, w/hoop handles, France, 19th c., 11" l. **1,495.00**

Red & Gilt Decorated Tole Monteith

Monteiths, tole, circular w/ornate
shaped rim, decorated in gilt
w/bands of stylized foliage on
a red ground, the sides w/ring
handles, fitted w/a beige
liner, minor chips, 8¼" d.,
pr. **805.00**
(Illustration: one of two)

Monteiths, tole, scalloped oval
form w/bail handle at each end,
decorated w/gilt leaves against
a red ground, France, 19th c.,
13" l., pr. **6,900.00**

Mug, tole, cylindrical w/tightly
rolled rim, original red paint
w/"My Boy" in gold stenciling,
2" h. **49.50**

Mug, tole, cylindrical w/narrow
rolled rim, strap handle, very
worn original dark brown japanning w/stylized floral decoration
in red, yellow, white & olive
brown, 4½" h. **302.50**

**Tole Mug with Starflower
Decoration**

Mug, tole, cylindrical w/large
side handle, decorated w/a single red starflower w/yellow &
white on a dark brown
japanned ground, 5¾" h. **742.50**
(Illustration)

Pail, cov., tin, worn old white
paint w/black smoked graining,
9½" d., 7¼" h.........................**104.50**

Allegorical Painting on Tin

Painting, tin, allegory on the
Westward movement w/Indians,
settlers, railroads & various other
subjects, probably an artist's copy,
21" w., 14¼" h., in modern frame,
overall 23" w., 16¼" h. **880.00**
(Illustration)

Panel, tin, punched Masonic
design composed of two arches, compass & other symbols,
in a red grained wood frame,
17" w., 13" h. (light rust) **275.00**

Sign, tin, "AC Spark Plugs,"
embossed & painted in orange,
blue & cream, 41" w., 13" h.
(scratches, rust & denting) **132.00**

Sign, tin, "Amalie Pennsylvania
Motor Oil," painted red, black &
cream, 10" w., 40" h. **99.00**

Sign, tin, "Champion Spark
Plugs," embossed & painted in
red, black, cream & blue,
applied w/a coat of clear lac-
quer, very minor paint chips to
mounting holes,15" w.,
5½" h. **412.50**
(Illustration: top next page)

Sign, tin, "Chevrolet," embossed
& painted blue & white w/cen-
tral logo, 23½" w., 12" h.
(scratches, denting & rust) **159.50**

Sign, tin, "Coca-Cola," bottle pictured w/"Drink Coca-Cola" to
right, framed, embossed &

'Champion Spark Plugs' Tin Sign

painted red, yellow, green & cream, "Made in U.S.A. Robertson Springfield, Ohio, 1934," 36" w., 13" h. (very minor scratches to edges).....**451.00**

Sign, tin, "Invincible Motor Insurance," depicting a beam of light focused on a classic car, painted in cream, green, orange, yellow & blue, 20" w., 9½" h. (minor scratches).......**231.00**

Sign, tin, "Lacquerwax," embossed & painted yellow, blue & red depicting can of product superimposed on an automobile, 19½" w., 13½" h. (soiling, scratches & minor paint loss)...........................**187.00**

'Sterling Oils' Tin Sign

Sign, tin, "Sterling Oils," rectangular, embossed & painted in cream, red, yellow & black, minor soiling, paint chipping & denting, 13½" w., 19½" h. ....**154.00** (Illustration)

Sign, tin, "Veedol 30¢ a Quart," painted black, orange & cream, embossed, 9¼" sq. (minor soiling & scratches) **231.00**

Sign, tin, "Vernor's Ginger Ale," self-framed, embossed & painted picture of bearded Irishman wearing knee britches & stradling a keg & holding a large bottle of the product, yellow, green, blue, brown, red & black, "Donasco 8-50 Form No. 50 Made in U.S.A.," 18¼" w., 54" h. (scratches) **275.00**

Sign, tin, "Wheat's Ice Cream Co., The Home of Quality Ice Cream," self-framed, scene of large four-story building w/trucks in front & product in upper & lower corners, orange, green, blue, black & white, gold slug plates w/black lettering, "Haeusermann Metal Mfg. Co. N.Y.-Chi," 26" w., 18¼" h. (some fading & scratches) **467.50**

Spice box, cov., tole, rectangular w/six interior canisters, old black w/stenciled design, brass bail handle, 9½" l. (minor wear) **93.50**

Sugar bowl, cov., tapering cylinder, original floral decoration in red, yellow & green on a dark japanned ground, 3¾" h. (minor wear).........................**192.50**

Sugar bowl, cov., tole, flaring cylindrical body w/matching fitted lid, decorated w/red & yellow fruits & flowers on a black ground, some paint losses, probably Pennsylvania, mid-

'Roadside Rest Service Station' Tin Toy

19th c., 4½" h. **402.00**
(Illustration: left, with coffeepot p. 209)

Syrup jug w/hinged lid, tole,
tapering cylindrical form
w/strap handle, decorated
w/brightly colored red, yellow &
green stylized floral decoration
within yellow scallops on a
black japanned ground, some
paint loss, probably New
England, early 19th c.,
4" h. **2,875.00**
(Illustration: left, with coffeepot p. 209)

Tea caddy, cov., tole, hexagonal
body decorated w/stylized gold
flowers on a black ground,
France,19th c., 5½" h. **176.00**

Tea caddy, cov., tole, cylindrical
w/sloping shoulder, original
dark brown japanning w/floral
decoration in red, green & yel-
low, 6⅝" h. (wear) **104.50**

Tole Tea Canister

Tea canister, cov., tole, rectangular w/rounded front & back
panel, slightly tapering shoulder & short neck, original
black decorated w/a stylized
floral design on both sides in
orange, yellow, green & white,
6" h. **319.00**
(Illustration)

Tea canister, cov., tole, cylindrical w/sloping shoulder & flat
cover, worn brown japanning
decorated w/stylized floral
design in red, yellow, green
& white, 6½" h. **330.00**

Toy, tin, 1955 Buick convertible,
friction mechanism, yellow
body, rubber wheels, plastic
interior, made in Japan, 1950s,
11" l. **121.00**

Toy, tin, two children on teeter-
totter, polychrome paint, Gibbs
Toys, Kenton, Ohio,
14½" h. **302.50**

Toy, tin, "Cities Service" station,
battery-operated, lithographed
details, w/car, instructions
inside box lid, Line Mar Toys,
Japan (tears to box) **522.50**

Toy, tin, gas pump, "Crank it and
it will give you gallons," price
is turned by finger, complete
w/hose, some minor rust
& soiling, The Gong Bell Mfg.
Co., East Hampton,
Connecticut, 13" h. **495.00**
(Illustration: top next page)

Early Tin Gas Pump Toy

Toy, tin, "Goofy the Gardener," wind-up figure of Goofy pushing a wheelbarrow, lithographed details, Marx, Great Britain, 7¼" h. (very minor scratches) **522.50**

Toy, tin, hill climber trolley, friction mechanism, yellow, red & green, "Patd Nov. 21, Made in U.S.A.," 16" l. (scratches & minor fading of paint) **88.00**

Toy, tin, "Roadside Rest Service Station," comprised of small building, two gas pumps, lubster cart & water can, lithographed details, one pump hose missing, rust, scratches & minor fading, Marx, 10" deep, 14" w., 4½" h. ....**440.00** (Illustration: top previous page)

Toy, tin, scale, lithographed details, rectangular base supporting round dial & platform for goods to be weighed, orange, green, red, gold & blue, made in Japan, 6½" w., 5" h. (very minor rust)..............**27.50**

Toy, tin, taxi, 1959 Buick, friction mechanism, lithographed interior, yellow & black checkerboard roof & side stripe, yellow body, bubble on top indicates amount owed for ride, made in Japan, 8½" l. (minor scratches & wear)..................................**110.00**

Toy, tin, "Tin Trik Auto," open two-door automobile w/driver, No. 53 on back, painted red & yellow, Ferdinand Strauss Inc., New York, New York, 6½" l. (driver touched up, scratches & very minor fading) **93.50**

Tray, tip, tin, lettered "Jenney - Aero - Gasoline" over picture of an airplane, orange, black & cream, "Pat. Applied for H.D. Beach Co., Coshocton, Ohio," 4" d. (scratches & very minor rust spotting) **132.00**

'Sunlight Oil' Tin Tip Tray

Tray, tip, tin, center lettered "Use - Sun - Light Oil," golden yellow, orange, blue, cream & black, Kansas City Oil Co., Independent Refinery, Kansas City, Kansas, scratches, paint chipping & soiling, 4" d. ....**60.50** (Illustration)

Tray, tole, miniature, rectangular w/rounded corners, worn gold japanning over crystallized ground, rim w/a yellow border w/red & black trim, 4¾" l. **33.00**

Tray, tole, octagonal w/narrow turned up rim, worn original brown japanning w/wide border design in yellow, red & green, 9" l. (some areas of flaking down to bare metal) **412.50**

Tray, tole, octagonal, painted black w/a border of red berries & green leaves on a yellow

Tole Tray with Family Scene

ground, New York, first half
19th c., 8¾ x 12⅓" **115.00**

Tray, tole, octagonal w/flaring
rim, decorated w/polychrome
swags & leaves on a red
ground, minor wear,
Pennsylvania, early 19th c.,
8½" w., 12¼" l. **1,840.00**
(Illustration: with coffeepots, p. 208)

Tray, tin, "Burden's Ice Cream,"
square w/scenes of product,
blue, green, cream, red, pink,
yellow & gold, "Copyright 1925
The American Art Works, Inc.,
Coshocton, O. 151," 13¼" sq.
(white paint speckles overall,
scratches) **330.00**

Lovely 'Anheuser-Busch' Tin Tray

Tray, tin, "Anheuser-Busch,"
oval w/beautiful lady center
surrounded by colorful
cherubs, "Standard Adv. Co.,

Charles X Period Tole Tray with Scene

Regency Period Tole Tray

Coshocton, O.," 13½ x
16½"......................................**715.00**
(Illustration)

Tray, tole, octagonal w/narrow
turned up rim, worn original red
paint w/stylized floral decoration in red, black & white,
17¾" l. (wear & scratches) **137.50**

Tray, tole, rectangular w/round-
ed corners, stenciled Biblical
scene center entitled "Contract
between Jacob and Rachael,"
England, 19th c., 14⅞ x 19⅝"
(some damage)......................**115.00**

Tray, tole, octagonal w/reticulat-
ed sides & a beaded border
w/handholds, the central scene
depicting a family within an
interior w/gilt foliate borders,
losses to painted surface,
some repainting, George III
period, England, ca. 1800,
25½" l. **1,955.00**
(Illustration: top previous page)

Tray, tole, two-handled, oval,
painted w/a central oval
reserve of a boy w/a flower
chain, stenciled grape leaf border, Victorian, mid-19th c.,
26" l. (losses) **431.00**

Tray, tole, stenciled multi-colored
bronze powder scene of early
train in a landscape w/people

within a floral border on original
black painted ground, 20 x 28"
(wear & light battering w/rust
spots on rim)........................**275.00**

Tray, tole, George III style, rectangular w/canted corners,
decorated w/a central allegorical scene within gold leaf floral
borders, all against a black
ground, 19th c., 28⅛" l.
(some damage)....................**862.50**

Tray, tole, oval, decorated w/a
chinoiserie design within a floral trellis border, painted on a
black ground & highlighted
w/gilding, raised on an X-form
black stand w/gilt trim,
22¼ x 28¾" **3,450.00**

Tray, tole, rectangular w/rounded
corners, central allegorical scene
depicting an elderly bearded
man w/a young child, within a
Greek key border, painted in
tones of orange, green, yellow,
cream, grey, brown & highlighted w/gilding, restored, Charles X
period, France, 30" l. **1,035.00**
(Illustration: bottom previous page)

Tray, tole, rectangular w/serpen-
tine sides, enameled w/a floral
cluster surrounded by gilt
scrolling foliage, Victorian,
19th c., 31½" l. (chips) **1,150.00**

Tray, tole, original black paint w/chinoiserie decoration in red & gold, 32¾" l. (minor wear)..**825.00**

Tray on stand, octagonal w/handholds, the center w/a polychrome scene of a family in a pastoral setting, the sides painted *en grisaille* w/geometric designs, Regency period, England, early 19th c., now on a later faux bamboo stand, 21 x 30", 17½" h..................**3,680.00** (Illustration: top previous page)

Urns, tole, each w/a flared tapering body decorated w/a chinoiserie design painted in polychrome & highlighted w/gilding, raised on acanthus-cast paw feet on a square plinth, 11¼" h., pr. **2,300.00**

Mirror-inset Tole Sconces

Wall sconces, tole, two-light, the concave back inset w/mirror panels surmounted by a painted tin shell, the pendant in the form of foliage w/scrolling candlearms, Continental, 20½" h., set of 4 ....**6,900.00** (Illustration: two of four)

ZINC

Zinc is a bluish-white metal which is never found in a pure state in nature, but must be refined using great heat from such minerals as sphalerite, calamine or zincite.

In the past, the main use of zinc has been to form other useful alloy metals such as brass (an alloy of copper and zinc) and bronze (an alloy of copper, tin and zinc). By the 19th century, it was also discovered that zinc could be used to coat iron and steel, which *galvanized* them, thus preventing rusting. Today, all sorts of utilitarian items - from nails to roof gutters - are galvanized for durability.

Although zinc is too brittle in its natural state to produce useful objects, we list below a number of zinc-coated antiques which have sold in recent months.

Price Listings:

Figure of a cigar store Indian princess & cigar lighter, the full-length standing figure of the princess wearing a feathered headdress & a layered skirt & holding a lamppost staff in one hand, the whole mounted on a green-painted circular base above a turned wood base inscribed "Princess Red Dot Cigars," attributed to William Demuth & Co., New York, New York, ca. 1880, overall 84" h. **$31,625.00**

Roof ornament, modeled in the form of an eagle, America, late 19th c., 18¼" h. (imperfections) **230.00**

Weathervane, modeled to represent a roadster in low-relief, cast-iron & copper base w/arrow, now mounted on a wooden base, 22½" l., overall 21" h. (car has bullet hole) **77.50**

Weathervane, the molded cast silhouette of a quill pen w/molded point, possibly J. Howard & Co., Bridgewater, Massachusetts, third quarter 19th c., now mounted on a black metal base, 50" l., 15¾" h..............................**1,725.00**

GLOSSARY OF SELECTED METALWARES TERMS

Acanthus - A type of decoration taken from the acanthus leaf.

Alloy - A combination of two or more metals, usually achieved in a molten state.

Applied - Parts such as handles, finials and spouts are sometimes made separately and applied by soldering.

Assay - The qualitative or quantitative analysis of a substance, especially of an ore.

Base metal - An alloy or metal of low value which is applied with a plating, as in silver plating.

Beading - A decoration, usually used for borders, composed of small continuous half spheres.

Bell metal - An alloy of tin and copper, used to make bells.

Bleeding - Description of a piece of plated ware with the copper base exposed.

Bobeche - The flat saucerlike ring on candlesticks to catch the wax drippings from candles.

Bright-cut - A type of decorative edging cut into silver to form facets.

Britannia standard - The higher standard for silver, required in England from March 1697 to June 1720. It consists of 958 parts of silver per 1000 or 11 oz. dwt. per 12 oz., an increase of 8 dwt. pure silver per pound over sterling standard.

Buffing - Removal of the outer layer of metal with an abrasive rotating wheel in order to polish the article to a high finish.

Burnishing - Light polishing to increase the luster, entails the use of a hard, smooth, curved tool.

Carat - Measurement of the weight and purity of gold meaning the twenty-fourth part of weight of the whole; pure gold is 24 carats.

Cartouche - The enclosure for inscriptions, initials or ornamental designs, often very intricate.

Casting - The pouring of molten metal into a frame containing casting sand.

Chasing - The technique of modeling the metal's surface by use of a punch and hammer.

Coin - Used to indicate 900/1000 parts of silver and 100/1000 parts of copper, the standard used for coinage in the early 1800s.

Date-letter - Letter stamped on silver indicating the year the article was made or assayed. This systems was required by the Assay Office in London; not used in America until the 19th century and then not consistently.

Diaper - Decorated in a continuous diamond-shaped pattern.

Die - A metal stamp struck by a hammer to impress a maker's mark.

Dramweight (Dwt.) - see *Troy weight*

Embossing - Forming raised designs on the surface by hammering on the reserve.

Engraving - The technique of cutting designs into metals with a scorper or graver, removing metal in the process.

Escutcheon - A shield-shaped form surrounding heraldic devices and coats-of-arms; also the area surrounding a keyhole.

Finial - An ornamental terminating part, such as on a lid.

Flange - A projecting rim or edge of an item.

Flat chasing - A low-relief surface decoration.

Flatware - A term generally referring to knives, forks, spoons and serving pieces; also plates and other flat table items.

Fluted - A form of ornamental parallel, vertical, half-round grooves.

Forging - The technique of shaping metal by heating and then hammering.

Gadrooning - An ornamental band embellished with fluting, reeding, beading or other continuous pattern.

Gilding - The process originally entailing coating the surface of the metal with gold and mercury which was then heated to evaporate the mercury; more recently accomplished by electrolysis. Parcel gliding is partial gliding by covering parts not to be gilded with a resistant substance.

Goldsmith - An artisan capable of making articles of gold or silver.

Guilloché - An ornamental border formed of two or more bands interlaced in such a way as to repeat a design.

Hallmark - A mark used in England to stamp gold and silver articles that met established standards of purity.

Hollow handle - A handle made in two sections and soldered together.

Hollowware - Serving pieces such as bowls, pitchers, goblets and the like.

Japanning - A black enamel or asphaltum finish of a type originally used in the Orient as a background for painted decoration.

Maker's mark - The identifying mark or device used by an individual artisan.

Matte finish - Roughened texture or dull finish obtained by chasing or dotting punches struck closely together.

Oxidizing - The technique of darkening certain areas of silver to emphasize the design, accomplished by the application of a sulfur compound.

Parcel gilt - see *Gilding*

Patera - A stylized petaled design in either an oval or circular form.

Pennyweight - see *Troy weight*

Pierced work - A decorative method in which the metal is cut away to form a design.

Pricked work - A decoration formed by needlepoint engraving.

Rattail - A means of reinforcement or decoration in which two pieces of silver are joined by a spiny ridge, especially the join between the bowl and handle of a spoon.

Reeding - A convex decorative ornament having parallel strips resembling thin reeds. The opposite of fluting.

Repoussé - A decorative relief device accomplished by hammering from the reverse side, frequently further enhanced by surface chasing of detail.

Reticulated - Pierced designs or patterns that have a netted appearance.

Rococo - Characterized by elaborate profuse designs intended to produce a delicate effect. The word is derived from the French *rocailles* and *coquilles*, meaning rocks and shells.

Scorper - A small chisel used for engraving.

Serrated - Having notched, toothlike projections.

Strapwork - An applied decoration consisting of interlaced bands and scrollwork, or pierced scroll and ribbon patterns, often enclosing floral motifs and other devices.

Touch mark - An impressed maker's mark.

Troy weight - Standard weight system in English-speaking countries for gold, silver and precious stones; 5760 grains or 12 oz. to Troy pound.

Vermeil - French gold-plating technique from the mid-1700s that was banned early in the 19th century because of the danger from the mercury used. Vermeil today is produced by an electrolytic means.

BIBLIOGRAPHY

Aluminum

Woodard, Dannie A. *Hammered Aluminum Hand Wrought Collectibles, Book Two.* Weatherford, Texas: Aluminum Collector's Books, 1993.

Woodard, Dannie A. and Billie J. *Hammered Aluminum Hand Wrought Collecibles.* Weatherford, Texas: Aluminum Collector's Books, 1983.

Brass, Copper & Bronze

Burks, Jean M. *Birmingham Brass Candlesticks.* Charlottesville, Virginia: University Press of Virginia, 1986.

Gentle, Rupert and Rachael Feild. *Domestic Metalwork, 1840-1820.* Woodbridge, Suffolk, England: Antique Collectors' Club Ltd., 1994.

_____. *English Domestic Brass, 1680-1810 and the History of its Origins.* New York, New York: E.P. Dutton & Co., 1975.

Kauffman, Henry J. *American Copper and Brass.* Camden, New Jersey: Thomas Nelson & Sons, 1968.

McConnell, Kevin. *Heintz Art Metal Silver-on-Bronze Wares.* West Chester, Pennsylvania: Schiffer Publishing, Ltd., 1990.

Chrome

Kilbride, Richard J. *Art Deco Chrome - The Chase Era.* Stamford, Connecticut: Jo-D Books, 1988.

Sferrazza, Julie. *Farber Brothers Krome Kraft, A Guide For Collectors.* Marietta, Ohio: Antique Publications, 1988.

Iron & Others

Mitchell, James R.. *Antique Metalware.* New York, New York: Universe Books, undated.

Revi, Albert Christian, Editor. *Spinning Wheel's Collectible Iron, Tin, Copper & Brass.* Hanover, Pennsylvania: Everybody's Press, Inc., 1974.

Southworth, Susan and Michael. *Ornamental Ironwork, An Illustrated Guide to Its Design, History, & Use in American Architecture.* Boston, Massachusetts: David R. Godine, 1978.

Pewter

Cotterell, Howard Herschel, Adolphe Riff and Robert M. Vetter. *National Types of Old Pewter*. Princeton, New Jersey: The Pyne Press, 1972.

Ebert, Katherine. *Collecting American Pewter*. New York, New York: Charles Scribner's Sons, 1973.

Laughlin, Ledlie Irwin. *Pewter in America, Its Makers and Their Marks, Volumes I & II*. Barre, Massachusetts: Barre Publishers, 1969.

_____. *Pewter in America, Its Makers and Their Marks, Volume III*. Barre, Massachusetts: Barre Publishers, 1971.

Montgomery, Charles F. *A History of American Pewter*. New York, New York: E.P. Dutton, 1978.

Moore, N. Hudson. *Old Pewter, Brass, Copper, and Sheffield Plate*. Rutland, Vermont: Charles E. Tuttle Company, 1972; original edition by Frederick A. Stokes Company, New York, 1905.

Nadolski, Dieter. *Old Household Pewterware*. New York, New York: Holmes & Meier Publishers, Inc., 1987.

Scott, Jack L. *Pewter Wares from Sheffield*. Baltimore, Maryland: Antiquary Press, 1980.

Silver - Sterling & Coin

Belden, Louise Conway. *Marks of American Silversmiths in The Ineson-Bissell Collection*. Charlottesville, Virginia: The University Press of Virginia, for The Henry Francis du Pont Winterthur Museum, 1980.

Bentley, Jane, Editor, *Early American Silver and Its Makers*. New York, New York: Mayflower Books, Inc., 1979.

Carpenter, Charles H. with Mary Grace Carpenter. *Tiffany Silver*. New York, New York: Dodd, Mead & Co., 1978.

_____. *Gorham Silver, 1831-1981*. New York, New York: Dodd, Mead & Co., 1982.

de Castres, Elizabeth. *Collecting Silver*. London, England: Bishopsgate Press, Ltd., 1986.

Ensko, Stephen G.C. *American Silversmiths and Their Marks - The Definitive (1948) Edition*. New York, New York: Dover Publications, Inc., 1983.

Fales, Martha Gandy. *Early American Silver*. New York, New York: Funk & Wagnalls, 1970.

Fennimore, Donald L. *The Knopf Collector' Guides to American Antiques - Silver & Pewter*. New York, New York: Alfred A. Knopf, Inc., 1984.

Green, Robert Alan. *Marks of American Silversmiths Revised (1650-1900)*. Key West, Florida: self-published, 1984.

Hood, Graham. *American Silver.* New York, New York: Praeger Publishers, 1973.

Kovel, Ralph and Terry. *Kovel's American Silver Marks, 1650 to the Present.* New York, New York: Crown Publishers, 1989.

McClinton, Katharine Morrison. *Collecting American 19th Century Silver.* New York, New York: Charles Scribner's sons, 1968.

Rainwater, Dorothy T. *Encyclopedia of American Silver Manufacturers, 3rd Edition.* West Chester, Pennsylvania: Schiffer Publishing, Ltd., 1988.

_____. *Sterling Silver Holloware - Gorham Manufacturing Co., 1888 - Gorham Martelé - Unger Brothers, 1904 - American Historical Catalog Collection.* Princeton, New Jersey: The Pyne Press, 1973.

Poole, T.R. *Identifying Antique British Silver.* North Pomfret, Vermont: David & Charles, Inc., 1988

Turner, Noel D. *American Silver Flatware, 1837-1910.* Cranberry, New Jersey: A.S. Barnes and Co., Inc., 1972.

Ward, Barbara McLean & Gerald W.R. Ward, Editors. *Silver in American Life - Selections from the Mabel Brady Garvan and Other Collections at Yale University.* Boston, Massachusetts: David R. Godine, Publisher, 1979.

Wyler, Seymour B. *The Book of Silver - English, American, Foreign.* New York, New York: Crown Publishers, 1937, Twenty-fifth Printing, April 1972.

Silver Plate

Davis, Fredna Harris and Kenneth K. Deibel. *Silver Plated Flatware Patterns, 2nd Edition.* Dallas, Texas: Bluebonnet Press, 1981.

Hagan, Tere. *Silverplated Flatware, An Identification and Value Guide, Revised Fourth Edition.* Paducah, Kentucky: Collectors Books, 1981.

Rainwater Dorothy T. and H. Ivan. *American Silverplate.* West Chester, Pennsylvania: Schiffer Publishing, Ltd., 1988.

Snell, Doris. *American Silverplated Flatware Patterns, A Pattern Identification and Reference Guide.* Des Moines, Iowa: Wallace-Homestead Book Co., 1980.

The Meriden Britannia Silver-Plate Treasury - The Complete Catalog of 1886-7, with 3,200 Illustrations, by The Meriden Britannia Co. New York, New York: Dover Publications, 1982.

Victorian Silverplated Holloware - Rogers Brothers Mfg. Co., 1857 - Meriden Britannia Co. , 1867 - Derby Silver Co., 1883 - American Historical Catalog Collection. Princeton, New Jersey: The Pyne Press, 1972.

APPENDIX

Guidelines to Markings on Common Metalwares

Until the arrival of the Industrial Revolution and the mass-production of metalwares in the late 19th century, most quality hand-crafted metal objects carried only simple stamped markings, if they were marked at all. With mass-production it became important for manufacturers to have their products recognized by the buying public; therefore, stamped and incised marks became commonplace on everything from humble pots and pans to exquisite silver centerpieces.

The following guidelines should prove helpful recognizing typical markings found on antique and collectible metalwares.

Aluminum

Because the mass-production of aluminum didn't begin until the early 20th century, most items will be clearly marked. Shown above are the marks of the three major makers of hammered and stamped aluminum products of the 1930s-1950s era.

Brass, Copper and Bronze

Heintz Art Metal Shop Mark

Very early examples of hand-crafted brass, copper and bronze were seldom marked by the maker. English and European pieces before the 19th century are more likely to be marked than American-made pieces and because American makers were copying English and foreign styles it can be very difficult to determine where an unmarked piece was made. By the early 20th century more mass-produced kitchenware pieces were being marked and there was a revival of hand-craftmanship during the Arts and Crafts Movement. Arts and Crafts artisans such as Dirk Van Erp and the Roycrofters often stamped logos or special marking on their best wares. One marking to become familiar with is that of the Heintz Art Metal Shop of Buffalo, New York. They produced a wide range of decorative bronze items featuring sterling silver inlay beginning in 1915. Their logo, shown above, is a diamond surrounding the initials "HAMS." This logo is sometimes found in conjunction with additional wording or patent information.

Chrome

Chrome plating became widespread in the 1920s and 1930s when it began to supersede silver plated and nickel-plated wares; therefore, most pieces are clearly marked. The two major producers of chrome wares were Chase and the Farber Brothers with their 'Krome Kraft' line. These firm's marks are shown above.

Pewter

John Danforth's lion mark
ca. 1773-93

Ashbil Griswold's eagle mark
ca. 1807-15

R. GLEASON

Roswell Gleason's name
stamp, ca. 1821-71

Pewter has been one of the most popular and commonly used metalwares for hundreds of years in the Orient, as well as Europe, England and America. As far back as the 15th century there have been strict controls on its production in Europe and England, where years of training as an apprentice were required before one became a 'master' and could apply one's own 'touch' mark to his pieces. In early times only very simple symbols such as a crown, rose or lion were used to denote quality because most people were illiterate and any wording would have been meaningless. However, by the 18th century most English and American pewterers were also including their name or initials as part of their personalized 'touch' mark. Prior to the American Revolutionary War, American pewterers used symbols similar to their English counterparts and after the Revolution most such symbols were replaced with our patriotic eagle. By the first quarter of the 19th century, the final period of true pewter production, often just the maker's name and city were stamped on pieces. Most early pewter marks were stamped in *intaglio*, which means the background is recessed with the symbol or letters raised in relief.

Above we show copies of three typical American pewter marks of the late 18th and early 19th century. Remember, pieces stamped "Genuine Pewter" will date from the Colonial Revival era of the 1920s when antique pewter was widely copied.

SILVER

British Silver

| Leopard's head (London mark) | Date letter | Lion passant (England) | Monarch's head |

Sterling silver produced in the British Isles, especially in England, is undoubtedly one of the easiest types of antique metalware to identify and date. This is because the English require that each piece of sterling silver be carefully assayed and marked with a series of simple markings called *hallmarks*.

The use of hallmarks in England began in the late 15th century. Pieces of sterling produced in London were required to be stamped with a small leopard's head mark (a symbol for London) and a date letter indicating the year of production. By the mid-16th century another marking was added, the *lion passant* (a side view of a walking lion). The lion passant became the symbol for sterling silver produced in England, while in later years a *thistle* mark was used to indicate silver made in Scotland and a *harp* was used on silver produced in Ireland. Over the centuries, silver assaying offices were opened in the English cities of York, Sheffield, Birmingham, Chester and Exeter. Each city was assigned a town symbol to use in place of the leopard's head used on London-made products. The English have been very strict about upholding the sterling silver standard (925/1000 pure silver) and every piece of English sterling silver will carry the markings described above, as well as the initials of the individual maker.

For collectors of antique English silver the date letter is especially of interest and there are reference books which illustrate these series of letters used since the 15th century. The letters appear in a reoccuring cycle running from A to Z, but omitting the letter J and each letter represents a new year in the chronological series. For each complete series of date letters the style or form of the letters was changed. Therefore you will find Gothic letters in one series and Roman style letters in another and one series will be in all caps while the next will have them all in lower case.

Finally, another hallmark was added to this series during the period from 1784 to 1890. This was a duty mark and was represented by the use of the profile bust of the reigning monarch's head. Thus any silver made during Queen Victoria's reign from 1837 to 1890 will include a mark showing her profile.

An example of a typical series of English hallmarks is illustrated above. It represents a piece of sterling silver assayed in London in the year 1876-77. No maker's mark is included with this series although most pieces will also include such a marking.

English Sheffield Plate

A series of marks used by Sheffield plater J. Rodgers & Sons, ca. 1822

As explained in the text, Sheffield plating was an early process of laying copper with a thin layer of pure silver to produce a cheaper version of sterling silver objects.

Although the process was developed in the 1740s it wasn't until the 1780s that many English Sheffield platers were allowed to mark their products. The English government did not want these markings confused with the hallmarks used on pure sterling silver. Illustrated here is a series of marks used by Sheffield plater J. Rodgers around 1822. Note that there is no lion passant mark or city mark as found on sterling hallmarks. Also, the individual letters are *not* date letters.

Remember, in the late 19th and early 20th century many American and English silver plating companies would include the phrase "Sheffield Silver" or "Sheffield Plate" in their markings. These pieces were not produced using the early Sheffield process because neither the words "Sheffield Plate" nor "Sheffield Silver" ever appeared on the early Sheffield plate pieces.

American Silver

Early American silver is not as easy to identify and date as old English silver because our silversmiths were not allowed to use the

English system of hallmarks. American colonial makers could only mark their wares with a name or initials and because these tiny markings are often badly worn after several years, it can be difficult to attribute surviving pieces to a specific maker.

American silver was not held to the same standard of purity as English wares therefore it is generally referred to as "coin" silver, approximately 900/1000 parts pure silver. The term "coin" derives from the fact that in Colonial America the wealthy sometimes had their silver coinage melted down and made into a useful and decorative silver object.

During the early 19th century some American silver maker's did attempt to mislead the buying public by using a series of "pseudo-hallmarks," somewhat resembling the true English hallmarks. Sometimes a series of these marks were used in conjunction with the stamped marker's name. Pseudo-hallmarks often included an eagle, a letter, a man's head, a star or an anchor. Today we have no way to determine if these markings had any real significance, but it is generally believed they were marketing gimmicks used to confuse the general public. A typical stamped marker's mark is illustrated here as well as a series of typical American pseudo-hallmarks from the early 19th century.

In addition to a marker's name and perhaps pseudo-hallmarks, some American silversmiths in the early decades of the 19th century would stamp their pieces with the words "Coin" or "Pure Coin," to indicate its quality. Some pieces of coin silver will also carry the stamped name of the *retailer*, rather than the actual marker of the piece.

J.LUKEY

**Name stamp of J. Lukey,
Pittsburgh, Penn., ca. 1830-40**

Typical American Pseudo-hallmarks

Around 1860, the American government adopted the use of the English sterling silver standard and American pieces made after that era will include the word "Sterling" with the maker's mark. It is important to remember that English sterling silver is never marked with the word "Sterling."

Illustrated here are three typical American sterling silver markings used by notable Victorian silver manufacturers.

R. Wallace & Sons,
Wallingford, Connecticut

Whiting Mfg. Co.,
Providence, Rhode Island

TRADE-MARK.

STERLING

Gorham Company,
Providence, Rhode Island

American Silver Plate

Very soon after the electroplating process for silver was developed in the 1840s, American manufacturers began to mass-produce plated wares, especially table flatware. By the mid-19th century large quantities of silver plated flatware and tablewares were available to the American buying public and most of it was clearly marked with a trademark. Illustrated here are three typical silver plate markings from the late 19th century. Note that each includes the term "Quadruple" or "Quadruple Plate." This refers to pieces which carried the heaviest plating of silver; slightly lesser wares might be marked "Triple Plate." "Quadruple Plate" does *not* mean that a piece was dunked four times in the plating solution as some sources have stated; the term was simply a marketing tool used by manufacturers to indicate quality pieces.

Barbour Silver Co.,
Hartford, Connecticut

Wm. A. Rogers, Ltd.,
New York, New York

Wilcox Silver Plate Co.,
Meridan, Connecticut

Some other markings which you may encounter on American silver plated pieces are a series of stamped numbers or the initials "EPNS" or "EPBM." The numbers having nothing to do with the date of the piece but were simply factory style numbers. The initials "EPNS" stand for "electro-plated nickel silver" while "EPBM" stand for "electro-plated Britannia metal."

A typical page of Victorian silver plate wares as shown in the 1886-87 catalog of *The Meriden Britannia Silver-Plate Treasury.* Courtesy of Dover Publications, New York, New York.

European Silver

Unfortunately for American collectors, the European countries did not use an easy to follow system of marking their silver. Each country or kingdom seemed to have its own version and deciphering these today can be difficult. Sometimes only a city stamp, emblem, or a maker's name or initials were used on early silver from regions of France, Germany or Northern Europe. The only overall reference book which offers assistance in identifying such markings is *The Book of Old Silver, English, American, Foreign,* by Seymour B. Wyler (Crown Publishers, 1972).

Where To Find It
&
A Whole Lot More!

4 WEEKS FREE
The Antique Trader Weekly

❏ Yes! Sign me up for 4 complimentary issues of **Antique Trader Weekly.** If I like it, I'll pay only $35 for a full year at only 65¢ an issue. (That's 48 issues plus 4 complimentary copies) and save 70% off the cover price.

If I choose not to subscribe, I'll simply write cancel on the invoice, and owe nothing.

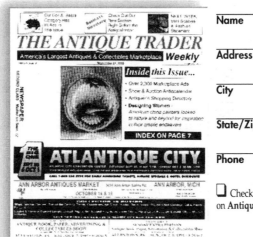

Name _____

Address _____

City _____

State/Zip _____

Phone _____

❏ Check here for advertising information on **Antique Trader** Weekly.

MB

---

2 Months FREE
Collector Magazine & Price Guide

Send your card in today for 2 months free to one of today's hottest Antique & Collectible magazines, **Collector Magazine & Price Guide**. Each issue contains a 25 page price guide plus a nationwide calender that is full of Auctions and Shows from the Antique & Collectible industry. Fill out the card and drop it in the mailbox to start your free 2 months.

Name _____

Address _____

City _____

State/Zip _____

Phone _____

❏ Check here for advertising information on **Collector Magazine & Price Guide**

MB

Antique Trader Publications

BUSINESS REPLY MAIL
FIRST CLASS MAIL   PERMIT NO.50   DUBUQUE, IA

POSTAGE WILL BE PAID BY ADDRESSEE

Antique Trader Publications
PO BOX 1050
DUBUQUE   IA 52004-9969

Antique Trader Publications

BUSINESS REPLY MAIL
FIRST CLASS MAIL   PERMIT NO.50   DUBUQUE, IA

POSTAGE WILL BE PAID BY ADDRESSEE

Antique Trader Publications
PO BOX 1050
DUBUQUE   IA 52004-9969